A THEOLOGY

FOR

URBAN YOUTH WORK

Dr Sally Nash

A THEOLOGY

FOR

URBAN YOUTH WORK

YTC Press

www.ytcpress.com

Monograph Series

YTC Press

An imprint dedicated to research on Youth, Theology & Culture

First published in 2008 by

YTC Press, Cambridge, UK

– A Division of Youth Focus –

www.ytcpress.com

www.youthfocus.biz

ISBN: 978-1-84799-505-6

Youth Focus

Youth Focus is a partnership dedicated to providing good quality resources for those involved in Christian youth ministry at an affordable price. We undertake this ministry by

- Training volunteer, part-time and full-time youth workers throughout the world through our accredited online Emerge Academy, www.emergeacademy.net
- Providing lecture resources (scripts, handouts and PowerPoint presentations) for those involved in teaching youth ministry and associated disciplines, www.youthfocus.biz
- Publishing books, with our YTC Imprint through www.lulu.com, on youth ministry, ecclesiology, cultural studies, theology, education and associated disciplines

Youth Focus is based in the UK but partners with organisations around the world.

For more information, please contact Steve Griffiths through steve@youthfocus.biz or go to the websites:

www.youthfocus.biz
www.emergeacademy.net
www.ytcpress.com

This work is dedicated to Paul

for his continual love, support and encouragement

Contents

Acknowledgements

With thanks to the workers who participated in the study, for their openness, honesty and commitment to their work. Also, to Ian Duffield and Loveday Alexander, my Supervisors, who challenged and encouraged me. Also to all those who provided financial support to enable me to undertake the research.

Thank you to the Urban Theology Unit, Sheffield for developing an innovative course based around Action Research Projects such as the one described here and to Youth for Christ for being the subject of my project.

Chapter 1

Youth for Christ
in its Jubilee Year

Young people matter to God but the Churches have not always
shown by word and example that they really believe it. I am
happy to commend the work of Youth for Christ because they
are committed to relating the Gospel to the culture of young
people today. May its work help to transform the Church as
well as young people (Rt Revd George Carey, in Bartlett 1996:
3)

Youth for Christ (YFC) was started in Britain in 1947 but
originated in America in the 1930s. It grew to become an
international organization. Youth for Christ International
(YFCI) specialises in communicating Christian faith to young people.
The mission statement of YFCI is 'to work with the Church in
responsible evangelism of young people, communicating to them the
person, work and teaching of Jesus Christ and discipling them into the
church.'[1] It is described as a parachurch organization that was 'raised
up by God to exist alongside the local church and to fulfil a special

---

[1] See Kesler (1985) for a full explanation of this statement.

task. This task is to reach, with the gospel of Christ, youth who would not be reached by the normal channels of evangelism made available by the church' (Fernando: undated).

American evangelists Billy Graham and Torrey Johnson were the catalysts for the organization to start in Britain. Many older people still associate YFC with the main thrust of the early years, the Saturday night rally. By the early 1960s, there were monthly rallies in over one hundred towns and cities across Britain. They were successful in attracting unchurched young people, a main focus of the ministry of YFC. Other activities of the early years included a film ministry, Choir Festivals, and a 'National Keen Teen's Bible Quiz'. A commitment to train young people to evangelise their peers, an essential element of YFC today, was initiated in 1959. This took the form of a National Youth Week that brought together 300-400 young people for training, evangelism, teaching, and support. The first British YFC worker, Leslie Edgell, had a philosophy of ministry that still holds true today:

> There is a need for total dedication to the Word of God, prayer and a heart for people and evangelism. A burden for young people is right as long as it is balanced with a passion for Jesus. The methods may change but the message never changes (Bartlett 1996: 5).[2]

The early 1960s were a high point for the movement. Monthly rallies, coffee bar outreaches, and film nights were happening all over Britain. This momentum did not last. The late 1960s were a time of decline for Youth for Christ. By 1970, the situation was serious with the organization in debt and with low morale around the country. It was in this year that Phil Vogel was appointed to the post of National Director. He laid the foundations for the refocusing and rebuilding of YFC. The main change was from a monthly outreach, the rally, to the idea of daily evangelism with a focus on reaching young people where they were. This led to the development of YFC's work in schools. This was a pioneering move with YFC being the first organization to have full time workers in schools, involved in lessons, assemblies, and extra-curricular activities.

This time of rebuilding continued throughout the seventies. A significant event took place in 1976 when Clive Calver, who had been working as an itinerant evangelist for YFC, was invited to replace Vogel as National Director. This led to a time of growth for YFC. When Calver first became National Director, there were only four or

---

[2] The quotations are from interviews conducted for YFC's Jubilee year publication.

five staff. By the time he left, there were eighty staff and over sixty full time volunteers. An important development at this time was the establishment of Spring Harvest (a teaching and worship event held at Easter) in partnership with Buzz magazine. Creative Arts were a feature of this period too, as Geoffrey Stevenson recalls:

> From the early touring days of our music and mime act, Kendrick and Stevenson, I have known and appreciated YFC for its commitment to relevant and exciting forms of Christian communication. Matching a passionate concern for the youth of our country with an appreciation of the difficulties in reaching them, they have not shrunk from bold artistic initiatives (Bartlett 1996: 14).

In 1982, Calver left YFC and Rob White replaced him as National Director. White had a pastoral emphasis and sought to build YFC into a 'family'. Part of this vision led to YFC buying Cleobury Place in Shropshire. This was to be both a residential centre and Head Office. Many staff relocated to the area with a number living on site. Having a residential centre meant that it was possible to run camps. Fort Rocky, an evangelistic weekend for youth workers to bring their youth groups to, started in 1989. During White's time as National Director, the range of training opportunities for young people widened with an emphasis on discipleship and the creative arts.

Lowell Sheppard, a Canadian Evangelist, joined YFC in 1985 as Director of Evangelism. He continued in this post until 1992 when he became National Director after Rob White moved on to local church ministry. Sheppard brought a focus on analysing and responding to the changing youth culture. He also initiated a major, consultative, strategic development of the movement. The organization explored again its theology of evangelism and refocused the vision. This was a positive step for YFC as Sheppard sought to unite the whole movement behind one clear strategy. During this period, YFC sold Cleobury Place as it became clear that it should focus on its strength in youth evangelism rather than running a large centre that drained finances. Sheppard had an interest in both Europe and the wider international scene and was heavily involved in setting up work in Bosnia and supporting work on the continent. A series of events led the Sheppard family to relocate to Japan where he took up an international post with YFC.

His replacement as National Director was another evangelist, Roy Crowne. Crowne had worked for YFC since 1980 and had been heading up a range of evangelistic projects as Director of National Ministries. A restructuring of the movement began to take place that involved a relocation of the Head Office to Halesowen in the West

Midlands. The strategy, developed under Sheppard, was revisited and revised to reflect the changing priorities of the late 1990s.

Youth for Christ Today

The mission statement of YFC in Britain is, 'Taking good news relevantly to every young person in Britain'.[3] The statement was developed as part of the strategy process in the early 1990s. It reflects part of YFC's uniqueness as an organization; it focuses solely on young people. Other organizations who do some similar work such as Scripture Union, Youth with a Mission, or Oasis all work with a range of people groups, not just youth. Others, such as Crusaders, work with children as well as young people. Another unique characteristic of YFC is local ministries, known as 'centres'. The word 'centre' in this context does not usually mean a building but a group of local people who have a vision for youth work. This group usually represents a range of churches and together they have a strategy for youth evangelism in a local area. Often one or more workers are employed full time and there are many volunteers, some full time, others doing a session a week or month. Each of these local ministries is locally funded and managed, they are charities in their own right, but are linked to the national organization. Currently, YFC has in the region of fifty local ministries in villages, towns, and cities across Britain. They are involved in a wide range of work with both church and unchurched young people. Activities include schools work, events, supporting youth leaders, advocacy, taking Church services, networking with other youth workers and agencies, and discipling and mentoring young people. Some of the more unusual tasks undertaken include being Pastoral Advisors at a city centre night club, a night club for under 18s, working in a youth court supporting young offenders, and acting as health advisors in the local area.

This local work is supported by the national organization. Including both local and national workers, YFC have over one hundred staff and countless volunteers including over eighty on full time training programmes. All of YFC's support departments, which include finance, personnel, training, and communications are based at the Head Office in Halesowen.

The Head Office is also a base for a number of projects. These include creative arts and sports training programmes such as Activate, a theatre company; TVB, a band; Fly and Kick, the former a basketball project, the latter involving football. There are also youth work and discipleship training programmes running that encourage a specialism

---

[3] This statement is found on the letterheads and on YFC publicity.

such as urban work or evangelist training for those that stay beyond one year. A new development is a Church Resources Department that includes such projects as Fort Rocky, an activity based residential programme, and Rock Solid Clubs, a life-skills programme for unchurched 11-14 year olds.

Alongside local work and the national organization, YFC is also involved in a range of partnerships. These include the Centre for Youth Ministry which has established a Christian, professional youth work training course in Bristol, Cambridge, Nottingham and Oxford as well as volunteer courses, and Spectrum, an ecumenical initial youth work training programme. A relatively new partnership is with World Vision and their 24-hour famine project. World Vision was originally part of YFC in the United States, so this is restoring a historic link.

A New Approach to Youth Evangelism

Early in the 90s, work was undertaken, as part of a strategic review, to explore what evangelism means for YFC today. Out of this the concept of 4D evangelism was developed.[4] It can be described as a holistic approach to evangelism incorporating four factors: demonstration, declaration, decision, and discipleship. *Demonstration* incorporates social action work and an incarnational approach to youth work. It is an area where YFC has been weak in the past. *Declaration* involves the work done in proclaiming the gospel. This ranges from large-scale missions to training young people to share their faith with their peers. *Decision* suggests the need for a clear choice to be made to accept or reject the gospel. However, it is acknowledged that for many this is a process not a clearly definable moment. *Discipleship* involves work done both before and after people have made a decision. It includes developing understanding and faith in young people and helping them see the relevance of Christianity to their lives.

Part of this new approach involved identifying strategic priorities for YFC's work. In 1993, a major document *Where Faith and Strategy Meet* (Sheppard: 1993) was produced. This was the strategy that YFC were following when the research project described in this thesis was started. The document included eight priorities:

1. Effective work in schools
2. Reaching young people at a younger age (a focus on work among 11-14s)
3. Mobilisation of volunteers both nationally and locally, some full time and others working regular sessions

---

[4] See Sheppard (1993) for an explanation of this development.

4. Mega Missions – large-scale town wide missions incorporating both pre- and post-mission week activities
5. Helping the Church to keep young people
6. Caring for poor and marginalized young people
7. Being a voice to and for young people
8. Developing a dynamic infrastructure to support the work

These priorities provided a helpful focus for both local and national YFC to unite behind. At a local level the priorities were expressed in different ways according to the vision for that place. For example, one Centre had work in schools as its main priority and another caring for the poor and marginalized. A review of the strategy, towards the end of the five-year period of implementation, revisited these eight areas of work. This revision acknowledged that it was not possible to be involved in all facets of youth work and that YFC needed to concentrate on youth evangelism. Apart from a clarification of the task, the main change that the list below reflects, has been to clarify priorities in relation to the 4D approach to mission.

1. Work with young people 11-25 with an increased emphasis on 11-14 year olds
2. Schools. Principally 11-16 but developing work in Junior Schools, FE Colleges and Universities
3. Demonstrating God's compassion to young people who are marginalized
4. Developing good discipleship practice, models and materials
5. Motivation, mobilisation and the deployment of volunteers
6. Declaring the good news to young people

As with the original eight, these six priorities are implemented in very different ways. As a national organization, YFC could not hope to do all six effectively. Local ministries around Britain consider the six areas and work out the priorities for the specific situation they are in. Each local ministry is not expected to give equal time and resources to all of the areas. In this respect, calling them priorities may be misleading. They are the activities that are to be the primary focus of the work of YFC at present. In each local centre there will be a plan that relates some or all of these six areas of strategy to the local context.

Introducing the Author

When starting this research project, I was YFC's Training Manager, based at the Head Office. This role was a wide ranging one, as per the job description. First, it involved developing strategy and policy for training within YFC. This included a major focus on gaining accreditation for courses we run. Second, the role required the promotion of training issues and the implementation of training programmes primarily within YFC. This was predominantly with staff but included some joint projects. A third area involved helping to plan National Events where a training element was involved. Primarily, this meant an annual staff conference but could involve one off events as well. Fourth, the role involved co-ordinating training initiatives within YFC. This included overseeing the content of volunteer training programmes. A fifth responsibility was to keep up to date on training issues including appropriate professional development. This involved conferences, journals and academic study. Sixth, I was expected to be a resource to other areas of YFC and the wider Christian Community. An example of this is membership of the Executives of Frontier Youth Trust and Brainstormers. Lastly, I represented YFC externally in training related issues. I was the YFC representative on the Spectrum Management Group and for the Centre for Youth Ministry. Where YFC is referred to in the above list this includes both local ministries and the national organization. I reported to the Executive Director of YFC and was part of the Senior Managers' Team. Three years into this research project my role within YFC began to change and I made the transition, over a two-year period, to being the Director of the Midlands Centre for Youth Ministry (MCYM), a partnership with St John's College, Nottingham.

I first joined YFC in 1982 as a volunteer on a one-year youth work training programme. In May 1984, after a time back in teaching, I was invited to join the staff of this same training programme. Shortly after this I pursued an option to join a new community based youth work team in London, a project that YFC eventually decided not to start. A vision to be involved in this sort of work has never left me and I approach my work with a bias towards this ministry. Partly in response to this, we (my husband also worked for YFC) moved to Birmingham in 1989 to live and worship in an Urban Priority Area. After taking on various roles within the area of short term training programmes, I began to take on some responsibility for staff training in 1994 and became full time Training Manager in September 1995. I was working full time in this role and was salaried although I was responsible for raising fifty per cent of my salary costs. It was at this time that I began to review the work of YFC.

Working Together
Collaboration was vital to the development of the action research project that is described later in this book. It needed more than one person to get a broad overview of the current situation, analyse it, and

identify potential problems that YFC faced. One person working alone is likely to have too narrow a perspective, so I began to establish a group to work with me. In YFC, collaboration is sometimes easier said than done! Although based at the Head Office at this stage, I usually only visited it once a week. Many staff visit Head Office only occasionally, which means that they face many conflicting demands on their time when they are there. Also, I wanted to get a perspective from the whole organization and thus, somehow, needed to include workers based in local projects, rather than solely those working for the organization nationally. The nearest local ministry was about forty miles away, so meeting in person was unlikely to be the solution.

Finally, a compromise was reached with two separate groups working with me on the project. I will refer to these groups as support teams. The first was a small group of Head Office staff, Rick and Karen Bartlett are an American couple who worked with YFC in the area of missions and communications respectively. They both have Masters degrees and a varied experience of youth work and have now returned home to the United States. Judy Lloyd is a long time YFC worker, who manages a variety of short term and mission related projects. Peter Massey is an ex-head teacher who had worked closely with me when I was running short-term projects. Peter left YFC in December 1996. He is now working in Adult Education for the Hereford Diocese. Paul Nash was then the Director of Personnel Development, a member of the YFC Leadership team, my line manager, my husband, and also training as an ordinand. Paul left YFC in July 1997 to pursue ordination in the Church of England and is now Senior Chaplain at Birmingham Children's Hospital.

The other support team functioned via e-mail. They were able to take part in various pieces of work by this medium. These people included Dennis Birch, a leadership team member responsible for the South of England and for urban initiatives. This post was made redundant in 1996 and Dennis set up Worth Unlimited, a project associated with YFC that works with disadvantaged young people. Dennis moved on from Worth Unlimited to work as a consultant on urban and youth issues. Another person was Warwick Danks who then worked with YFC in Gibraltar. He had previously been on a short term YFC team as well as working at Head Office. David Howell was approached too. He was a long serving Director of one of our local centres and, at that time, a part-time Leadership team member. David left YFC in September 1996 to become Project Director for the Centre for Youth Ministry, a partnership involving YFC, which was establishing training programmes for Christian youth workers. I still work with David as one of the regional staff in the Centre for Youth

Ministry. I also recruited Nick Shepherd, the Director of Bath Youth for Christ, one of our local centres with a wide range of youth work. Nick moved to Greenwich YFC in November 1997 and is currently a doctoral student at King's College, London. At various times other staff were consulted on e-mail as appropriate to the task.[5] I have included the job changes of staff above to try and give some idea of the ever-changing nature of the organization and the problems that can exist in doing long-term work collaboratively.

The first task that we undertook was a survey within YFC. A questionnaire was devised which related to YFC specifically, as well as youth culture and young people. This task was completed in autumn 1995 and gives a clear idea of how staff perceived the organization at that time. It was sent to seventeen individuals or groups that represented a cross section of YFC staff and projects. We then spent three meetings analysing the results of this questionnaire. First, this involved identifying the strengths and weaknesses of YFC. Second, we sought to identify trends in youth ministry over the last five years and those we expect over the next five to ten years. We also considered areas that encourage or discourage us concerning youth culture. The last part of the analysis was to identify barriers, problems, and issues relating to the spiritual growth of young people. Some of the main findings of this questionnaire are summarised below giving the context for an action research project in YFC.

Understanding the Context - Young People
In this section, I will outline some of the major issues that relate to working with young people today. Alongside the information gained from the questionnaire, the results of other research that YFC has done is included to give a broad understanding of the context that YFC works in.

The emergence of youth as a specific phase of life is a relatively recent phenomenon. However, its origins are hard to trace. It is generally agreed that, in Britain, a youth subculture did not really emerge until after the Second World War, although in America there were youth movements emerging in the 1930s. Howell writes, 'The roots can be seen in such things as the gradual raising of the school leaving age which has generated a group who are becoming physically and emotionally mature but who have not got the responsibility of earning a living' (Undated b: 1). Definitions of what 'youth' is vary. The United Nations, for example, describes it as the period between 15

---

[5] I collated information from both groups and when I use the phrase 'support team' it includes contributions from both of these groups.

and 24 years of age. Professionally, youth work involves young people aged 11-25. Legislation gives a range of ages of transition: you can leave school and get married at 16, learn to drive at 17, vote at 18 but cannot stand as an MP until you are 21. As an evangelical organization, there is a desire to identify a biblical basis for the ministry. In surveying some of the biblical material on youth, Howell concludes that there is a mandate for organizations such as YFC to focus on youth evangelism based on Paul's practice of approaching different people groups in a relevant way (Undated b: 2).

Research has been undertaken which shows the importance of evangelism among young people because this is the period when individuals are most likely to make a Christian commitment (Brierley 1993). It suggests that the average age at which someone becomes a Christian is 14.9 years and that this process has taken an average of 3.8 years. With the average length of service for YFC staff being less than that, many will not see the harvest of seeds that have been sown.

Cultural conditions affect the work of YFC. The initial survey identified aspects of youth culture that aid the work. One such aspect is the spiritual openness and search for purpose and meaning in life of young people. Another is their flexibility to adapt to a changing environment. The importance of the peer group and commitment to friends can be helpful in evangelism as personal contact is often the most effective way of communicating the gospel. However, the peer group can have a negative impact on the task. For example, young people are reluctant to show an interest or respond to a gospel challenge in front of their friends.

Some cultural conditions can make the task of the youth worker or youth evangelist more difficult. A lack of purpose and apathy can make it difficult to interest young people in activities or relationships with youth workers. Young people can also choose to escape from the difficulties of their lives through substance abuse. Communicating to anyone who is intoxicated or influenced by drugs is very difficult, and the sorrows often outnumber the joys in these instances. The breakdown in family and society structures has led to a lack of trust and a negative approach to authority. This can affect the perception of a young person towards a youth worker and make it harder to build relationships.

As an evangelistic organization, it is important to look at reasons why young people do not become Christians. Those reasons that can have a direct affect on the work are discussed below. Others are shared with all ages such as the diversity of activities now possible on a Sunday and the pursuit of other types of spiritual experience that are available. One reason suggested in our survey was the perceived irrelevance of the church and Christianity to many young people. The way the church is portrayed in the media, particularly on television programmes popular with young people, can contribute to this. An example of this is the portrayal of Christians on the television soap *Eastenders*. A petition was started by two youth workers, supported by the Evangelical Alliance, complaining about media portrayal of Christianity (*Church Times* 30.1.98: 6).

The attitude some in the church have to the issues raised by youth work and outreach can make it difficult to run effective youth work for those outside the church. An example of this is problems caused by vandalism that makes churches wary of working with young people. Some work is stopped prematurely and this leaves the young people feeling betrayed and dismissive of the church.

For some young people, the cost of becoming a Christian in terms of a changed lifestyle can make them reluctant to do so. In the past, there has been a tendency to focus on what Christians should or should not do and to be legalistic in presenting Christianity. A fresh approach may be needed in a changing culture.

This brief review has mainly focused on young people generally. Research that looks at young people from a specific Christian context is also useful. A survey by Agape, an organization that works with young people and students, highlights ten important findings about church going young people today.[6] Three of them are very pertinent to YFC. These are that young people are uncertain about absolute truth, they may not pray and probably do not read the Bible, and they may leave church in the next few years. YFC tries to support the church in working with young people and these findings suggest that the organization needs to be more serious about discipleship. As an evangelical organization, the concept of truth and the importance of regular prayer and Bible reading are fundamental. Without an understanding of these aspects of Christianity, it may be more difficult for young people to sustain faith into adult life. These findings may suggest that, for some, church going is just a developmental phase, not a life-long vocation. This is an area of concern and needs to be addressed. Whether YFC is the organization to do this is a different issue, others may have more experience and skills in this area such as the Church Pastoral Aid Society, whose main emphasis in youth work is supporting church-based work.

However, YFC's holistic approach to evangelism does incorporate discipleship. Some of the successful strategies for discipleship include the growing emphasis on one-to-one relationships

---

[6] See *Quadrant* Autumn 1997 for full details (Brierley *et al.*).

in youth work. Some describe this as discipling, others would talk about mentoring. These approaches would include a worker being a role model and providing support. Giving young people the means to make life choices consistent with their faith helps spiritual growth. Seeing how adults do this can be helpful. Encouraging young people to find a meaningful spirituality and outworking of their relationship with God is important. There is an increasing experimentation in worship with young people using images, meditation, silence, and active responses. As well as developing relevant worship, young people need to be incorporated into the life and ministry of the church. They also need to be challenged and given exposure to wider issues in the community and beyond.

Understanding the Context - YFC

In looking at the results of the questionnaire, YFC's strengths and weaknesses were considered. Strengths were identified, by the support team, in four main areas. The first is the credible youth work done through local ministries. Another is schools work, which includes assemblies, lessons, clubs, Christian Unions, and relationship building. A commitment to young people outside of the church, seen in a variety of youth work projects, is a third. The last is the focus on discipleship, particularly for volunteers on training programmes.

The support team then identified the main organizational weaknesses out of the many mentioned. It was interesting to note that it seemed much easier to identify weaknesses than strengths. There was a strong feeling from some that there has been a lack of emphasis from the national movement on relational youth work. The term relational youth work in this context means an approach to youth work based on individual relationships with young people, usually with the young people themselves setting the agenda for the content and progress of the relationship. A specific term YFC uses to describe this sort of work is 'incarnational'. In YFC, this term has often been applied specifically to workers who live alongside the young people they work with, rather than travelling in to do a certain number of sessions per week. It is the type of work envisaged by YFC's 'Demonstration' category of evangelism. As the strategy document states: 'Demonstration covers the incarnational nature of evangelism. To be where young people are; to love unconditionally and to serve; to be the people of God; to be living sacrifices' (Sheppard 1993:14). The two other organizational weaknesses identified were a lack of follow up and failure to turn evangelistic success to lasting discipleship and the setting of unrealistic objectives and targets. This has often been the case with new projects and, unfortunately, with the finance for them!

The last major weakness identified was an emphasis on 'grasslands' not 'jungle'. This phrase is used to mean that most work tends to be in suburban areas rather than in the inner city or outer urban estates. The terms 'grasslands' and 'jungle' are from the strategy document of 1993 which states that:

> We believe God is calling us to the hard work of entering the jungle of youth culture and establishing there the Kingdom of God. This will mean a bias to the poor, to the needy, to the under-privileged in our society, seeking to develop a radical new edge to the work. This will require us being pro-active in choosing inner-city and urban ministries (Sheppard 1993: 6).

The early history of YFC in Birmingham is a good example of this issue. In the past, there have been two local ministries, one in Sutton Coldfield and the other which started in Kings Norton, both of which are predominantly pleasant outer suburbs. In recent years, work has developed in urban priority areas. This is an historic issue rather than a policy one. YFC has usually only started work where there has been a local initiative to initiate such work. It has been easier to start a new YFC project in the grasslands because there is more finance to be found in such areas. In recent years, this has changed a little as YFC has, in some instances, been able to access money from Government initiatives such as the Single Regeneration Budget. In the past, a Leadership Team member was responsible for urban areas and there are now some pioneer initiatives in such areas with some national funding. This post was made redundant in a restructuring programme in 1996, and a project linked to Youth for Christ was developed to continue trying to initiate work in urban areas with disadvantaged or excluded young people. This was an example of the way such work was not seen as core to the objectives of the organization.

As an organization that works with people, personnel are the main resource that YFC needs. The survey would not have been complete without considering this aspect. However, this has to be set against a high staff turnover and lack of bonding to the movement. At the end of 1995, the average length of service of staff was 3.5 years. This is not long when compared with the length of time a minister would stay in one church or the demands of relational youth work. Unfortunately, staff do not always feel they have a conducive working environment. Among weaknesses highlighted were poor support and pastoral care, lack of accountability, poor supervision, and an ineffective approach to equal opportunities. This can mean that staff are not fulfilling their potential and YFC may be wasting some of its most valuable asset. This is particularly a problem in urban areas. Staff initially go intending to stay for five to ten years. This is seen as a reasonable length of time by local people and churches, but workers often give up before they have reached this goal. The failure to sustain such work and workers is a valid and real concern.

1997 was YFC's Jubilee Year,[7] and staff were asked to think through how YFC's ministry could celebrate this. There was a desire to see some of the Old Testament principles of the Year of Jubilee applied to YFC, and the lack of work amongst the poor and marginalized was noted as an issue to be considered. Alongside this, the desire to be effective in the urban 'jungle' as well as the 'grasslands', YFC needed to consider its responsibility to urban young people. YFC has very little work solely focused in urban priority type places and those who are based there are often self-funding. The organization has not been successful in retaining staff long term in such situations and has not been good at supporting such staff. If YFC is to fulfil the mandate to bring good news to young people in Britain effectively then an ability to do this in the city needs to be demonstrated. In the current culture, YFC cannot expect young people to come to events, there is a need to go and search them out.

Concerns Arising from the Questionnaire
It became clear, as we looked at the results, that people were both the strength and the weakness of the organization. We felt that further work should have a focus on workers. One of the problems highlighted was that of managers being absorbed with the vision at the expense of pastoral care of workers in their department. Another was the relatively short-term nature of many workers commitment to YFC. Stress and burnout is an identified problem. We were keen to look at ways that people could be helped in addressing these factors.

From exploring personnel weaknesses came a desire to explore what was necessary for workers to be effective. We were concerned that the short stay of staff may relate to structural issues in the organization rather than the actual work that staff are involved in. We chose the term 'fruitfulness' as one which adequately reflected our concern about the effectiveness of workers. Wanting to gain a biblical perspective, the parable of the sower was used as a starting point for helping to identify what makes a ministry fruitful. This exercise was also undertaken with a wider group of YFC staff as part of a training event. Out of this study, we identified conditions that were helpful or necessary for continued fruitfulness in ministry. This was an area that we identified for further work to be done, as we saw that YFC could

---

[7] Celebrating fifty years of ministry.

benefit from some of the insights gained.

Another area of concern raised was how to respond to the new emphasis on a local focus to the work. The strategy discussions of the early-90s had identified a need to be effective in supporting local ministries. In the last couple of years, the issue of what to call Head Office has been raised. Some felt that 'Service Centre' more accurately reflected what was done. The name has not totally been accepted but the spirit of the term is being adopted. A history of local/national tensions was identified, along with a lack of resources and communication problems. Again, this was an area where further work could be helpful. How could Head Office, and in this instance the Training Department in particular, be more effective in serving local needs?

In this exploration of the work of YFC, some things stood out. 1997 was the jubilee of YFC and staff were encouraged throughout 1996 to look at ways in which our work could reflect some jubilee principles. YFC's current emphasis was on the 'grasslands' and not the 'jungle', which had led to an under-emphasis on relational work that was our main way of making contact with the poor and marginalized.

These were the issues and challenges most concerning us arising from the questionnaire that we might be able to address in a project originating from the Training Department for which I was responsible.

Once the questionnaire and the analysis was completed, formal collaboration of the support team within YFC ceased. At this time, YFC moved offices from Cleobury Mortimer to Halesowen and working patterns changed which meant that there were fewer opportunities to meet. There was also a restructuring of staff responsibilities that led to key members of the support team leaving YFC. I continued to have individual discussions and consultations on various issues both face to face and by e-mail. Collaboration has happened throughout the project but not in the sense of formal meetings as originally envisaged.

The situation within YFC had been analysed and a range of cocerns identified that were challenging and worthy of further investigation. The next step was to refine these into a specific problem that could be explored through an action research project that fell within my remit as the Training Manager of YFC.

Chapter 2

Identifying the Problem:
The Struggles of Incarnational
Youth Workers

> Effective Christian worship and witness requires an understanding of our cultural context, sensitivity to the needs of people, awareness of the radical demands of the gospel and a willingness to commit ourselves to it (Drane 1997: 55).

From our initial exploration, described in Chapter 1, certain key concerns emerged. These concerns included a lack of emphasis on relational work,[1] the setting of unrealistic targets and objectives, and an emphasis on 'grasslands' not 'jungle'. Other concerns were the short average length of service of staff, the need to have a specific focus on the poor and marginalized in YFC's Jubilee year, and the importance of understanding the cultural context of youth work. Consideration of these concerns led to the identification of a problem that could be addressed.

The problem, which crystallised many of these concerns, was around YFC's support of urban youth ministry. The problem related to YFC's core vision, the ability to 'Take good news relevantly to every

---

[1] This involves long-term relationship building with young people.

young person in Britain'. It covered the personnel issues raised, involved work with the poor and marginalized, was based in the 'jungle', and was an area of work where often unrealistic objectives have been set.

YFC has some workers involved in what is often known (within the organization) as incarnational youth ministry, meaning that workers have chosen to move into an urban priority area to live and work amongst the young people there. This group of workers particularly focussed the major issues that had been identified. These workers had been a cause of concern for some time. There was a failure to retain and sometimes recruit such workers, and it was acknowledged they had feelings of isolation. Through consultation with colleagues, the problem was defined more precisely as:

> Youth for Christ is failing to support and retain sufficient workers to be involved in long-term incarnational urban youth ministry.

This gave rise to a project title of *A Theology for Urban Youth Work*, which seemed to be the heart of the issue: the lack of support giving rise to the problem of retention can only be addressed from a strong theological basis.

Why this Problem?

There were several reasons for choosing this problem, some of which began to emerge from the questionnaire as reported above. Other factors contributed to a sense of this being the right problem to consider. The main factor was that YFC was in the process of restructuring the national organization. With a primary focus on the Head Office and national work of Youth for Christ being there to facilitate the work of YFC locally. This introduced the concept of a Service Centre. With this in mind, focusing on a problem where a national ministry could facilitate local ministry seemed to be important. Focusing attention on one particular type of local ministry could enable results of a project to be more clearly evaluated. It could also establish an approach that would benefit other areas of local ministry.

As described earlier, the concern that YFC's work was based more in the 'grasslands' than the urban 'jungle' was one that ran across the organization, particularly as YFC looked to celebrate its jubilee with a concern for the poor and marginalized as implied in the biblical concept. Moving the Head Office in May 1996 from the Shropshire countryside to the Black Country was seen as symbolic of this desire.

YFC have had a limited amount of work in urban priority areas. The main project set up by YFC nationally has struggled with recruiting and retaining staff. Several people left before their original commitment had elapsed. With increasing urbanization, it was vital that YFC learn how to effectively resource and equip staff for urban ministry.

The last reason for choosing the problem of supporting and retaining incarnational youth workers was that it could be addressed through my role as Training Manager. Other problems that may have been good to pursue, such as those around the conversion and follow up of young people, are the responsibility of others. I work in a Human Resources Department and this problem has implications for training and personnel, which is within my remit and which may give the opportunity to broaden the understanding of the job as it currently exists.

Clarifying the Term 'Incarnational Youth Ministry'

In the context of this book, incarnational youth ministry refers (as it did historically at that point in YFC) to workers who live and work in urban priority areas involved primarily in relational youth work. Gerali provides a definition or description of 'incarnation' that could be owned by such workers:

> Incarnation is a cornerstone of God's program for the world. God took on flesh. Without incarnation we have no salvation, no relationship with God, no church, and no ministry. We cannot attempt to create strategies around incarnation without clearly seeing that incarnation – for those already clothed in flesh – is about invading, understanding, and becoming a part of a social context known as a community. Incarnation cannot be understood apart from the context of community (2001: 285).

Whilst one may want to disagree with Gerali about the possibility of a relationship with God outside of the incarnation, or of a term such as 'invading' used in connection with youth work, this definition does emphasise the contextual nature of the work and the importance of understanding this as a basis for developing youth work.

The term 'incarnational' is used to describe other types of youth work outside that being explored in this book. This is done most notably by Pete Ward, in *Youthwork and the Mission of God* (1997c) who uses the term as part of a discussion of an approach to relational youth work. He describes a five stage approach to relationship building but this is not dependent on living in the area where one is working, it is about building relationships and seeking to present the gospel in a culturally relevant way (1997: Ch. 3). A very good exposition of what incarnational youth work is in practice is to be found in Bob Holman's

Kids at the Door (1981), which was written up as part of a series of
social work practice books.[2] Although the book does not give details of
Bob's Christian faith as a motivation for the work, the methodology of
moving on to an estate and creatively hanging around and building
relationships is at the heart of incarnational youth work.

Detached youth work is the term given to an approach where
youth workers go and meet young people on their patch and let the
young people set the pace of the relationship and often the agenda of
the contact. Incarnational youth workers may well use this as one of
their approaches to youth work, but it is only a part of what they do.
They go to 'be' in an area as well as 'do', and seek to identify the needs
and issues of young people and develop provision or interventions in
response to this. They become part of the community rather than
professionals who visit it during work hours and then retreat to their
homes.

Incarnational Youth Ministry in YFC

Establishing incarnational urban youth ministry in YFC has not been
straightforward. There are various reasons why there is a problem with
the way that incarnational urban youth ministry is perceived.
Historically, YFC has been an organization that has been involved in
big missions and proclamation evangelism, expecting people to come
and hear the gospel. This approach does not work in urban priority
areas. Here, long-term relationship building is seen as paramount, and
this is done on the young people's turf. As this is not high profile work,
it does not always get recognized in an organization like YFC. There
are also problems in the way that some of the urban projects have been
set up. Workers in these projects were, in the past, expected to be self-
funding, whereas other YFC staff were on a salary (although often
raising a significant percentage of that salary themselves). When
projects have been set up nationally, there has also been a problem in
determining whether workers in such projects are national or local staff.
This status determines who pays for their attendance at national events,
for example, which has an impact on the amount of money to be raised
and project budgets. It also affects perceptions of who or what should
be involved in the support of the project. National Directors of YFC
have often set up projects in areas where they have had a keen interest.
Thus one National Director set up an urban priority area project, but
when he moved on, its status as a national YFC project became
uncertain. It is now perceived as a local ministry. The national situation
changed since this thesis was started and a growing awareness of the

---

[2] Bob Holman had previously been an academic training social workers.

need for work in urban areas has led to YFC nationally appointing staff to work in two major British cities facilitating a range of youth work although with a hope that in the longer term local funding will be found.

A sign that incarnational youth work was moving on to the national agenda in YFC was the establishment, in 1997, of a 'demonstration' group to contribute to national strategy. As a member of YFC's National Strategy Group, I was part of the demonstration sub-group. As our vision statement we said we wanted 'Demonstration to be firmly established as an equal partner within the 4 D's'. Demonstration work was defined as that which is relational, is with those who are marginalized, and includes social action. The type of youth work discussed in this thesis, living and working within a community, was defined as presence/incarnational/lifestyle. A wide range of proposals was made by the sub-group and some of them were taken forward as part of the national strategy, for example a special training programme for volunteers wanting to work in an urban setting.

Insights into the Youth Workers' Situation
Before responding to the problem, I reflected on some of the concerns that arose from the questionnaire or through personal contact with incarnational youth workers. Most workers in urban projects are not local people, they have relocated. Many are also middle class and are choosing a location and lifestyle very different to that which their peers have. The issue of classism is an interesting one in this context. It adds to the cross-cultural nature of the mission that is being undertaken: not only is the local youth culture different to that of the worker, often there is a middle class worker relocating to a working class area. Classism is also very relevant when considering self-funding workers. If you come from a family and church who are poor then where does the finance to live come from? It is very easy to tell people to trust God and then accuse them of lack of faith if the finance does not come in. Such accusations can come from those who just need to drop a subtle hint to parents or the Church Secretary to obtain the finance they need. This is not meant to query the ability of God to provide for individuals, but reflects the actual experience of workers. Issues of class also affect what identification with the local community means. If you have the resources to leave any time you want to or the ability to get places in the better schools, for example, how does that affect the level of identification?

For workers who have chosen a different lifestyle, there are still the social, economic, and psychological consequences of that choice to be faced. It is important that these are taken into account when YFC looks at how to prepare and resource workers for such a ministry. Socially, there is the difficulty of finding friendship and support in an area where you are perceived, or perceive yourself to be, different from your neighbours. Often, in these areas, churches are not strong and the few who could offer some support have many demands on them. When workers have young children there are such problems as language and accents, the schools they attend, the opportunities they may be missing. Personal safety is a concern that is very real, particularly for women and children. How can supportive relationships be built and maintained? Who is there to 'off load' on, to talk through doubts with? Who pays the telephone bill when support is most readily available many miles away?

Economically, if you are raising your own support you could potentially be better off than someone on a low YFC salary. In reality, a lot of time is being devoted by workers to ensuring that this money comes in. While some would argue that it keeps a worker dependent on God, there is the other problem that it distracts the worker from their work and can keep them permanently anxious. The possibility of claiming social security benefits is one to be considered, also. It is a culture shock for many. For some, it is an ethical problem; should the church or state support me? Historically there has been little theological reflection to help workers think through or resolve some of these complex issues.

Psychological pressures will vary from individual to individual. However, it is hard for most of us to continue when we feel misunderstood, and undervalued. Identifying ways to mitigate this will be important. Others will think they are seen as somehow second class because they have not preached to five hundred people this week, recorded a CD, or whatever is the current measure of success within the organization. This highlights the importance of finding ways of measuring and valuing the work done by incarnational urban youth workers.

Researching the Problem

Part of this problem discernment process involved some background reading, research, and discussion on relevant topics that went on alongside the action research project contained in the next chapter. Here, a range of topics relating to the identification and exploration of the problem will be considered. The purpose of this was to try to identify some of the resources that would help a fuller understanding of the problem, as well as identifying potential responses and areas for further exploration. Further theological research was undertaken subsequently to the action research project, as the realization developed that a fuller theological rationale for incarnational youth work needed developing. This work is contained in the latter chapters of this book. In the rest of this chapter the topics of mission, jubilee, urban, incarnational ministry, and incarnational youth ministry will be briefly considered.

Mission

Mission is the main activity of YFC. As an evangelical organization, a biblical perspective on mission is important in shaping its understanding. 'Taking good news relevantly' usually means telling people about Jesus, through words or actions. It is the reason why incarnational urban youth workers are there. To be there effectively, they need to have a good understanding of Christ's mission and methods. Previous theological training is not a pre-requisite of becoming a YFC staff member and sometimes staff are sent out without the theoretical and theological underpinning of their practical skills. An explanation of the importance of this understanding is provided by *Youth A Part*:

> The Church's mission must always be focused on our understanding of Christ. Christ reveals the true nature of the relationship of God, the Church and the gospel to the world. The nature, needs and dignity of human (in this case young human) life are established by reference to him. His incarnation, ministry, death and resurrection establish both the content of the Church's mission and the methods by which it carries out that mission (Church of England 1996: 34).

More specifically, YFC is involved in evangelism. Basic teaching for anyone involved with YFC should be to understand what evangelism is and what it is not. Experience from a cross-cultural perspective brings insight for YFC's incarnational urban youth workers. Donovan makes the distinction between evangelization and propaganda that seeks to make clones (1982: 189-93). It is important that staff respect the right of individuals to make their own choice in response to the gospel. Marginalized young people are a vulnerable group and there can be a danger of manipulation or other forms of spiritual abuse. This is an issue that is increasingly being recognized by the introduction and development of child protection policies. Connected to this is the need for incarnational workers to distinguish the non-negotiables of the gospel from the cultural version often presented. Sometimes what is rejected by young people is the context or medium the gospel is presented in, not the gospel itself. YFC workers need to be equipped with the ability to communicate the gospel effectively in terms of the culture they are working in. A starting point for this was identified in conversation with Margaret Walsh, a nun who has been involved in urban incarnational ministry for over ten years. She believed that there was a need to immerse oneself in the local culture first before beginning any activities.[3] Obviously, to communicate within a particular culture requires an understanding and sensitive appreciation of that culture as a prerequisite. This may need to be part of a research phase for a new project being established and induction for a worker joining a project.

Jubilee

Jubilee is still a concept that is used today in relation to celebrating anniversaries and was prominent in 2002 because of Queen Elizabeth II's Golden Jubilee. Outside of this the most significant use of the term recently was in the campaign to release third world countries from debt as a celebration of the year 2000. This latter use related to a biblical understanding of the term and was picked up by by YFC during preparations for their jubilee year in 1997. Four things were supposed to happen in a jubilee year, according to the Pentateuch. They were: to leave the land fallow; to release people from their debts; to free slaves; and lastly to return family property.[4] The aspect that YFC chose to focus on was releasing people from their debts, and ex-volunteers who still owed YFC money were written to and released from what they owed.

What was interesting, during this period in YFC, as discovering that some commentators believed that the concept of jubilee contributed to the theology of Jesus. Sloan writes:

> The Year of Jubilee figured significantly in the theology of Jesus as it is related in the Gospel of Luke. The rejection of Jesus in Nazareth (4:16-30); an event which is programmatic for the Gospel of Luke, makes extensive use of themes related to the OT prescription of a Year of Jubilee (Ex 21:2-6; 23:10-12; Lev 25; Deut 15:1-18; 31:9-13), especially as those themes were already incorporated into Isaiah 58:6; 61:1-2, the text which was read and sermonically elaborated by Jesus (4:18-21). The Jubilee year is best understood as an intensified Sabbath Year, announced on the Day of Atonement every fifty years as a sabbath year of sabbath years (1992: 396).

---

[3] An account of her experience can be found in Walsh (1997).
[4] See, for example, Lev 25; Deut 15; 31:9-13.

One way in which these elements of jubilee are relevant to incarnational urban youth workers can be seen when Sanders argues that the use of these passages quoted in Luke 4 enabled the hearers to identify with them and understand that the gospel was for them. He writes: 'They would have identified, in their turn, with the poor (for they were poor), the captives (for they felt themselves captive to the Romans), the blind (for they felt like dungeon inmates who were blind), and the oppressed (for they surely were oppressed)' (1993: 22). The inference for incarnational workers is that they too have to make the gospel seem real to those who hear it from them. They need to enable young people to make connections with the gospel and to see that it has relevance to them. This would be worth developing further but is outside of the scope of this research, which is primarily focusing on supporting the workers rather than exploring the work. However, the fact that YFC were looking at ways to celebrate its jubilee added to the relevance of the project at the time. There was little work going on among the poor and the marginalized and a project that may facilitate such work fitted in well.

Urban

Urban is a term that means different things to different people. In this book, the word relates to those working in an urban priority area (UPA). These places suffer multiple deprivation and low income. Inner-city is a term that some use but this does not cover the large housing estates sometimes found on the edge of cities, such as Easterhouse in Glasgow. The main characteristics of UPAs are economic decline, physical decay, and social disintegration.[5] Harrison describes the situation:

> The poor, wherever they live, carry their own inner city round with them, like snails their shells, and every urban area has some district of some size, even if it is a single housing estate that shares the interacting problems of concentrated poverty, unemployment, bad housing and crime of the larger inner city areas (1983: 24).

This can help explain why there was a YFC long term incarnational urban youth work project in Cheltenham as well as Manchester. It can be easy to make assumptions about a geographical area, but everywhere there are pockets of deprivation that may need a different approach to youth work and mission than other places around it. This is a challenge

---

[5] An introduction to the topic of UPAs is provided by chapter 1 of *Faith in the City* a Report of the Archbishop of Canterbury's Commission on Urban Priority Areas (1985).

to YFC in each of its local ministries.

For incarnational workers in urban priority areas there are, therefore, pressures just because of the environment they are in. Bradbury describes the situation facing people who live there:

> Those who have no choice but to continue living in our inner cities can clearly expect little relief from social and political institutions in the foreseeable future for their feelings of anxiety, hopelessness and anger and that is a measure of the immensity of the pastoral task which faces the churches in UPAs (1989: 18).

This task is faced by YFC workers too. It is possible that the realities of the urban environment will not be fully understood by those who move there. It is very easy to be full of enthusiasm, particularly when you are young, for what appears to be a tough missionary situation. However, this initial zeal does not sustain a long term commitment, and YFC needs to review the ways in which it recruits and inducts workers into these situations. This pressure affects families also; Laurie Green writes of his experiences as a Vicar in inner city London:

> It is difficult to describe the terror and fear in some of these areas. My daughters have been mugged, my wife once hit rock bottom despairing of the filth and concrete facades of the place. I, like most, have had physical abuse and personal intimidation. Living in the inner city is not a romantic experience unless you find a way of cutting yourself off from its realities (1993: 5).

As well as a difficult living environment, the youth work in urban priority areas will be tough. Although published in 1983, many of the comments made in David Sheppard's *Bias to the Poor* seem as relevant today as they were when written. He comments that traditional approaches to Christian youth work that rely on commitment or issue-based work are not relevant to many urban youth. What is needed is relationship building. He observes that often the church does not understand what such youth workers are trying to do (1983: 211). It is not just the church, it is often friends and family as well, and this brings another pressure to long term incarnational urban youth workers. The experience in YFC suggests that this pressure can rarely be alleviated. Working with young people brings little status, and choosing to relocate to an urban priority area is understood by few Christians, let alone by those who have no faith. Having a clear biblical and theological rationale for the work is imperative to help sustain those who make this choice.

Incarnational Ministry

There are now few role models for 'incarnational' workers to observe. At one time a range of professionals were to be found living on the job. Sheppard believes that it is probably only the church, and I would add religious organizations, that continue to do this. He suggests that while this provides helpful opportunities for work, it does result in strain on partners and families. Sheppard also believes that workers should not be alone in such an environment (1983: 205). These suggestions of Sheppard are helpful to note. Within YFC, the families of workers usually fall outside any support mechanisms perhaps attention needs to be given to how support could be provided. In relation to the second suggestion, that workers should not be alone, the building of teams in areas is also wise. As a pioneering organization, YFC can have the tendency to forge ahead with new projects and all the consequences of the project may not be thought through. It may be helpful to take time to learn from the experience of others in similar fields.

One organization that has a long history of incarnational type work, although not specifically youth work, is the Salvation Army. They use this term of themselves, as Hick reports:

> Recently General Eva Burrows of the Salvation Army said in a BBC radio programme (1 July 1990), 'We want to be an incarnation of Christ in the world.' She did not mean that we want to be 'of one substance with God the Father' but to be Christ's dedicated servants, carrying out God's purposes on earth (1993: 104-5).

I had the opportunity to observe one of their incarnational works a few years ago and YFC could learn some principles from the work on Easterhouse. Two main things impressed me: the breadth and quality of relationships that Captain Eric Buchanan had with local people, and the presence of Christ that he brought into the situation. Particularly vivid was a sense of joy that seemed out of place in what is the most deprived area I have seen. This joy must come from his own relationship with God. It can be easy to be affected by the spirit of the local community, and YFC needs to continue to impress on its workers the absolute necessity of a relationship with God as the source of strength for the work. Another facet of Buchanan's work is described in a book about the Salvation Army:

> Their very modest little apartment is above the two halls - one for meetings, a kind of chapel and the other for various gatherings. Although it is their home, it is in fact open house to lots of people - though most folk are seen, counselled and given practical help downstairs. When they come it is always, 'A

cuppa?' - for tea is constantly available in the tiniest of kitchens (Gauntlett 1990: 204).

Having an open house is something that is debated by incarnational youth workers. The question could be asked if your home is not accessible at all to those in the community then why live in the area? Many very effective urban youth workers travel in to do their youth work. However, if the desire is to be incarnational, then surely a young person needs to be able to see a worker in a range of settings, including home, to get an idea about what Christianity really means. The disadvantage of an open home is the additional pressure this can put on a worker and their family, particularly if they have children. How can family life be maintained and availability to young people offered? There are no simple solutions to these dilemmas but they need to be worked through by incarnational workers. This is another instance where a team can be beneficial; time off can be structured while still having workers available to young people. Whatever approach is chosen, twenty-four hour availability will probably lead to burn out and this issue of accessibility needs much thought and wisdom.

As well as learning from those currently involved in incarnational work, insight can also be gained from the past. It is helpful for YFC to see female pioneers of incarnational work, as some of those who have been involved for the longest are women. Role models are an encouragement; Jackie Pullinger who worked with drug addicts in Hong Kong would be someone who inspires.[6] Another example is Dorothy Day, a journalist who converted to Catholicism and established the Catholic Worker movement. She is now being considered for canonization.[7] I have chosen to mention her in more detail because, as an evangelical organization, YFC knows little about the contribution of Catholics and the Roman Catholic Church to an understanding of mission. As an evangelical agency, there was in the past a suspicion of Catholicism that is now not nearly as apparent. A growing diversity in the spirituality of many YFC workers has led to an increasing exposure to Catholic writers such as Henri Nouwen. It is important that prejudice does not stop us from learning from those who have much to teach. Callahan provides a summary of Day's mission:

> Her call was to speak the word of God's love in deeds of love. Her solidarity with poor people was not a condescending method of handouts; she lived with them as they lived, eating

---

[6] See, for example, the new edition of her autobiography *Chasing the Dragon* (2001).
[7] See Berger (2000: 13).

food cooked for them with them and wearing the clothes donated to them. Her own concerns were socio-political; unemployment, poverty, racism and war .Her clear vision of the cost of discipleship can shed light on our efforts to bring the gospel to bear on the reality of our daily life. She inspires us to see Christ in others. Her compassionate love of neighbor is her passionate love of God (1992: 57).

Dorothy Day clearly made sacrifices because of her faith and beliefs. Her experiences can help YFC understand the nature of incarnational ministry and to explore motivations and rationale for involvement in such work.

Two main challenges arise from the statement above. The first is that 'she lived as they lived.' What does this statement mean to incarnational workers today? One example for youth workers is clothing. Even in our most deprived areas young people are still to be found wearing designer label trainers, for example. This may seem a trivial example, but a survey showed that nearly half of those 15-16 year olds interviewed believe that wearing the right clothes makes you popular.[8] Does 'living as they live' mean identification in this way or would the gospel be better served by workers not wearing expensive trainers? These are the sort of ethical decisions that face individual workers as they seek to be authentic witnesses of Christ and also culturally relevant to the young people they work amongst. The second challenge is the socio-political concern she expressed. Historically, YFC has concentrated on evangelism leaving social action for others. However, in urban priority areas, the socio-political problems can be such that they provide a real barrier to the gospel. Workers may need to address issues such as debt or racism, and need to be equipped to do so.[9] At the time this research began little training was provided to equip workers to be involved in social action. Subsequently, an annual module for urban workers was included in staff training that initially arose as an outcome of this project.

Incarnational Youth Ministry

One of the most important points to acknowledge is that incarnational youth workers are missionaries. As Borthwick says:

Imitating the incarnation means that we go into their world, listen to their cares, attempt to understand their perspectives,

---

[8] The actual figure was 49%. This statistic is from a research project called 'Himmelweit, reported in *The Sunday Times* 8.3.98: 4.

[9] This connects to the theme of jubilee and could have been another way for YFC to respond to including jubilee principles in their ministry.

join them in their pain. The incarnation of Christ establishes the model of compassion, loving others so much that we give ourselves on their behalf .Incarnational ministry towards youth means coming into their environment - family, social, educational, economic. It involves intense listening and approaching youth culture as missionaries: seeking to understand and then looking for Gospel entry points. It means 'contextualization' so as to communicate in culturally relevant ways (1997: 11-12).

Missionaries never seem to be sent straight into a new environment to work. There always seems to be a period of training and familiarisation. There is often a thought-through structure for communication and support, even if it does not always work effectively. Lessons may be learnt from established missionary agencies as to how YFC should prepare and train its workers for contextual ministry.

The benefits of long-term incarnational youth work are described by Bob Holman. These benefits include being available when the young people wanted to see them; being able to respond quickly in an emergency; gaining local knowledge about residents which gave helpful insights into the work; being close to what was happening; having frequent contact over a long period of time and being able to offer a variety of different options to the young people (1981: 79-82). These benefits would be familiar to workers on similar projects in YFC.

To be involved in long term missionary work it is important to have a strong rationale for incarnational youth ministry. Those consulted felt that a lack of a rationale can contribute to a short stay in this type of work. This helped us to see the importance of a theological dimension to YFC's work. Allan Pettie provides a very helpful explanation of what this means and the reasons it is so important: 'For me, personal theology is not a matter of choice as a frontier worker. It is a matter of survival, of identity, of motivation and of authenticity and authority' (1993: 5-6).[10] Workers need to have worked out how they deal with these areas of survival, identity, motivation, authenticity and authority in their ministry, a gap in meeting any of them may well cause problems for the worker, particularly when encountering difficulties.

---

[10] The term 'frontier' reflects the context of the work as part of a series of papers for Frontier Youth Trust. It would be seen as referring to work amongst young people who are poor and marginalized.

From Problem to Project

The point reached thus far was the identification of the problem to be investigated, that of supporting and retaining incarnational urban youth workers. Some preliminary background research had been done looking at theological and other material that related to the main issues thus far identified. The next stage was to design and implement an action research project designed to explore and address the problem. Theological material would be revisited at a later date to help put the findings of the action research into context and to develop some implications of, and insights from, the research.

Chapter 3

Moving from Reflection to Action: Exploring how to Support Incarnational Urban Youth Workers

Urban theology is also a form of practical theology because it takes the current situation with all its complexities, structures, and ambiguity seriously, and begins to fashion relevant, practical and systemic action (Duffield 1997: 22).

It is clear that the task of reaching young people in urban priority areas is an urgent one; supporting and retaining the workers to achieve it is what YFC have found difficult. This problem, having been identified, needed addressing. It was to be addressed through a six-month project that was designed to try to change the current situation. Three goals were set to help this process:

Goal 1: to identify the needs of those involved in long term incarnational urban youth ministry

Goal 2: to respond to the needs of those involved in long-term incarnational urban youth ministry within the remit of the Training Department

Goal 3: to help workers in the field develop a personal theology that sustains fruitfulness in long-term incarnational urban youth ministry

Goal 1

The first goal, to identify the needs of the target group was chosen in order to gain an idea of what was required by long-term incarnational urban youth workers. Identifying their needs would be crucial to supporting and retaining such workers. Apart from wanting to respond from a place of understanding needs, a main purpose of this goal was consciousness-raising within the wider movement. Although YFC talk about the difficulties of being involved in ministry and particularly about working in our inner cities, for example, not much time is spent appreciating the needs of these workers. Without being aware of the needs of workers, it is difficult to have appropriate support mechanisms in place. There have been structural problems in some of the urban projects. Sometimes, focusing on these has obscured some of the wider issues pertinent to the specific sort of ministry that they are involved in. Identifying the needs and getting some mutual agreement about them would give us a basis to develop a way forward. If YFC is to support and retain workers then identification of and a response to their needs is necessary.

Within the time-scale of the project, what could realistically be hoped for was that the issues be clearly identified and this information disseminated. Focusing on two local projects representing different approaches to incarnational urban youth ministry within YFC could accomplish this. This gives a specific field in which to research.

We sought to identify the needs of the target group by facilitating a dialogue. This was to be done by drawing up a questionnaire as a framework for discussions. This questionnaire would be distributed to relevant parties. They included the National Director, a worker at a project close to one that we were working with, an urban specialist, and a support team member. In order to get more detailed feedback from incarnational urban youth work projects, I would visit them with a support team member. It was decided to use a questionnaire to make the results of the survey easier to compile and to ensure that each person and project consulted had the opportunity to respond to the same range of questions. The idea of taking a support team member with me was primarily to help with recording, to ensure that all the relevant information was noted for later reflection. Using e-mail in YFC usually ensures a response, and that is why this method of distributing the questionnaires was used.

We also sought to pursue our first goal by collating and disseminating the results of the dialogue. This was to be done through writing a report and distributing it to relevant parties. Once the information had been collected, it was important to see that it was collated and given to the appropriate people. The report was to be compiled by me, after receiving feedback from the support team who saw a first draft.

Goal 2

The second goal, followed on from the first. It was to respond to the needs of those involved in long term incarnational urban youth ministry within the remit of the Training Department. This goal was particularly related to my job within YFC. As I had taken on this role relatively recently, I also wanted to have the opportunity to explore and possibly refine or develop the role.

The second goal sought to respond to the needs of workers by engaging in a training needs analysis of the workers. In order to identify potential areas for training, a group brainstorm with each project would be done to identify the skills/knowledge/attitude necessary in incarnational urban youth ministry. The second goal also involved writing a training policy for staff involved in this ministry. This was to be done by analysing the results of the training needs analysis and drawing up a training needs matrix. A training needs matrix identifies the areas staff need training in. Information obtained from work towards Goal 1 would be incorporated where necessary.

Our plan was to ensure that the Training Department made an effective response to some of the issues identified. It would also establish a clear framework by which new workers could be assessed for training needs and a relevant training programme devised for them. It was hoped that the system would be appropriate for other groups of workers. As all this was clearly within my job responsibility, I undertook to do the work.

Goal 3

The third goal was to help workers in the field develop a personal theology that sustains fruitfulness in long-term incarnational urban youth ministry. In concrete terms, it sought to explore a more holistic approach to effectiveness in ministry. This would involve seeking to identify a theology, and from this a framework for ministry that facilitates long term fruitfulness in this work. The average length of service of YFC workers at the time this research project was started was three and a half years. This is not long in the context of building relationships with young people and winning the trust and respect of people living in urban areas. If this is to change, then YFC need to look and see if there are things that can be done that will help workers stay longer.

Whenever people are engaged in ministry, it is important that they have a theology that sustains their continued involvement. This should have an outworking in the way that ministry is approached. It is also important for workers to be able to communicate to managers and supporters the choices that they make and the reasons for them, so as not to be misunderstood or misinterpreted. If choices are based on a theological understanding of what they do then this should help workers have a clear rationale for their involvement in the work. Having a clear theological understanding of the work also helps with recruitment. This is because projects have a clear vision to impart and a thought-through strategy for encouraging long-term involvement in ministry. This is seen as particularly pertinent for those involved in long term incarnational urban youth ministry, with the many pressures and difficulties they face. If it were not for a strong sense of God's call, and a clear theological understanding of what they do, some of the workers who have remained in long-term incarnational urban youth ministry would not be there now. It also gives the opportunity to develop materials and approaches that can again be applied to other groups of workers.

So, in our third goal we sought to help workers in the field develop a personal theology that sustains fruitfulness in long-term incarnational urban youth ministry by identifying what fruitfulness means in this kind of work. This was to be done through Bible study and discussion, starting with the parable of the sower. A brainstorm with each project would be done exploring how fruitfulness can be measured in their context. This would cover their youth project, their work with young people and the workers themselves. Others would also reflect on fruitfulness. All this would be summarised in a paper on fruitfulness in long-term incarnational urban youth ministry.

We also sought to achieve the third goal by reflecting on biblical and other models to enable individuals to develop their theological understanding of incarnational urban youth ministry. This was to be accomplished through biblical and theological study and consultation with experienced practitioners. Material would be provided to help workers develop a personal theological statement. A forum to raise issues identified was proposed.

Evaluation Procedures

The last stage of our project plan was to identify ways of evaluating goal achievement.

Goal 1 was evaluated by the production of a report summarising the findings of the research. The completion of each of the strategies could be measured quantitatively in terms of the process outlined. Qualitative evaluation could be done by asking participants to give feedback relating to the specific activities they were engaged in.

Goal 2 was evaluated by analysing current training provision and policy in respect of needs identified and then comparing this with policy and training available after the project had finished. This enabled us to see to what extent the Training Department had been able to respond to needs identified.

Goal 3 was evaluated by personal interviews and written statements at the end of the process.

An Initial Hurdle

Having planned the action research project and worked out how to evaluate it, the next stage was to begin. However, the story of the project reflects something of the problems that YFC face in long-term incarnational urban youth ministry. Although the plan was to do a case study based around two projects, there were unexpected difficulties with this. I had hoped to work with a project that a close colleague of mine was to join. She was exploring the restructuring of her current national post to include some locally based work. She made the decision not to proceed with this plan when the team leader moved on because of difficulties that it did not seem possible to resolve. The team leader who left was the other person I knew relatively well: in an unstable situation, where the future of that local project was being re-evaluated, it was inappropriate for our team to be involved there. Another project was one of the earliest incarnational youth work projects established by YFC, but unfortunately there were structural problems there with some differences of opinion between workers and managers. I decided to continue with this project because some of the workers were interested in the research, but expected that things would not go according to plan. This project will be referred to as Forgreen.[1] Their mission statement declared that, 'We work with young people to bring wholeness into every aspect of their lives, through encouragement and teaching, as we believe Jesus would. In particular we target young

---

[1] I am using false names for the projects and pseudonyms for the workers. This is to protect the confidentiality of workers involved, who spoke freely and honestly to me.

people who are disadvantaged and marginalised by society.'[2] A third project, where the workers had trained with YFC, but were now church based, was identified. This project, based in an urban priority area parish, will be referred to as All Saints. They summarised their purpose and aims as 'To serve young people at their point of need' and 'To encourage their full development'.[3] Work was primarily done with these latter two projects, but workers from similar projects in YFC contributed in other ways through both personal conversation and e-mail. Some of the difficulties experienced reflect problems that led us to identify these groups of workers as a target for the project in the first place.

The Story of Goal 1
The task began by seeking to identify the needs of those involved in long-term incarnational urban youth ministry. I devised a questionnaire that looked at the needs of projects, workers, recruitment, retention, the role of YFC and the Training Department. This questionnaire was circulated to a cross section of workers who were involved in, or had management responsibilities for, this work as well as my support team. Visits were made to Forgreen and All Saints to look at the questions in detail. Generally, people like to be asked their opinion on issues. This helped ensure a high response rate.

Some responses to the questionnaire showed a clear understanding of the issues. For one senior YFC worker, there was an understanding of some of the pressures faced: 'Urban work is very different to other sorts of ministry, and I think they are dealing with so many social issues that are very real that often they pick up the culture they are living in which can be very depressing.'[4] The need for facilities for retreat and spiritual and emotional refreshment were added to this remark. However, at that time YFC had no policy about or way of responding to that need. One person commented that the work

> wears on a person emotionally, physically and spiritually. If there isn't a clear calling and a place to 'recharge' then it would be difficult to stay. Also, since most of the workers are young, they marry, think about kids, etc. and leave because of the

[2] This is found on a strategic plan dated 12.2.96 prepared by the project leader. For reasons of confidentiality it is not included in the bibliography.
[3] From an A5 flyer sent by Morag on 21.3.96.
[4] Questionnaire response. For reasons of confidentiality, names will not normally be identified. This was part of the agreement to enable people to speak freely.

pressure of work.[5]

YFC needs to ask if it is being realistic in whom it expects to do this sort of work, in what conditions, and for how long. Ways of encouraging potential workers to think through what is involved in being committed to such work need also to be considered. The difficulty of the work situation was such that another worker commented that people leave 'Because they get burnt out through too much to do and so little support.'[6] Other reasons for workers leaving were identified. These included deficiencies in the initial briefing and selection process; being disheartened by limited success; lack of finance; no long term strategy for the work; little attention given to personal development; limited or no spiritual support, leaving the worker open to fall into temptation.[7] It is sad that many of these difficulties could be addressed by better management and a more thorough process of establishing projects. A pioneering spirit can be commendable but pioneers can 'die' if adequate preparations have not been made to meet the conditions. One of the issues contributing to this was the lack of understanding and recognition from churches for long term incarnational urban youth ministry. A support team member commented that:

> Many local churches or 'The Church' would not give a person a sense that their work is needed. A church would need to be looking beyond the end of their pews to be willing to make the sacrifice and commitment for a long-term work. There are not quick results and our society is accustomed to that.

Using the questionnaire format, discussions also took place about the issues with those involved in long term incarnational urban youth work projects. 'Sustainable Infrastructure', was a phrase used by the project leader at Forgreen which sums up much of what was felt to be needed by the projects. This embraced such things as an effective and active management, and non-managerial support and encouragement. In Forgreen, much of this needed to come from outside the immediate work area, because people where they were working did not have the necessary skills. At All Saints, there were church members who could offer such support.

As well as practical support for a project, a network of support

---

[5] Questionnaire completed by support team member.
[6] Questionnaire completed by worker with some responsibility for an urban project.
[7] Questionnaire completed by urban specialist.

for workers personally is also important. One of the workers at All Saints had grown up in the area and this was seen as a distinct advantage. She already had a network of support and friendship, including parents, who could assist with childcare, for example. At Forgreen, the full time workers moved into the area and this friendship and support had been hard to find. This need was described by a worker at All Saints who had relocated from a couple of hundred miles. She described it as finding 'A place of security and secure relationships when everything else is insecure'.[8] How projects are set up will influence the extent to which this is possible. It is important that YFC try to identify how to go about facilitating a support structure and learn from previous mistakes. Having one strong supportive church, where there is fellowship and some understanding, does seem to provide a degree of security and stability to work out from. It also means that there is a church structure that can facilitate the integration of young people who are exploring the Christian faith.

The story of one worker who found herself involved in this sort of work shows how it is not always a conscious decision to end up there.[9] Morag felt that she had made a series of small decisions, which were part of a journey that resulted in her being involved at All Saints long term. It was not a job she applied for, but a process including a YFC Training Programme. YFC need to be aware of the different ways people arrive in this work. Support should be given in their decision making to enable them to be realistic about the consequences of their choices. Morag described an aspect of this. She commented that she had not made a vow of voluntary poverty, it was just a consequence of other decisions. That can be hard to cope with, particularly when peers are in successful jobs and the worker's family do not share their beliefs and values. In this sort of situation, a project may just evolve around a worker, rather than being more formally established. This makes deficiencies in support more likely as things happen on an ad hoc basis.

Even if workers are clear about their needs it does not always mean that they will be met. Pastoral care is a problem with one family member expressing the view that no one wants to take responsibility for this.[10] The outcome of lack of pastoral care was not feeling valued for what they did. Eventually, this couple found some support outside of the area, but it was several years before this happened.

At both Forgreen and All Saints, there was a strong feeling that

---

[8] Comment made on a visit to All Saints in February 1997.

[9] Comments in this paragraph taken from a conversation at All Saints in February 1997.

[10] Comment made by a spouse on a visit to Forgreen in April 1997.

it was not the work with young people that was stressful; it was the lack of adequate support and management. One worker was looking for a management committee who had 'fire in their bellies for the kids', who were stakeholders in the work.[11] Some of the difficulties in recruiting such people for the committee were perceived to relate to the way the Forgreen project was set up. There had been too little consultation with local churches, who then felt no ownership of the work. This was not a problem at All Saints where the project was an integral part of the church.

The main outcome of this part of our project plan was that the workers felt listened to and able to express their joys, concerns, and frustrations. It enabled them to step back and reflect on their situation. It can be helpful having a neutral party involved facilitating discussion and introducing a structured time to reflect on the work and how workers are perceiving their own ministry. One worker wrote: 'We have struggled over many issues over the last year! Although we are moving positively on many of them it was good to talk through and assess where we were on some of this stuff.'[12] Involving others not directly involved in the work, in the information gathering process, meant that a broader perception was gained. This also meant that some of the comments from workers were put into a wider and fresh perspective.

A report was written which summarised the dialogue from both the questionnaires and the visits. The main points are outlined below. The key issue relating to projects was the need for effective local management. This raises questions for YFC of how it trains and equips those, often volunteers, who provide management in these settings. A wider management issue is what support national YFC can offer in these situations. For workers, the main concern was pastoral care in the widest sense. Included in this was the need to receive encouragement and affirmation in a situation where this does not always come from the work. This again demonstrates the need for establishing a range of support options for workers, which should include home church, local church, and someone from outside to act as an independent support – non-managerial supervisor in youth work terms.

Motivation for entering this sort of work and the sense of call are factors that influence recruitment and retention. Discerning this call and motivation is not always easy. YFC has a clear policy for recruitment, but there is more work to do in assessing people's

---

[11] Comment made by the project leader in Forgreen on a visit in April 1997.
[12] This and the next comment are from Evaluation Sheets completed after initial visit to All Saints.

readiness for long-term incarnational urban youth ministry. However, deficiencies in both management and pastoral care have led to workers leaving despite still feeling a vocation to the work. It was felt that there were unrealistic expectations of YFC from some projects but also that promises had not always been fulfilled. Being listened to and raising the profile in national publications and at events were issues that were important in taking the concerns of workers forward. Those involved in long-term incarnational urban youth ministry generally appreciated what the Training Department was doing. However, there was a desire for it to be more pro-active in identifying suitable opportunities and resources.

The benefit of the report that was produced was that it will assist YFC in learning lessons for new projects that are being set up; particularly looking at the needs of the workers and the way that management should be structured.

The Story of Goal 2
We next considered how the needs of the target group could be met within the remit of the Training Department. The first goal had highlighted needs relating to all aspects of the work, this goal was looking specifically at training related needs. The first task in achieving this goal was to conduct a training needs analysis. An approach was chosen which focused on identifying the necessary competencies under the headings knowledge, skills, and attitudes. This is a widely accepted way of analysing a youth worker post.[13] This method for an analysis had been identified from some work I had done on a course on 'Business Success Through People'.[14] I had piloted a Training Needs analysis with secretarial staff in YFC that began by analysing the skills and knowledge needed for the role[15] and then asking staff to assess their ability in relation to the elements identified. Attitudes were not included in this training needs analysis because it was felt that this was not an area where formal training could be offered.[16] Brainstorming

---

[13] Used, for example, by Brunel University and the Centre for Youth Ministry.
[14] This was a course funded by the local Training and Enterprise Council.
[15] Information was taken from job descriptions, managers and the secretarial staff themselves.
[16] However, we did talk about appropriate attitudes, and those identified on visits in February and April 1997 included: a genuine concern for young people; a non-judgemental servant attitude; a non authoritarian approach; commitment to long term relationships; giving young people a voice; sharing your life, not just one night a week; getting things wrong doesn't have to be a bad thing; tolerance of people and their backgrounds. These may be criteria

sessions at both projects were analysed and compiled into a list. A key was devised to enable workers to indicate their training needs and existing competence. This approach was adopted as it is one that could be used for any group of workers and is based on job specific skills and knowledge. To determine a list of skills and knowledge for incarnational youth workers, a brainstorming session was undertaken on the two visits mentioned above. The lists were then collated and a list of skills and knowledge relating to the role of incarnational urban youth workers was then available to use in the Training Needs Analysis. For participants the process seemed to be easy to understand and straightforward to do. The method involved the staff choosing a range of responses for each knowledge or skill. These were:

◆ Could train others in this area
◆ Competent in this area
◆ Some further training needed (specifics given if possible)
◆ No experience - training needed
◆ Not appropriate in my role

A key was developed so that workers just needed to put a symbol by each aspect. It also meant that it was easy for someone to complete if it was being done on an interview basis.

This mechanism for identifying training needs was used for a new worker at Forgreen so his line manager would know what training he needed. It provided a useful opportunity to pilot the mechanism. It worked well as a user-friendly way of raising a range of elements in which the worker needed training. The whole process of introducing the mechanism has also enabled me to identify training expertise amongst those involved in this sort of work, which will be helpful in planning training events and practical placements.

The next stage was to draw up a training policy for staff involved in this work. What was attempted in doing this was to draw in many of the suggestions made by the workers I had visited and to take note of some of the points arising from the original questionnaire we undertook as part of Goal 1. The hope was that there would be a greater awareness of the pressure of incarnational youth work and a willingness to look at ways that policies could help address this. In many respects the policy that was drawn up goes beyond training, it looks at personal development in a holistic way. The major suggestion, that would perhaps be controversial within YFC, was that of making provision for

---

that would be used in selection, modelled by workers and discussed in supervision sessions. They are just as important as the knowledge and skills but not something to be included in formal training.

family members who were not formally part of the youth work project team. The issue is more one of available finance than an unwillingness to acknowledge the role played by a worker's family in this ministry. Historically, YFC had run a family weekend each year to include the worker's wider family within the YFC family. However, given the financial constraints faced by some incarnational youth workers, funding some personal development for spouses of workers where it was needed would have been a formal recognition of the contribution they made to the work and to the worker being able to pursue their ministry.

The training policy itself has two parts: national YFC Training Department responsibilities, and recommendations to local management committees. One of the difficulties faced with the latter is that each YFC local project is autonomous. Although suggestions can be made at a national level, this does not mean that they will always be adopted.

A main problem with the first part of the policy relates to its financial implications. It has been possible to get some trainers to give their services free, or on an expenses only basis, and this has been helpful in meeting specific needs. Other times, it is possible to offer subsidised places on courses.

There were various aspects of the second part of the policy that were important to the workers. When meeting with them, it was clear that they really valued the opportunity to get away. This enabled them to meet others involved in a similar sort of work and to get fresh input. The need for regular spiritual sustenance was also vital, particularly for those who did not find it in their local church. Both these concerns were incorporated into the training policies recommendations to local management committees. Another concern was for spouses and families. With incarnational urban youth work, families are subject to many of the same pressures as the workers. Allowing a spouse to attend one conference a year at the project's expense was seen as one way of acknowledging their contribution.

It was helpful for me to identify a training needs process and mechanism that I could use with different groups of workers. This will be of value to me in my job and of wider benefit to others in YFC. I feel a degree of frustration in that I can work hard identifying needs and developing policies, but our structures do not give me the authority to have them implemented. However, my experience within the organisation of being involved in setting up new projects is that ideas are sometimes readily taken on board and, therefore, a quality training policy and programme can be set up. The YFC Youth Worker Apprenticeship Scheme would be one example of this. Here, YFC have set up a programme that involves both theological and youth work accredited training as well as practical youth work. Often volunteers have benefited from well thought out policies that take longer to be accepted by staff and their management committees. Appointing a professionally qualified personnel manager has helped this process.

The Story of Goal 3

The third element of the project was a major piece of development work. We were exploring the areas of sustaining fruitfulness in ministry and the personal theology that enables this. To begin, we had to identify what we meant by fruitfulness'. The term fruitfulness was chosen because it is a word that can be looked at from a biblical perspective and embraces a range of outcomes. 'Success' in youth work can be very difficult to define and, in an evangelistic organisation, it is often measured in numbers. There is independent research done into the work of YFC regularly, and the way this is written up tends to emphasise the number of young people YFC are contacting. For example, a Christian Research Association FactFile [sic] from Summer 1998 was based on an audit of contacts for Youth for Christ in November 1997. Under the heading 'Main Findings', the first two points read:

1. Youth for Christ reaches a huge number of young people every week. In the last week of November 1997, 48,000 young people were contacted, 29% for the first time. This proportion was the same as in 1995.
2. In an average week a YFC centre/worker contacts 900 young people, 250 for the first time (Brierley et al. 1998: 1).

Point 10 was the one most relevant to incarnational youth workers. It said that, 'The longer an opportunity, usually the greater the spiritual depth of the meeting.' Reading the report one would be unaware that YFC engage in the sort of work undertaken by incarnational urban youth workers: the only two headings under the list of contacts that the work could be included in are 'Casual contacts' or 'Unspecified'. Neither of these categories give a flavour of the work. It was partly to try and offer an alternative to the numbers based approach to success that the idea of fruitfulness was explored.

Henri Nouwen draws a helpful distinction between the ideas of success and fruitfulness:

> There is a great difference between successfulness and fruitfulness. Success comes from strength, control and respectability. Fruits come from weakness and vulnerability. And fruits are unique. A child is the fruit conceived in vulnerability, community is the fruit born through shared brokenness, and intimacy is the fruit that grows through

touching each other's wounds. Let's remind one another that what brings us true joy is not successfulness but fruitfulness. (1996:12)

This passage suggests what ministry is about and can help incarnational youth workers see what they are doing as a valid form of ministry. Nouwen's honesty and own vulnerability in his writing provides a helpful model for workers and encourages them to be real about who they are, the problems that they face, and the work that they are doing. This can sometimes be at odds in what feels like a numbers based success culture in YFC referred to above. Coupland, discussing John 15, provides a helpful reminder that although 'there is a warning that fruitlessness is not acceptable to God, [it is] coupled with the reassurance that fruitfulness comes from him' (2002: 30). He goes on to point out that when Moses caused water to gush out from the rock at Meribah that may have looked like a ministry success but in God's eyes his disobedience was a failure (2002: 30).[17] Pursuing the will of God is what will bring fruitfulness. Merton offers a helpful insight into the beginning of fruit, seeds. He writes: 'Every moment and every event of every man's life on earth plant something in his soul...If I were looking for God, every event and every moment would sow, in my will, grains of His life that would spring up one day in a tremendous harvest' (1972: 12-14). At the outset of considering the concept of fruitfulness it is important to emphasise that it is to be found in pursuing God's will.

Measuring Long-Term Incarnational Urban Youth Ministry
An issue that had not been planned for in the original research arose early on in the quest to explore fruitfulness. It was the relationship between fruitfulness and measurement of the work. To assess if a worker or a project was being 'fruitful' there needed to be some sort of criteria to assess this by. I pursued identifying methods of measuring incarnational urban youth ministry.

Most people need to see fruit of some kind from their work. They need some sort of measure of progress. This can be very difficult with long-term incarnational youth work. That is why it was important to try to identify some ways of measuring the outcomes of the work. This needed to be broader than merely numbers contacted, for both those involved in the work and people who support and fund it. Conversations with workers in two YFC Centres led me to discover existing models of measuring progress in the youth work being undertaken. Along with these two models, a visit to All Saints led to me

---

[17] Numbers 20:1-13.

writing up an informal approach to measuring the way relationships with young people can develop and become closer, that had evolved in their situation. The three different ways of measuring this work are described below. The first is a method that looks at stages relating to detached work, this I will call a *developmental* model. The second looks at stages of relationship with individual young people, this I will call a *relational* model. The third looks at the young people's behaviour, attitudes, etc. and how they relate to the workers and the extent to which workers allow the young people into their lives, this I will call a *responsive* model.

A Developmental Model of Measuring Incarnational Youth Ministry

The developmental model[18] has a seven-part strategy for developing work with young people. This enables workers to measure where young people are and to set targets to be achieved. These are:

1. **Cold contact** - an initial meeting with a young person or group where there is no previous relationship.
2. **Area based work** - initial work in a clearly defined geographical area.
3. **Peer Group work** - working among a specific group of young people. At each stage, there is what they call a 'mechanism', a more usual youth work term would be 'intervention'. This is the event, issue, hobby, trip, etc., that enables work to progress from stage to stage. It is something that enables the relationship to develop at a deeper level.
4. **Basic small group work** - with key young people as they are identified. At some stage during this group work an appropriate intervention will be identified with the aim of taking the group to the next stage.
5. **Risky small group work** - moving work and relationships forward, more informal. Again, an intervention will be identified that will seek to move the work on to the next level.
6. **Exposure and exploration of spirituality** (includes declaration of the gospel). At this stage, the individual may or may not make a decision to become a Christian. If they do, they move on to the final stage.
7. **Relational based expression of church**. This may mean a small group that meets together for worship.

---

[18] Scale developed by Richard Passmore and team at Cheltenham YFC.

Workers would use this model as a planning tool in their work with young people and, at a team meeting, for example, explore how to move their work with young people on to the next stage. In its original form it was a measure for detached youth work but can be applied to incarnational youth ministry. With some young people the final stage would be reached but with others the workers never get beyond the early stages.

A Relational Model for Measuring Incarnational Youth Ministry

The relational model[19] includes an expectation for people to become Christians. It asserts that, 'The work of God is this: to believe in the one he has sent' (John 6:29). It involves identifying nine stages that reflect how a relational based approach to youth work might achieve that. An individual's progress is monitored over the following stages:

Stage 1. Introduction (the first contact with young people). This might just be saying hello a few times as you pass them in the street before moving on to the next stage.

Stage 2. Conversation - make personal contact with potential 'people of peace'.[20]

Stage 3. Relationship assessed through prayer and discussion with the team.

Stage 4. Deepening of friendship.This may include meeting friends and family, serving their needs as we see them, doing things together and introducing Jesus as appropriate. During this time we will pray to identify 'hooks', the issues that will help unlock people spiritually.

Stage 5. Open and positive discussions about God.

Stage 6. Commitment to God.

Stage 7. Meet with other young Christians for worship, teaching and fellowship.

Stage 8. Introduction to the local Church.

Stage 9. Active in Christian service.

The final stage would be the hoped for end result, but would not be expected in many cases. However, such a model does give a focus to the work and a structure for planning work with individuals.

A Responsive Model for Measuring Incarnational Youth Ministry

This model was worked out in the context of All Saints where there is a

---

[19] Model developed by Gavin Coxhead and team at Kenilworth YFC.

[20] Taken from the story of the sending out of the seventy two by Jesus, Luke 10:5-6.

drop-in centre on the ground floor of a building where two of the workers live with their family upstairs. They have a series of steps that they use informally to respond to callers, but the response that is made enables them to assess the level of relationship they have with individual young people, and the changes in these over time can be monitored. It is an informal way of approaching the task of measuring the work but reflecting on the response to callers does enable one to make an assessment as to how you see them. The steps are:

1. Don't answer the door when you see who it is! (There may be a good reason for this)
2. Stand at the door and chat.
3. Invite to come in to the drop in.
4. Go down and invite to come up stairs to the home area.
5. Call them directly up stairs.
6. Give them phone/mobile number.

This shows the degree of relationship a young person has with a worker, as well as reflecting a level of trust. Although it is a simple way of looking at a relationship it does give a snapshot of the depth of relationships that exist. Furthermore, it can be helpful to trace over time, the progress of individual young people up and down the scale, as unfortunately relationships can deteriorate as well as improve.

The main weakness of all three models is that they are quite subjective. They all depend on the worker assessing where the young person fits in their model. They also require that individuals have some idea of what the different terms mean, particularly outside of the original contexts in which they were devised. Nevertheless, a use of all three models would provide some helpful insights. The *responsive* model enables the workers to use their expertise and instincts to identify where a young person is at in their relationships with them. The *developmental* model provides a plan for the workers with different approaches to group work. The *relational* model works well for individuals. It brings in prayer and the team in the assessment of an individual and looks clearly for individuals to become Christians. Some further work could be done in refining these models into an holistic approach.

The collation of three different models for measuring long term incarnational urban youth work was not part of the original plan. When I began, I thought we would be more likely to end up with a series of criteria but not a model that would be easily adapted for use elsewhere. There has been a useful spin off from this research in that YFC have set up a new strategy making process. I have been involved in looking at the topic of Demonstration that incorporates both social action and relational youth work. One of the strategies the group identified was a need to help workers and projects measure what they do for accountability as well as encouragement for workers and churches involved. The material from this project has been used for this.

People of Peace
At All Saints, too, they use the concept of 'people of peace' that was mentioned in the relational model of measuring the work. The term is derived from their understanding of Luke 10:6 and, according to Marshall, was 'an idiom found in Classical and Hellenistic Greek but also frequent in Semitic' (1978: 419). They see that this applies to people in agencies as well as the young people they work with. Although they work with all who come to the drop in, they are aware that some are 'people of peace', people who are receptive to hearing the message of salvation. This is not a linear based measurement. Young people can manifest different characteristics at different times and then fail to manifest any, but change again six months later. Who are perceived to be 'people of peace' can be a fluid thing. It focuses on the young people themselves, rather than what the worker is involved in.

Recognising 'people of peace' is not always easy. Sometimes it is intuitive, a spiritual response. Others show some signs that indicate they may be a 'person of peace''. These signs include young people who take the initiative in relationships with workers. Often in long-term incarnational urban youth ministry, it is the worker who takes the initiative. When it is the young person, this is a positive sign. This may take the form of more or less inviting themselves round for a meal, for example. Other indicators include those who are not negative or people who influence positively rather than being influenced. A move from disruption to insight/attention is also something to look for. Showing respect and consideration for the worker and property, perhaps by making the worker a drink, is another sign. An apology for inappropriate behaviour and an awareness of the care being shown may indicate 'people of peace'. In discussions about spiritual matters, grasping a concept and feeding it back can happen at unexpected times. Participation in Christian activities, e.g. praying out loud, articulating the gospel in their own words, recalling teaching input and applying it are all signs of hope. All of the above characteristics have been observed in young people who would not normally be called Christians, if one uses a narrow evangelical definition around a conversion experience. However, they are signs of fruit in the work.

Others have mentioned different aspects that could be part of the process of identifying 'people of peace' or seeing progress in relationships. These include harm reduction (e.g. taking a less harmful drug or using a condom when having sexual intercourse); honesty and openness in conversation; curbing bad language; treating each other better; valuing themselves more; believing there is a future; believing they have something to offer; finding a purpose in life.

Fruitfulness

After considering practical models of measuring or assessing progress in relationships with young people as developed by different projects, it was important to consider in more depth what 'fruitfulness' might mean in measuring long term incarnational urban youth ministry. I sought to do this in a range of contexts, with YFC staff, the support team and workers. The work with YFC staff happened at a staff training week that I was co-leading. With the support team, I used a long lunch break one day when many of us were in the office. In respect to the workers, I was only able to complete the exercise at All Saints but had a productive time there with the help of a support team member who joined me for that trip. Getting a perspective on the topic from three different groups with a variety of experiences helped me to develop a paper that drew on a wide variety of expertise and thought about the topic.

Fruitfulness – a YFC Staff Perspective

The parable of the sower from Luke 8:1-15 was chosen as a well known biblical story that would resonate with workers because of its obvious connections with the concept of fruitfulness. An interesting observation about the passage was made by a Management Trainer, who works with YFC occasionally. Does it mean that we can only expect success twenty five per cent of the time? For some involved in this work that would be very fruitful! Pip Wilson records his experiences of incarnational youth work in East London: 'Why, I was asking myself, after seven and a half years of personal commitment and team work, are there so few individual Christians, and certainly no group of young Christian people as a result of our work?' (1985: 115). That is why it is important to have more subtle ways of measuring the work. The usual evangelical numbers game does not work here and can be disabling to the worker who does not feel their contribution is esteemed in the same way as, for example, a preaching evangelist who can talk of the many who made a commitment under their ministry.

A Bible Study on the parable of the sower was devised, based on Walter Wink's approach to Bible study as an agent of transformation (1990: 128-29). I introduced the material to a Youth for Christ Staff Training session as a time when workers could reflect privately on their work, their relationship with God, and their personal life. The idea was to begin to encourage people to think about, and use the concept of fruitfulness in their ministry. The hope was a degree of awareness raising in respect of how workers looked at their lives and work. This was done as a private exercise to encourage honesty.

We then moved on and made use of a well-known biblical phrase, 'the fruit of the Spirit' (Galatians 5:22). Using the example of 'The Fruit of the Spirit is .', we asked workers to complete the following statement: 'A fruitful worker is .' This is what was recorded: approachable; dependable/reliable; take risks; honesty; wisdom; give time; vulnerability; humility; integrity; a friend; trustworthy; challenging; encouraging; example – lifestyle; unconditional love; accepting. Looking at this list, it would seem to be from the perspective of what a young person would look for in a youth worker. This may reflect the fact that this is what workers perceive to be the most important thing about their role. There is little in the list that would reflect the ability to do a school assembly or complete administrative tasks, for example. It would be fair to say that the list represents an organizational bias where support staff skills such as secretarial work or accounts are not valued as highly as ministry skills.

The last part of the session involved completing the statement 'YFC will be fruitful if .' The group decided that the core thing needed was to live by the Spirit, with a special emphasis on the fruit. Out of this living by the Spirit, other things were necessary. Included was acceptance and respect for people; relational living; consistency in behaviour and attitude; a positive and joyful attitude; good communication - internal and external; listening to each other; accountability; good management and supportive godly leadership; taking time out to pray; seeking God's face and will; an attitude of humility. This seems like the sort of qualities your ideal manager would have! It is interesting to consider this list in the light of recruitment strategies. These qualities can be quite difficult to measure but they make such a difference in a ministry environment. How do you encourage the development of such attitudes and how can you recognise them? These are tough questions for a Human Resources Department and probably outside the scope of the project.

Fruitfulness in Ministry – Support Team Perspective

Between them, the support team have over seventy years experience of working with young people. When they looked at what was needed to be fruitful in ministry, they identified two sets of things to consider. The first involved us as individuals and the second our context. What do we need personally to be fruitful in ministry? Before identifying what these things may be, the team noted that we always need to bear in mind that God may choose to alter our circumstances and that we are called to a life of denying ourselves and following Jesus. We were not equating what we needed for fruitfulness in predominantly material terms. We began with a general brainstorm and then identified various categories that we could use to group ideas together.

The first category was those that related to our personal lives, and our understanding of, and approach to, ministry. The terminology used at times reflects the evangelical roots and traditional biblical understanding of both the organisation and individuals. We began with our spiritual lives. The first quality that was identified was the need to be in love with Jesus. The second was a knowledge and love of God, self, and others. Out of this would come obedience, faithfulness, prayer, personal spiritual disciplines, and faith. It was expected among workers that they listened to God and sought to be guided by him. A Spiritual Director, a discipler, or perhaps a Paul and Timothy[21] type relationship was seen as desirable.

The next category identified was called an 'Understanding of what ministry is'. The primary quality here was serving and servanthood. This could be explained further by saying that we should imitate Jesus and prefer each other's needs.[22] The other main concern in this category was the need for stewardship of time, resources, gifts, and abilities. These are all pertinent issues in YFC where burnout is a danger.

Working relationships was a third category explored. One example give was the idea of looking out for and being looked out for, as in the example of Jethro and Moses.[23] Allegiance and loyalty to those who we work with and for was commended. Joseph demonstrated this loyalty that we were seeking.[24] This includes a first loyalty towards God.

The next category the team explored was called 'personal'. This included an accurate self-awareness and assessment. Another category was a knowledge of calling and gifting in the way that Isaiah and Jeremiah had.[25] Connected with this is anointing: this idea was

---

[21] See 2 Timothy Chapter 1, for example.

[22] Philippians 2:1-11 was a passage mentioned which elaborates these ideas.

[23] See Exodus 18:17f where Jethro suggests to Moses that he gets others to help him.

[24] See, for example, Genesis 39 where Joseph rebuffs the advances of Potipher's wife.

[25] See Isaiah 6 and Jeremiah 1.

taken from the story of Samuel anointing David.[26] Two other issues raised in this category were self discipline (reflecting a traditional evangelical approach to alcohol, tobacco, drugs, sex, and money, etc.) and manage oneself well which means good time and resource management, or to use another term, good stewardship.

Character was another word that the team chose to group together a range of items. This included a willingness to suffer and to act with integrity, also, the need to be godly, teachable, leadable, accountable, holy, and humble.

Lifestyle issues were identified next. The first was a balance between the so-called Mary and Martha attitudes of being and doing.[27] Also mentioned was the need for the right amount of food, exercise, and sleep. The importance of taking time off and regular holidays as well as retreats and spiritual sustenance was noted. The need for hobbies, for a more balanced lifestyle, and the opportunity to switch off from work was mentioned. Linked to this is the need for some sort of social life. Ministry can be quite isolated and sometimes effort is needed to do other things. A releasing into ministry by the family – wider, as well as nuclear, was the last thing mentioned in this category. Time and financial pressures are often acute in ministry so the immediate family need to be supportive. However, the wider family can be either a positive or negative influence depending on how they view the work. Workers whose family are not supportive of their work, and this includes those with Christian families, can feel particularly isolated when times are tough.

The team then moved on to the second section of the brainstorm and identified a range of factors relating to our context that help us be fruitful in ministry. The first factor mentioned was working relationships. We saw the importance of having a sense of belonging and being part of a team. Along with this, we identified a need for mentoring and development. We saw this as a two-way process, with us mentoring and assisting in the development of others as well as others doing this for us.

Good management was something identified as a necessity by the projects. The team saw the need for it as well. A very basic requirement was an accurate and up-to-date job description. This happens for all national posts, and YFC's personnel manager is trying to ensure that this happens for other posts. An appraisal or review system is also needed. Some posts can be quite isolated and it is good

---

[26] See 1 Samuel 16.
[27] See Luke 10:38-42.

to have the opportunity for two-way feedback in this process. Another task of a good manager is to help the worker understand the purpose of what they are doing. Even mundane tasks can be satisfying if you understand where your role fits in the bigger picture. The need to set realistic and achievable goals and objectives was another role of good management. Connected with this is the need to hold a worker accountable and for them to be accountable themselves. Encouragement was also mentioned; some times staff feel taken for granted and need to be encouraged and know that they are valued. The last item in this section was a good salary and adequate expenses, which is one mechanism that people use to assess their value. We made a distinction between management and leadership. We saw management as relating to the day-to-day work and leadership the vision for the organisation. The team wanted leaders who were prophetic, envisioned and who listened to God. Prophetic in the context of YFC means what God is saying to us, rather than lifestyle or challenging in the social-political sphere.

It is part of the expectations of YFC staff that they are members of a local church. This was added to our list because we saw that it was an important source of support and accountability. The ideal would be a recognition from the church of the ministry a worker was involved in, as we find in Acts 13:1-3 where Saul and Barnabas are set apart and sent out. In reality, it is more often the potential worker who initiates the discerning of their call. However, being formally commissioned for ministry is seen as beneficial for the worker. Many workers hope for both prayer and financial support from a local church. Prayer support is usually available but financial support depends on other commitments the church may have. The benefit of having a point of reference and accountability within a local church was seen as helpful. There are times when it is beneficial to talk to someone whose main concern is you, not the work. To some this could sound like rather a selfish list. However, it is written from the context of what a worker needs to be fruitful. It would be accepted that a worker would seek to give to the local church as well as receive from it.

Fruitfulness – the Workers' Perspective
It was at this stage of exploring the notion of fruitfulness that it became difficult to work with Forgreen. For various reasons, it was not possible to find a mutually agreeable date to visit, and although the project leader said that he would try to do the exercises, this did not prove possible and difficulties continued. However, it was possible to visit All Saints and get a local perspective on fruitfulness in long-term incarnational urban youth work. Many of the points made at All Saints,

when looking at the conditions needed personally to be fruitful, were identified by the support team. However, some of the terms and phrases used bring a slightly different perspective and they are listed below.

Peer support was mentioned. For the workers at All Saints, a regular gathering of Christian youth workers in the town over a pub lunch meets much of this need. Relationships are developed and this support is then available. It is important that this is seen as 'work', as it fulfils an important need in a situation where managers may not fully understand the pressures involved.

Another phrase used was 'sounding board'. This was understood as someone to talk to about the different things that happen, new ideas, and so on. In professional youth work terms this may be known as non-managerial supervision and involves someone not directly involved in the work meeting with a worker regularly. It is something some workers have adopted in YFC, whereas others have focused more on spiritual support and input. It generally happens in an ad hoc way but a more structured approach may benefit workers.

The importance of 'team' was emphasised. In this particular situation, team relationships are generally good and supportive. It has been interesting to note that some of the difficulties in other projects have been exacerbated by interpersonal team problems. YFC have tried to provide training modules to develop skills in this area and one module on conflict management is being planned as a consequence of some of the issues identified overall in this research project.

Another term used by workers was 'perspective'. This was a helpful comment because a lack of perspective is something that can quickly bring despair. This is where peer and other support can be so valuable in helping to get a realistic grasp of the situation. It is important not to let a lack of perspective influence decisions. When a worker loses perspective, there needs to be support to enable them to regain perspective. This may involve time out or away from the situation, and YFC need to be aware of places people can go to do this. Workers may also need authorization to do this. Those who lack perspective may need to be instructed to 'go away'.

Having time for your relationship with God was seen as important. Often the busyness of youth work means that this is an area that can get neglected, so some time out can be helpful. It may be necessary to provide help and support in this. For some people the idea of a quiet day or retreat is unfamiliar. Opportunities need to be presented to facilitate this. The opportunity to receive input was seen as important as it can seem like a worker is always giving out. What this needs to be depends on the individual and their needs. It may be spending time with friends or going to a different church tradition -

whatever refreshes someone. Time out somewhere different is sometimes necessary. This is part of a need for taking appropriate time off and holidays. Going away somewhere can recharge and refresh a worker even if it is just a weekend. Finding low cost places to enable this is important and can be a role for a management committee or wider group. One of the dangers is feeling guilty when taking time off or not doing much. A more holistic approach to ministry is needed where each element is seen as important. This would include sleep! Sleep can be very important for a youth worker who may face many late nights. Youth workers should not be made to feel guilty over having a lie in.

'Space for me' was another concept that was mentioned. This is vital in an incarnational setting where home can be part of work. Again, how that space needs to be created depends on the individual. When a family is involved this can become more complicated, particularly when childcare is not readily available and when a couple feel they need space to be together. The benefits of working where a network of family and friends already exists is obvious.

The final thing that was considered on the visit to All Saints was how they measured fruit in their own lives as workers involved in long term incarnational urban youth ministry. This was probably the most difficult question to consider. One reason it is difficult is that there are no guidelines. Many situations urban youth workers face are grey areas where there is no right or wrong answer. It is an area where one can see personal change and significant growth that reflects a maturing faith and an unwillingness to accept simplistic answers or solutions to problems. One of the workers said that she asked herself, 'Am I getting liberal?' Working for an evangelical organisation, being liberal is not a sought after label. This perception is part of the post-evangelical debate initiated by Dave Tomlinson. He writes, 'It never ceases to amaze me how paranoid evangelicals are about liberalism' (1995: 60). What is regarded as liberalism does seem to vary culturally from a particular doctrinal position to 'liberal' attitudes towards alcohol, tobacco, sex or whatever. Youth groups in evangelical churches today would not have the same list of dubious activities best avoided, as in the past. The cinema, for example, was banned for some young people of my generation but is generally acceptable now. However, feeling you are becoming liberal is an issue relating to fruitfulness. What is often behind it is a growing compassion for young people in difficult circumstances. This can lead to difficulty in reconciling work with them and traditional evangelical views on such areas as sexual orientation. More work needs to be done in offering workers a theological framework within which to assess their work and make decisions. It is an issue that will be raised at a future staff training. This is perhaps one of the most serious implications of incarnational urban youth ministry. Facilitating workers' explorations in their faith and enabling them to work through some of the difficult questions that their ministry brings must be a priority for YFC.

One sign of fruitfulness, identified at All Saints, is being able to accept the way people need or want to be discipled, and how they see being a disciple. Sometimes it feels as if there is an image that you have to conform to or encourage young people to become like. Pete Ward has talked about the 'tribes of evangelicalism' that have been built around some of the major Christian festivals and events such as Spring Harvest and Soul Survivor (1997b: 19-34). While this sense of belongingness is good, we need to appreciate that many of the young people we meet in long-term incarnational urban youth ministry may not fit into this scene and alternatives need to be sought. Our own experiences of being a young Christian may influence us as well. Work needs to be done on identifying what (if any) are the non-negotiables of the gospel and trying to divest our form of discipling from any additional cultural baggage.

Self-perception can sometimes be a sign of fruitfulness. 'Do I feel like a good youth worker today?' If the answer is yes then that is likely to mean that the worker is being fruitful in their work because so many things can occur to dent that confidence. Knowing whether you are a good youth worker or not can be hard when there is not a proper job description or supervision structure. Sometimes workers need others to tell them that they are doing a good job. Also they need something against which to measure their performance. The information we have collated above on measuring long-term incarnational urban youth ministry may help in this respect. However, the ideal is to get to the stage where a worker is not dependent on the views of others to know that the work they do is of value. It is also important not to have a self-perception focused solely on work, as people need to know their worth as individuals in their own right. If they are able to know this for themselves then this enables them to be themselves and not to try to be different for the sake of the work. This does not mean that, at times, a worker does not adopt different roles, but that they can be themselves without fear.

The perception of others can reinforce a sense of fruitfulness or not. It can be difficult for people who have been used to one style of youth work to accept a very different style. One way this manifests itself is that the local community want to see programmes run, they want to see more than relationships being built. However, although it can be easy to have a fruitful programme if it is measured in terms of numbers, the impact for young people of being involved in that programme is more difficult to assess. This demonstrates the importance of communicating to the community, church, funders and other stakeholders what kind of work is being done. This communication takes time and commitment, and is sometimes seen as a low priority for the workers when compared with working with the young people themselves.

A range of other ways of identifying fruitfulness in the lives of long-term incarnational urban youth workers emerged from discussions. One was seeing hope in negative situations. For many workers this sense of hope is something to hold on to in an environment where many people feel hopeless and where breakthroughs come slowly. At times a negative reaction to a worker or a project can be a sign of hope as it means the work is provoking a response. Defensive reactions from young people are common and thus hope may emerge from what seems on the surface a negative situation. Along with this is learning from failure, which can be a regular occurrence in youth work. There are times when more can be learnt through failure than when things are going well, particularly about one's self and one's resources and support. It can make a worker more aware of what an appropriate way forward might be the next time.

Feeling more love towards those one works with is another sign of fruitfulness. Linked to this is the ability to be firm when this is needed. It needs to be the right sort of love that seeks to see growth in the young people, not an indulgent love that lets them do what they like. Workers seek to love the young people unconditionally but this does not mean they condone what they do. Loving them for who they are now, not who they could be is an aim. Linked to this desire to love the young people is demonstrating more patience and persevering with the young people even when they are difficult and no progress seems to be made.

Having not too many 'If onlys .' was another way in which fruitfulness was identified. This would indicate that workers were satisfied that what they were doing was right, even if outward signs were few. Linked to this is the idea of being able to fulfil calling as a measure of fruitfulness in their own lives. It was expressed as a, 'This is what I was made for' type feeling, and that helps them to feel they are being fruitful. Therefore, there is a dissatisfaction in not fulfilling one's calling. This emphasises the need for YFC and others to help individuals identify their call. Often it is an evolving process and someone only realises when they are doing something how this fulfils them.

The last way of identifying fruitfulness related to a person's relationship with God. Each individual would have a different way of doing this. However, there was a consensus that this involved having an idea of where someone wanted to be in their relationship with God, where they are now and seeing a progression. It was acknowledged that this was a difficult area in which to identify fruitfulness because it is often not until afterwards that someone can see what God has been doing in them. Desert or wilderness experiences are often more about growth than is realised at the time. A Spiritual Director or such like, may be helpful in enabling workers to understand what is happening in their spiritual life.

Fruitfulness – the Metaphor

The outcome of all this exploration was a paper on fruitfulness. YFC's strategic planning process led to the setting up of a group involved in relational youth work. It was agreed that the appropriate time to distribute the paper was when this group started to meet early in 1998. A brief biblical introduction to the metaphor of fruitfulness is provided here. This was completed as part of the original research in order to provide a biblical foundation for adopting the term 'fruitfulness' as an alternative approach to measuring work, as opposed to numbers of young people contacted, for example.

Before looking at some biblical material, the use of fruitfulness as a metaphor needs to be considered. Soskice, having discussed how difficult it is to define metaphor, offers this definition: 'metaphor is that figure of speech whereby we speak about one thing in terms which are seen to be suggestive of another' (1985: 15).[28] This is important to bear in mind when using a term such as fruitfulness. It is a helpful way of looking at things but its function as a metaphor or figure of speech should not be forgotten. One could imagine an unhelpful discussion as to what kind of 'fruit' is the best! Is it the 'fruit' that preaches to a thousand young people or the one that stays up until the early hours listening to a young person whose father has just walked out of home?

The most frequently used fruit image in the Bible is that of the vine and is found in both the Old and the New Testaments. The vine is a relevant metaphor for those in ministry because of the way it is usually used to represent God's people. Vawter and Hoppe, writing about Ezek. 15:1-8, suggest that:

---

[28] McGrath makes the observation that 'Perhaps the most attractive feature of metaphors for Christian theology is their open ended character' (1994: 138-39).

The first words that we read appear to be less allegory than they are a parable, a simple simile or a metaphor. Their allegorical character, however, derives from the vine-figure that represents Israel. It is not a figure chosen at random, but it is rather one that has a history in Israelite symbolism...we can note Num. 13:23, where the vine appears as a sign of the richness of Canaan; Jotham's fable of the noble vine in Judg. 9:12-13; Gen. 49:11, in which the vine represents the fullness of the blessing of the messianic age; the parable of the vineyard in Isa. 5:1-7; the lengthy comparison of Israel with a vine stock in Ps. 80:8-19; Israel the luxuriant vine in Hos. 10:1; and the imagery of Ezekiel himself in Ezek. 17:5-10 and 19:10-14 (1991: 91).

If the vine does not bear fruit, the vine is useless, the fruit is what it exists for; the wood from the vine is usually only useful for burning, not for building. Motyer, introducing his commentary on the unfruitful vineyard of Isa. 5:1-7, writes that, 'According to Ezekiel 15:2-5 a vine is either good for fruit or good for nothing. Since the Lord's people are his vine the same truth applies' (1993: 68). The rest of Isa. 5 describes some of the reasons for the bad fruit, as identified by Isaiah. They are summarised by Motyer as involving, first, the 'abuse of the material benefits of life' and secondly, 'failure in the moral and spiritual obligations of life' (1993: 70). The passage is in the form of 'woes' and the consequences of judgement. The work that was done on fruitfulness sought to identify what is needed in place to help resist following the example of Israel as described in this chapter. In considering what might contribute to good fruit, Isaiah 58 gives some idea of what was required of Israel, for example, verses 6-7:

> Is not this the fast that I choose: to loose the bonds of injustice, to undo the thongs of the yoke, to let the oppressed go free, and to break every yoke? Is it not to share your bread with the hungry, and bring the homeless poor into your house; when you see the naked, to cover them, and not to hide yourself from your own kin?

There is a challenge from the writer of Ezekiel in 17:10, the end of the parable of the eagles and the vine: 'When it [the vine] is transplanted, will it thrive? When the east wind strikes it, will it not utterly wither, wither on the bed where it grew?' Many incarnational urban youth workers are transplanted into a place; what is needed for that worker to be fruitful, to thrive, not wither? That is a challenge to YFC and to local management committees who have responsibility for preparing both the 'vine' and the 'ground' where it is planted. Those responsible for incarnational urban youth ministry may grow in their understanding of their role by means of this image.

A core New Testament text that uses the vine as a metaphor is John 15.This contrasts with the Old Testament passages where the vine is often used in the context of negative passages about Israel. Here, Jesus is introduced as the true vine. Smalley believes that there is a link back to the first recorded miracle in John's gospel. He writes: 'Thus the changing of water into wine may be linked with the saying, 'I am the true vine'. Not only is there superficial contact in terms of wine and grapes; more importantly, the manifestation of the glory of Jesus in his first sign (John 2: 11) makes clear that in him the life of the new Israel, the true vine, has come to birth' (1998: 133). Milne puts John 15 into the context of what he calls the 'second upper room discourse' (1993: 218). He believes that the gospel author in this passage 'confronts the disciples (and ourselves) with the cruciality of mission and some of the basic principles of its effective pursuance' (1993: 218). This is a helpful context for us to think of our image of fruitfulness. It is for the purpose of mission that workers seek to be fruitful, it is a continuation of the ministry of Jesus in the world. Michaels comments more explicitly on this: 'If remaining in Jesus is defined concretely as loving one another, the consequent bearing of fruit must be defined as reproducing oneself and one's relationship to Jesus spiritually in the lives of others – that is, as what later, and more ecclesiastically minded, Christians have called evangelism (cf. 12:24: a single grain of wheat 'dies' in order to produce 'many seeds', lit., 'much fruit')' (1989: 274). Not everyone defines fruit in such a narrow way. Morris suggests that, 'The action of the Father is such as to cleanse his people so that they will live fruitful lives. The 'fruit' is not defined here, but we need not doubt that qualities of Christian character are in mind as elsewhere in the New Testament (Matt. 3:8; 7:20; Rom. 6:22; Gal. 5:22; Eph. 5:9; Phil. 1:11, etc.)' (1995: 595). This approach has parallels with the research findings about fruitfulness many of which relate to a growing and maturing faith that will hopefully be attractive to young people and others in the community.

In what is called 'a psychological commentary' on John, Sanford stresses the importance of the inner life in helping us to abide in the vine. He writes, '...we must care for the living process that goes on within us. Like a good gardener who tills the soil of the garden and cares for the plants, so we must till the soil of the soul and tend to the inner life' (1994: 282). This reflects the tension between 'being' and 'doing'. It is difficult to abide in Christ without giving this attention to the inner life. Maintaining a relationship requires effort and is not without pain and workers may well be involved in the feeding, the watering, and pruning of themselves that is necessary to continue to grow and be fruitful. Once again, it is not too difficult to be able to make connections between the image of the vine and fruitfulness for workers.

Developing a Personal Theology

The final part of the third goal involved exploring the biblical and theological basis of long-term incarnational urban youth ministry. The process by which it was done involved personal study on my part and consulting practitioners in the field. By this time in the story of Goal Three, there had been major structural changes within YFC that meant that it was no longer practical for the support team to provide input.

One of the tasks that had been set was to enable workers to reflect on some of the material available and as a consequence draw up their own personal theological statement relating to their work. Again, this was possible to do with only one local project; and one of the workers completed the task.

I identified some significant statements or quotations under three key headings: incarnational, urban, and youth. Some comments from three practitioners consulted were added to this, which covered the ministry side of the work. All of these were given to workers along with a statement on developing a personal theology and some suggested headings to explore. In this way an attempt was made to stimulate the workers' thinking and provide some structure for their response in developing their own personal theology. Below I identify the material used and explain some of the reasons for choosing it.

Five statements on 'incarnational' were chosen. The first two, from Alan Pettie (1993: 7) and Paul Borthwick (1997: 11-12), relate directly to an incarnational approach to youth ministry and issue challenges as to the sort of youth work that is necessary if it is to be incarnational. The third quotation is from David Bosch and looks at the incarnation from the perspective of liberation theology. He writes, 'In this model, one is not interested in a Christ who offers only eternal salvation, but in a Christ who agonizes and sweats and bleeds with the victims of oppression' (1993: 512-13). This is how many of the youth workers feel about the work they are involved in. The aim was to give a theological background to this that some workers may not be aware of. The fourth quotation, from Driver (1993: 209), looks at the incarnation from the perspective of the community that Jesus built. This was chosen to encourage reflection on the wider context of the work and how an incarnational approach can be implemented in a way that has meaning to those the local project work amongst. The last quotation is from Luis Espinal and is a meditation/prayer of someone who lived an incarnational life (cited in Hebblethwaite 1993: 60). The purpose of this quotation was to encourage workers to engage again with their call and the consequences of it.

The next topic to reflect upon was 'urban'. Seven quotations were used. The first is from Harvie Conn and says that we should see cities as God's provision for our welfare (1993: 101). I wanted to start with a positive, biblical approach to the city to help theological reflection. The next quotation is from Jacques Ellul, whose writings tend to give a negative view of the city. However, this extract focuses on the mission there (1970: 181-82). It ends by asking whether the city will accept us and is included to help workers reflect on some of the difficulties of their work. Any personal theological statement will need to engage with the reality of suffering to reflect a rounded picture of experience in this work. The third quotation is from Rowland Croucher, who encourages evangelicals to see that they can make a difference, using the parable of the Good Samaritan as an example (1986: 53). Again, theological reflection is being encouraged and it is hoped that workers will make their own connections with passages of scripture that relate to their own situation. Thomas Merton is the author of the next extract and this focuses on Jesus who identifies with those who are marginalized (cited in Leech 1990: 32-33). One of the aims of this process is to encourage workers to see what they can learn from Jesus and the way that he engaged in ministry. This quotation aims to start thinking in this direction. The next quotation is just one line from David Ford and points out that many of the New Testament letters 'are written to small and fragile urban communities of Christians' (1995: 201). Unfortunately, many workers do not have a wide biblical or theological knowledge and this quotation was included to help them see the relevance of some of the New Testament writings for their situation. Peter Sedgwick comments on how deprivation makes the task of witness harder (1995: 213). Again, this is included to challenge workers to reflect on some of the difficulties associated with their work. The final comment comes from David Sheppard who makes suggestions about the terms and conditions of clergy in the inner cities. These comments may be helpful for workers and their management committees to take note of (1983: 205-206). It is important for the worker to see the wider implications of what they are doing and to identify their own needs for support and this quotation is included with the hope that this will happen.

The next set of reflections were on the subject of 'youth'. The first comes from *Faith in the City* and highlights the alienation young people feel (1985: 315). This is the context in which our workers encounter young people and sets the framework for the remaining quotes. Nelson Copeland Jnr. talks about the need to empower young people (1997). Empowerment is one of those words which youth workers use and over which there is not a clear consensus of meaning. However, in this context, it encourages workers to think about how they can facilitate young people to achieve their dreams. It is a key part of the long-term relational youth work that is done, and is included because of this. The next extract combines two quotations from David Sheppard and talks about the way that youth work needs to be constantly changing, the importance of being there for young people and the difficulty of building links from a Christian perspective (1983: 209-11). These quotations are included to encourage workers to review their work and practice in the light of a rapidly changing youth culture. The next quotation is also from David Sheppard and talks about the difficulty of getting the wider Christian community to understand the long term, incarnational youth work that is vital in urban areas. This was chosen to help workers see the rationale for long term work and to confront one of the major difficulties they face, lack of understanding by other Christians. The last quotation is from Pete Ward who was the Archbishop of Canterbury's Advisor on Youth Work. He talks about the difference between a call to incarnation and a call to the cross and the need of youth workers to choose between the two (1997a: 2). This is included to encourage workers to examine their theological rationale for their youth work.

A series of comments were then collated from responses to a questionnaire sent to those with expertise in this area, predominantly outside of YFC.[29] Consulting at least three outside practitioners was part of the strategy for this goal. Although questionnaires were sent to five people, representative of different experiences including an ethnic minority and female perspective, I received only three replies. The first was from an Anglican clergyman, Edward Furness, who had worked at the Mayflower, a large youth and community centre in the East End of London. The second from Bob Holman who lives and works in a large council estate on the outskirts of Glasgow and who has written extensively on topics related to the project. The third was from Keith White who lives in community with children and young people who are part of Millgrove, the charity he heads up. The questions sent to these practitioners were similar to those that had been asked in earlier parts of

---

[29] The source of the comments were not identified on the sheets given out, although I verbally explained who had contributed. I felt it was important for workers to be able to consider the comments given without having pre-set ideas about the sources. This can happen when you have formed an image of a particular type of work or worker.

the project and encompassed issues and needs, a biblical and theological basis for the work, as well as the whole topic of fruitfulness. Some interesting comments emerged with an emphasis on making sure that the right people are involved in the work and that they are aware of the costs that are involved. A need for team working and an integrated lifestyle were also highlighted. This material was included on the basis that it was from practitioners who had been involved in this sort of work long term, and whose contributions thus deserved to be taken seriously.

Raising the Issues

The last part of the project involved providing a forum to discuss issues raised through the work done. Unfortunately this did not happen because my role in YFC was changing and I was becoming more involved in the Centre for Youth Ministry. However, I have been able to raise many of these issues in other contexts such as Frontier Youth Trust where I gave an address to their conference on 'A Call to Incarnation', which touched on a range of topics I first encountered in this research project. This last goal was the most rewarding for me personally but had the least impact on others. This was because the work with Forgreen, the larger project, could not be completed. However, material has been collated that can be used in the future and the methodology could be adapted for other spheres of work.

Evaluation of all three goals appears in the next chapter following some methodological reflection.

Chapter 4

Benefits, Drawbacks
and Learning

> In its simplest form, evaluation seeks to identify good and
> interesting practice, and based upon that, use the findings to
> inform future policy and practices. It is important to recognise
> that learning from one's failures, as well as the things that were
> a great success can provide valuable insights into what works
> and what doesn't (Bowes 2001: 7).

The quotation above is from a Connexions publication. The book, on evaluation, was part of an attempt to help develop 'evidence-based practice'. Bowes writes that, 'The concept of evidence-based practice originated in medicine, and has now been translated to a number of fields of professional practice, including mental health, education and social work' (2001: 5). Although I was not aware of the term at the time I started my research, it sums up helpfully what I was seeking to do – look at current practice to try and find ways of improving it to help future workers in the field. This should then have an impact on the main focus for YFC – the work with young people. A better working environment for incarnational youth workers should lead to an improved service to young people.

Evaluation is both helpful and necessary. This project has taken up time and energy that might have been used elsewhere. It is important, for both YFC and for myself, to identify the benefits and the drawbacks of the project. Did we[1] achieve what we set out to? What did we learn in the process? The answer to these questions is sought below. However, the evaluation will begin by reflecting on the methodology used in the research project.

Methodology

The research design was largely determined by the programme I was following at the Urban Theology Unit. The prescribed process involved doing a situation analysis of YFC, identifying a problem, and establishing goals to address the problem with related strategies to achieve the goals. Within this framework there was scope to identify appropriate research methods.

Action Research

The research undertaken was qualitative rather than quantitative. Bell suggests that, 'Researchers adopting a qualitative perspective are more concerned to understand individuals' perceptions of the world. They seek insight rather than statistical analysis' (1993: 5-6). We were seeking insight into the state of incarnational urban youth work within YFC. Beyond this, the desire was to use any insights gained to affect what happened in the future and to address some of the difficulties that were apparent in this type of work. This approach to the research project means that it could be described as action research. Action research is summarized by Campbell and Berry as being:

   ♦ Purposeful – it should be carried out in order to make a difference or to contribute to effecting change.
   ♦ Challenging – it involves…questioning, exploring, going beyond face value or the obvious.
   ♦ Focused – it is an in-depth approach looking at specific issues for specific target groups.
   ♦ Small scale – it goes for quality rather than quantity, other approaches are best for large samples of target groups (2001: 7).

These terms reflect the process that was undertaken well. The project was purposeful, it was seeking to explore how incarnational urban youth workers could be better supported as an aid to recruitment and

---

[1] The term 'we' in this chapter refers to the support team and myself.

retention. It was challenging in that it sought to look at what could be as well as what currently was happening. Those participating in the research were encouraged to think beyond the present situation and imagine what might be done better in the future to help prevent problems that had affected people's ability to do their job in the past. The research was also both focused and small scale, predominantly working with two local incarnational urban youth work projects. In these respects, the project undertaken fulfils the criteria of action research.

Sampling

In the initial stages of the research project, a group of people were pulled together to help me with a situation analysis of YFC and to identify some initial thoughts about incarnational urban youth work. The approach I adopted in identifying who to include is known as *convenience sampling*. This is a type of non-probability sampling and is defined by Bryman as a sample 'that is simply available to the researcher by virtue of its accessibility' (2001: 97). This may not appear to be the most rigorous way of choosing a sample to get a representative response, but it is one that is commonly used, as Bryman notes:

> It also perhaps ought to be recognized that convenience sampling plays a more prominent role than is sometimes supposed. Certainly, in the field of organizational studies it has been noted that convenience samples are very common and indeed are more prominent than are samples based on probability sampling (2001: 97).

Convenience sampling was used as the most likely way to get a high response rate to the questionnaires and other activities that I undertook. The way I approached identifying the sample was predominantly to work with people with whom I had an existing relationship, who I anticipated would be willing to help with a piece of research. This was true both of those who were based in the same office as myself, and who I could meet with in person and those whom I contacted through e-mail. A potential limitation of a convenience sample is that it contains people who share similar views. I was aware of this danger and tried to make sure that people with diverse perspectives on YFC in general and incarnational urban youth work in particular were approached.

In doing the situation analysis I also employed *quota sampling*, which involves identifying characteristics of a potential sample to get a representative response. I identified a range of characteristics of people to be interviewed that included such things as position in the organization, geographical location, and pastoral responsibility for incarnational workers. Using these criteria I drew up a circulation list for the questionnaire. My long service in YFC and knowledge of a range of workers through my work with volunteers placed around the country meant there was a reasonable pool for me to draw from to obtain material for the situation analysis.

Questionnaires

One of the difficulties of analysing the information received through the situation analysis arose because I chose to use a questionnaire with open questions rather than any sort of coding. Because no way of categorizing the answers had been developed beforehand, some degree of interpretation was needed to collate the responses, otherwise there would have been a series of unwieldy lists that would not have given a coherent situation analysis. Again, I needed to be aware of potential bias in choosing to interpret responses in a way that corresponded with what I already thought. Working with a team in analysing the information helped mitigate against this. The advantage, however, of open questions was that people were able to respond with their actual thoughts rather than being limited to choosing one of a range that I had already identified. Again, because this was a qualitative piece of research where I was more interested in hearing what people actually thought than being able to present graphs or pie charts summarizing data, this was the right approach. On reflection, it might well have been more illuminating if there had been time to use the questionnaire to conduct one-to-one interviews or if there had been time to follow up the original questionnaires with some interviews to clarify some of the things that were written. The difficulty with this would have been the time taken to transcribe the interviews and even greater problems with data analysis because of the volume of data acquired. However, it would have resulted in a more in-depth situation analysis, because interviewers could have probed the answers given more fully. Most of the questionnaires went out by e mail and were likely to have been completed quickly as part of the process of dealing with one's inbox. Three responses: illustrate this 'Here are my off the shoulder replies to your questions'; 'Sally, these are just my thoughts as I sit here before lunch'; 'Just a few quick thoughts'.[2] As there was a time frame within which the situation analysis had to be completed the way it was

---

[2] The first response was from an urban specialist and others from the support team.

completed was probably the most viable.[3] However, this may have been advantageous as a swift response may reveal what someone actually thinks whereas, given more time, answers might have become more theoretical or long-winded!

Focus Groups
The other major area where methodology had to be considered was in the visits to the projects. We decided to see people in a group, partly because of the time factor but also because of the dynamics of interaction in a group. A group discussion may draw out a fuller understanding than is gained with one-to-one interviewing. This is because in a group discussion there may be a challenging of views and development of thought in discussion.

There is discussion in the literature as to the difference between a group interview or a focus group.[4] The term 'focus group' describes more accurately what we were attempting to do. Bryman defines it thus: 'The focus group method is a form of group interview in which there are several participants (in addition to the moderator/facilitator); there is an emphasis in the questioning on a particular tightly defined topic; and the accent is upon interaction within the group and the joint construction of meaning' (2001: 337). This was a particularly appropriate method for gaining effective responses from a local project.

Interviews
Because a focus group approach was used it meant that the interview was relatively unstructured with a list of topics to be covered, but no need to stick to the wording and question order as in a structured interview. This style of interviewing is 'sometimes called the 'informal', 'unstandardized' or 'unstructured' interview' (May 1997: 112). It is a style of interviewing commonly used in qualitative research. Within such interviews there is a much greater emphasis on the interviewee(s) and their perspectives compared with quantitative research where the focus is often the researcher's concern. With the interviews we did there was scope to follow areas of interest raised by the interviewee or to gain clarification on a point of view; each interview could be different without that impacting on the validity of the research. Because detailed answers were going to be of more value,

---

[3] The situation analysis had to be completed between scheduled seminars two months apart.
[4] See Bryman (2001: 110), for example.

a degree of rapport with those being interviewed helps. This was another reason for pursuing convenience sampling. I already knew the people in the projects to be visited and anticipated that they would be willing to participate fully in the focus group.

The potential problem of bias needs to be acknowledged in relation to how interviewees react to interviewers. Two of the interviewees at All Saints knew me as one of the people in charge of the project they had been volunteers on. However, I and the member of the support team who came with me, had good relationships with the two people and had used the project they ran as a placement for other workers. There was a degree of trust existing between us, and the answers reflected this. The previous power dynamic in the relationship did not appear to be a problem. We monitored their responses and were not aware that we were being given answers intended to please us.

The one thing that was not done, which on reflection would have been helpful, was to record the interviews. At that time I did not have access to equipment that could have recorded group interviews, and thus perhaps some important points may have been missed as notes taken of interviews rather than a transcription will not be complete. If doing a similar project again I would try to record the interviews. However, this would require gaining consent from the participants in the discussions and this might inhibit contributions because of the different nature of a taped conversation to one that is being recorded through notes. Inhibition probably depends on the likelihood of disclosures that people would be concerned about others hearing. This is an issue that would best be negotiated with an individual or group depending on the questions to be asked or areas to be covered.

Overall, the research methods used were appropriate to the kind of research undertaken. The main limitations in terms of effectiveness were more to do with unforeseen changes in YFC and the local projects selected as the focus of the research.

Evaluating Goal 1
Goal 1 was to identify the needs of those involved in long-term incarnational urban youth ministry. Overall this goal has been achieved and a report has been written that highlights the needs of workers in this target group. The report drew on material from a range of sources including the support team, the workers themselves and some staff involved in managing such projects. Thus, a report was produced that took into account a variety of views, not just those of the workers. This adds to the credibility of the report; merely taking into account the views of workers would mean that the report would be perceived as more subjective than objective.

The collation and dissemination of the report about workers' needs was completed. There has been subsequent interest in the report outside of those involved in the process. One person suggested that another agency, Frontier Youth Trust, might be interested in the findings as they relate to issues their workers face. There is also an option to write up the report in a slightly different format and make it more widely available.

One of the consequences of working on this goal was that my own personal and professional awareness of the issues facing incarnational urban youth workers was raised, particularly through the dialogue with project workers. There were two main areas where my thinking was particularly challenged and developed. The first is the whole process of how workers arrive in long-term incarnational urban youth work. Morag's description of her journey led me to see that YFC need to be involved in a process too. This will include more than getting recruitment, induction, and training right; there needs to be some ongoing reflection on a worker's job and the implications of it. This is particularly true where workers start as volunteers and end up as paid workers. YFC has a large number of volunteer or 'year out' programmes,[5] and it is not uncommon to see someone who originally joined YFC for a year out carrying on in youth work. Jenny was one such person. She worked in retail management when she joined YFC's year out programme but after two years with the organization she returned home to All Saints and worked with the church. She had none of the culture shock that some workers get because they relocate, but there were issues about a role change to being an incarnational youth worker and living on the job that may have been worth thinking and talking through. Andy and Julie moved from the home counties to the inner-city and were faced with a range of difficult choices, particularly in relation to the education of their children. Other workers in that situation had been childless, and this was a new issue to be thought through. Identifying these sorts of potential problems before they arise, or before final decisions about vocation are made, can help reduce the pressure and stress on workers.

The second area where my awareness was raised involved including a spouse in the wider training policy, because of the pressure they face due to the nature of incarnational urban youth ministry. Spouses need input, support, and encouragement, too, to enable them to sustain their role in their ministry. In these situations, the whole family

---

[5] These are opportunities for young people taking a gap year, usually after A levels to join YFC and work either on a national team in the area of sports or creative arts, for example, or with a local YFC centre.

is involved in some way in the call to ministry, not just the worker. I empathised strongly with Julie when she talked about this. She and her husband Andy had felt called as a couple to the work; but because of their two young children, he was seen as the 'worker' and she as taking primary responsibility for child care and only a volunteer at the project they worked for. However, I know from experience as a clergy wife, it is not that simple. Spouses are involved in answering the telephone, the door, welcoming visitors, and coping with the consequences of the pastoral emergencies that occur in this sort of work. Consequently, it would be good if provision could be made for the whole family, as appropriate. This may mean providing child care for those with young children, so a short retreat is possible, or including older children on a retreat so that they too get an opportunity to be spiritually refreshed. What should also be acknowledged is that not all families function like this; some partners pursue their own separate career and seek to minimize their contact with the young people. In this situation, it would clearly be inappropriate to expect someone to attend events or activities, but YFC need to consider making the option available to those who would value it.

We sought to pursue the first goal about the needs of workers by facilitating a dialogue and then collating and disseminating the results of this dialogue. It was possible to take a member of the support team with me on visits to both All Saints and Forgreen. to engage in face to face dialogue. This proved helpful, as they were able to ask the questions leaving me free to record answers for future collation. Having a support team member with me also helped in drawing out material from the visits because I was able to consult with them afterwards. Another person's insight was beneficial. This helped to prevent me putting my own interpretation on what people said to order to fit in with pre-conceived ideas of what I might find.

Feedback was received from All Saints; the two workers there were clearly helped by the process. As well as commenting further on issues raised, Jenny stated that, 'It helped to discuss things with people on the outside and positive ideas/suggestions came up'. Morag wrote that, 'We have struggled over many issues over the last years. Although we are moving positively on many of them it was good to talk through and assess where we were on some of the stuff'. Their comments made me aware that YFC should perhaps consider offering a project evaluation service. It is encouraging and stimulating for workers to talk to others about work and the process can crystallise thinking as well as suggest new ideas and directions.

Some of the material that was discussed in the visit to Forgreen was later included in a strategy document prepared by the then project leader. Under the heading 'Developing a 'sustainable infrastructure'', he wrote, 'There are a number of lessons that have been learned the hard way over the last 8.5 years that the project has been in existence. Over that time there has been a lot of struggles for the staff, particularly over lack of support at a variety of levels.'[6] He then goes on to list eleven ways in which a sustainable infrastructure can be delivered. This includes several points that arose in the process of achieving Goal 1, such as a recruitment strategy that delivers workers to do the job and an effective support strategy for workers to reduce stress and enhance long-term commitment.

I enjoyed the process involved in achieving this goal. One of the most helpful aspects was to be able to offer to listen to the projects. It was also good to be able to take into account a range of views when exploring related issues such as those in the next goal about training needs. Because I am involved in various other committees relating to youth work, the information obtained has also been useful in planning training or other events and having input into decision-making. An example of this would be involvement in Brainstormers (weekend training events for youth workers in which YFC was a partner) where I helped lead a retreat that encouraged workers to look at issues relating to incarnational ministry amongst young people. It also meant, at that time, that I was able to contribute to the development of YFC's national strategy in the area of urban youth work because of my perceived knowledge and expertise relating to the issues. A further benefit is that if YFC want to set up a new local project along similar lines, then there is a concise document that outlines the issues and needs of workers to be worked through. The report will also be helpful to management committees in looking at recruitment and ongoing support of workers. There is a clear need for a more thorough selection and induction programme to enable potential workers to explore some of the many issues before they take on such work and for appropriate support structures to be put into place.

This goal was the right starting point for the project. Without it we would have been looking at addressing a problem without understanding the perspective of those who are most affected. This research has also led to me being invited to join the Management Committee of a local youth project in the place where we now live.

Evaluating Goal 2
The second goal was to develop a response to the needs of those

---

[6] I have this document but have not fully referenced it to preserve the anonymity of the author.

involved in long-term incarnational urban youth ministry within the remit of the Training Department. We sought to do this by engaging in a Training Needs Analysis of workers as described earlier. As a method it works well within YFC. Because there is such a wide range of roles within YFC, a job analysis is the most effective way of identifying specific training needs that workers have. When I piloted it with the secretarial workers there was positive feedback because it enabled them to identify strengths and weaknesses as a team as well as individually and engage in some peer tutoring.

Soon after this work was completed, a new member of staff was recruited in Forgreen, and I was asked to use the Training Needs Analysis mechanism with him. The results of this analysis led to the setting up a short placement for him to develop awareness, recommending a secular youth work course, and having a list of things that needed to be covered locally for his line manager. This was a very helpful opportunity, and meant that the worker could have a more comprehensive induction. The individual is also able to begin training early on in their new post, when there is more time available as the slow process of building relationships with young people begins. This opportunity reinforced the importance of this element of my job as Training Manager. It also helped both the worker and his manager to understand where he was starting from in relation to his new post as an incarnational urban youth worker. Billy told me he found it helpful as part of gaining an understanding of his new role. It was particularly useful in identifying what some of his induction and initial training locally should involve. It has also been useful in identifying potential trainers amongst experienced incarnational youth workers, particularly for training within a local situation. This style of training can be more useful than the artificial environment of a training room for some of the skills and knowledge needed for incarnational urban youth work, as well as being cost and time effective. One of the spin-offs of this goal is that we now have a method of conducting a Training Needs Analysis that can be adapted to a range of roles within the organization, and one on which workers can measure their progress in relation to their training needs.

The second goal was pursued further by writing a specific training policy for this target group of workers. This was accomplished. It was a task that I worked on using comments and suggestions gained from the work for Goal 1. Comparing this new policy to the standard YFC one, it is clear that this is a helpful development for workers. There are several ways in which it is an improvement. The first is through the entitlement for retreats and spiritual support in work time. This moves away from the existing ad hoc arrangements for individual workers and raises an awareness of the importance of making time for this.[7]

Another improvement of the policy was realising that there are other places where those doing similar work meet up for conferences and that incarnational workers should be able to attend such conferences as well as those provided by YFC. The idea of including spouses in the provision was also flagged up as a possibility. The standard policy says that workers should come to three out of the first four staff training weeks in their first two years of service. Beyond this, they should then attend a training event every year, and every other year this should be a YFC staff training week. In contrast, the new policy for incarnational workers offers personally designed induction programmes, offers one relevant module per year on staff training and the opportunity to gain accreditation. It also includes a range of suggestions for local management committees to adopt. Elements of the policy are recommendations rather than mandatory requirements, because each local project is an independent charity and YFC cannot prescribe exactly what they should do in an area such as training. Suggestions include an annual training budget, retreats/spiritual input/external pastoral care, and an in-service training programme. Such a well thought through, broad and holistic training programme may help workers feel better supported.

Again, one of the benefits of developing a 'role specific' training policy is that the principle can be applied to other groups of workers in YFC. We can now pilot a more detailed training policy that should be better for all our workers and can provide a starting point for negotiation with local ministries involved in other types of work with young people. This was introduced in 1997 and was largely a consequence of engaging in the work for Goal 2, which highlighted the limitations of what was then the policy.

YFC offer a range of support services to their locally based ministries. This project has been useful in seeing how the input of one of these support services can be broadened and improved. There will hopefully be methods we have used that other support services can adopt if they wish to review what they do.

---

[7] This principle was later included in an update I did of the existing official YFC Training Policy, although with a reduced entitlement for work time to be used in this way. I was able to argue for its inclusion on the basis of my research and a revised Training Policy that I presented to the Leadership Team was accepted. This was a spin-off of the research rather than something that had been planned.

Evaluating Goal 3

The object of this goal was to help workers in the field develop a personal theology that sustains fruitfulness in long-term incarnational urban youth ministry. 'Fruitfulness' had been chosen as a term in preference to 'success, because the latter did not seem an appropriate term to use in measuring the development of relationships with young people. Furthermore, fruitfulness appeared to be more appropriate from a biblical and theological perspective.

We sought to achieve the third goal by trying to identify what we meant by fruitfulness in this context and by enabling individuals to develop their theological understanding of incarnational urban youth ministry. This latter element was the most difficult part of the project to implement fully and thus some of the evaluation that would have been desirable has not been possible. It was not intended to evaluate each person's theological understanding, as this would be inappropriate in my role. What I was trying to evaluate was whether or not workers engaged theologically in working out their understanding of incarnational youth work and if it was possible to support them with resources in this process.

The work on fruitfulness was completed as designed in the original project plan and a paper was written as a consequence of the work done. The only exception to this was that it was not possible to visit Forgreen. However, I had done work with both the support team and a YFC group on staff training. This meant that I had received input from a wide range of people. The feedback I had on this process was predominantly verbal. Most people involved enjoyed the task and found that it stimulated their thinking across a broad range of issues. Copies of material produced were asked for so that workers could think about the issues in more detail. The visit at All Saints was mutually helpful. They had a different perspective on fruitfulness and the process encouraged them to think about what they did in more detail. Morag wrote, 'We need to have some kind of 'measure' of the work we do to satisfy our funders and 'prove' that we do spend time with young people and serve them in different ways. This discussion has prompted us to 'get on with the job of how we measure.'

This was one part of the project where information was gathered more widely than originally planned and two models of measuring work currently in use by local YFC Centres were made known to me. This happened in the context of casual conversations and was a very useful addition to the work being done on fruitfulness. The final paper that was written included this information and thus presented three different perspectives on measuring work: a development model, a relational model, and a responsive model.

The issue of measuring work done in this context was also raised during the process of developing the new strategy for YFC in autumn 1997. It was helpful to be able to offer some models for workers to consider which will be developed into a training package for our staff and volunteers.

A completely unexpected spin-off from this work on sustaining fruitfulness was to be able to use it personally. My husband became a Curate in the inner city; he had intended to remain non-stipendiary but his post was made redundant by YFC. Although Paul is not predominantly involved in youth work, many of the other issues raised in looking at fruitfulness in ministry have been relevant to consider. Exploring these issues led us to developing a rule of life that enables us both to have some sort of framework within which we exercise our ministry. We both started with YFC in 1982 and were beginning to be some of the longer serving staff. The survey that I had done as part of the situation analysis showed that the average length of stay for a staff member was three and a half years. At the point this research project started we had completed thirteen years. We expected to be in ministry long term and the concept of developing a lifestyle that sustained fruitfulness attracted us. We have developed a rule and rhythm of life that has been influenced by both Benedictine and Celtic Spirituality. We devised a pattern based on daily, weekly, termly, and annual rhythms that fitted for us as individuals, but also as a couple. For example, I began to use a Celtic daily liturgy and Paul an Anglican one. We take termly retreats and have a variety of places that for us are 'sacred spaces' where we seek to encounter God. One of these places is Buckfast Abbey in Devon and one of the disciplines we use is to meditate on the stained glass window in the chapel of the Blessed Sacrament, which presents an image of Jesus celebrating the Eucharist, and ask what Jesus is saying to us today through this image. Paul used this rule and rhythm in talking to his potential training Vicar as an explanation of how he best functioned in ministry. It is still working for us five years on and is something that we introduced into our church as part of a spirituality course that we wrote and a tool that we use with people who come to us for pastoral support or spiritual direction. It has been a very practical and beneficial spin-off of this aspect of the research.

We also sought to achieve our third goal by developing theological understanding. Practitioners were consulted. Material in the form of an exercise to help develop a theological understanding of long term incarnational youth work was devised. Unfortunately, the only worker who engaged with the material was Morag at All Saints. As a pilot for the material it seemed to be useful, she writes, 'The whole exercise was helpful to know why I am where I am and how I am going to stay here. It is true that when any outer pressure comes I need to know the raw reality of why I'm here. I also recognized that through this I need to go back to the calling again and again and clear out the rubbish that accumulates'. One development of the exercise that she undertook could perhaps be a more comprehensive set of questions/issues to consider in identifying a personal theological approach to incarnational urban youth ministry.

I found the process of collating material to help people explore their theological understanding of incarnational urban youth ministry extremely beneficial. Ever since I first trained as a teacher, I have wanted to enable people to think things through for themselves. I taught young people with educational and behavioural difficulties and one of my aims was to seek to teach them how to think critically about issues ranging from images presented in the media to ethical choices facing them. I intuitively resisted the 'banking' concept of education and felt more comfortable with problem-posing education which Freire describes thus: 'In problem-posing education people develop their power to perceive critically the way they exist in the world with which and in which they find themselves; they come to see the world not as a static reality, but as a reality in process, in transformation' (1996: 64). It was sad, although understandable, that some of the young people I taught preferred to tackle less challenging tasks, where they could achieve success in terms of the education system rather than something more difficult that would help their learning longer term. The importance of teaching people to think is also seen in adult education. Brookfield makes this point strongly:

> Learning to think critically is one of the most significant activities of adult life. When we become critical thinkers we develop an awareness of the assumptions under which we, and others, think and act. We learn to pay attention to the context in which our actions and ideas are generated. We become skeptical of quick-fix solutions, of single answers to problems, and of claims to universal truth. We also become open to alternative ways of looking at, and behaving in the world (1987: ix).

It is a weakness of YFC that we do not always engage with the relevant theological and biblical material to critique and develop what we do. What I tried to do in this process was present a range of different perspectives on the work to help people make connections for themselves and to think about their own motivation, calling, and rationale for their work. It would be good to have the chance to use the material in a group and get a team perspective on the work that then became a shared vision. New workers particularly need to gain an understanding of the reasons why this approach to work has been chosen and to integrate some of these insights into their own thinking.

The evaluation for this goal led me to consider whether or not YFC should have more of a curriculum for training its staff. When I was responsible for volunteer training there were initial and ongoing training programmes with learning outcomes identified for the sessions. The training and development programme for incarnational youth workers devised as part of the second goal addresses this in part, but not fully. Within YFC there are small groups of workers who take responsibility for different areas of work. There is an urban workers' group and it would be useful for them to work on a more formalised curriculum than currently exists that would address some of the issues this research has raised. Again a comparison with those training for ordained Anglican ministry highlights some of the deficits in the YFC system. An Anglican ordinand will follow a prescribed course of training for a minimum of two academic years, or three years if under thirty, when training commences. This will involve both academic study and practice-based placements. During this time progress is reviewed which includes students being involved in self-assessment. After someone is ordained they will then follow a course of post-ordination training that involves corporate learning, individual study, and retreats. In Birmingham Diocese, for example, this lasts for four years and includes theological reflection on the arts, practical ministerial issues, and continuing to explore biblical and theological material. After curates complete this, there is also an expectation that clergy will be involved in continuing ministerial education in the future. While it may not be possible to copy this programme in full, the concept that there should be an initial period of intensive training followed by regular further input and reflection is one that merits consideration in greater depth by YFC.

I think it is fair to say, from responses that have been recorded throughout this chapter, that the project did change the thinking and practice at All Saints. There is now a more reflective approach to work that has been demonstrated by their feedback saying that they need to continue to think through issues that were raised on the visits. In a personal letter outside of the formal evaluation forms, Morag concluded that, 'It is really helpful for me to assess where I am, and what I need as well as think through the work issues. It is too easy to just do it and forget why and how and analyse what I am doing. So thank you for reminding me!' With Forgreen, there was always too much going on, and major issues to be dealt with, for any quality time to be given to the issues raised. Because of this, it has not been possible to measure any group growth or individual growth apart from that already mentioned. This is a disappointment but in some ways reflects the difficulties that exist in YFC. I hope that the information gained and resources developed will be helpful in the future in trying to ensure that workers are better prepared.

Reviewing the Evaluation Process

Evaluation has been a difficult process. The culture of YFC as an organization is more verbal than written, consequently it has not been easy to get written feedback. Where verbal feedback has been received, it has not been recorded systematically. I have included some of the comments made to me earlier in this chapter. However, in practice, I did not always write down what was said and my recollections, from the perspective of five years on, are unreliable. If I were to do this again I would aim for more feedback to be given at the end of an activity and perhaps get someone to collate verbal feedback for me or tape it for later transcription. The staff who would and could have done this left YFC at a crucial time, therefore the project evaluation is not as complete as it could have been.

A major problem was the difficulties that were happening locally in Forgreen. Having lost one potential local project when the leader unexpectedly moved on, it was discouraging to find major problems at one of the other local projects I was working with. There was a common issue between them, namely a breakdown in relationships between the workers and the management committee. In both cases it led to the workers eventually leaving the projects. It is not possible to go into the reasons why this was so because they are confidential matters, which I have not been given permission to write about. However, it highlights several of the issues that arose in the pursuit of Goal 1, particularly those relating to a sustainable infrastructure, adequate recruitment, selection and induction procedures, and support for workers.

Beyond the immediate causes, there were some issues arising from the initial establishment of the incarnational youth work project in Forgreen that contributed to the problem. Within YFC there had been a group looking at urban projects and a plan was developed for two families to move to a city close to the national head quarters and start an incarnational urban youth project. This would have given access to good quality administrative and pastoral support close at hand, as well as a centre to take young people. Unfortunately this plan was not carried out, and one of the couples was permitted to move and establish some work in Forgreen, where there was little access to the sort of support and infrastructure necessary to sustain such work. These decisions were made outside of the established structure with regard to urban work with the then National Director taking a lead in supporting the development of this project. This made the project somewhat vulnerable and isolated from the beginning, because a vision (that had not been fully tested) was implemented in a place where there was not adequate support to develop and sustain it. Andy and Julie had joined the project expecting to work with this initial couple who soon left the area and Christian ministry. They were then placed in a situation that they had not anticipated, with Andy taking on a leadership role that had not originally been envisaged in such a short time span. One hopeful thing to emerge from these difficulties is that the person now in charge of this type of local project believes 'what happened meant that the work in [elsewhere in the same city] became far more focused and able to learn from the mistakes elsewhere.'

Tackling Problems and Effecting Change
YFC is an organization where change happens rapidly. This can cause problems when trying to effect specific changes. Events can overtake you; and this happened with this research project. If beginning again, I would identify a wider pool with which to work. With two of the three potential local projects having internal problems, it was always going to be difficult to accomplish, as planned, some of the tasks. Learning from experience, the research project would have benefited from the inclusion of Senior Managers more fully in the initial project process. Although I was supported in my desire to undertake the project, I might have benefited from consulting them to a greater extent. Also, this would have aided implementation of the findings.

One thing that has been helpful is using technology to aid research. I have sent out numerous pieces of paper trying to get information from staff on various issues. Using e-mail, I received at least a 90% response compared with 25% with paper. Even people who regularly respond on e-mail, do not always do so on paper. If tackling problems in the future, I would consider how to utilise this further. However, since not all YFC staff are accessible on e-mail this could result in an unrepresentative sample, although this is less and less true as time goes on. Another approach is to telephone people and get the necessary information in that way. However, this is not a mode of communication that I favour and there was no one else to whom it could be delegated. The styles of communication that worked best in my work environment were face-to-face contact and e-mails. I found that people enjoyed being asked for their opinion and being listened to, and that, in itself, was a helpful and supportive task to undertake. It almost would not have mattered what the subject was; being listened to, and opinions being valued, can boost staff morale.

I began this section by saying that YFC is an organization where there are rapid changes. However, in some ways change happens slowly. This can be true in areas of work where you are trying to take a new approach and break down old barriers. Incarnational workers feel that they are involved in developing a new approach because proclamation evangelism has been the predominant style used in the past by YFC. Raising awareness of other methods has taken time. When 'big' changes are identified as necessary and there is only a limited time within a project to address them, there can be frustration. What I found was that although changes were not immediately apparent, I could put in place systems or policies that I hope will enable change to take place in the future.

Another unexpected point to emerge from this research is that so often there is helpful knowledge and good practice available, which has not been widely disseminated. An example of this from the project was the methods of measuring incarnational youth ministry. I came across two of the methods by accident. Being willing to share our expertise and experience is a great help. Reasons for not sharing include a lack of confidence that what one has to offer is worth anything. Workers need to get past a reluctance to share and realise that there are riches to be found in unexpected places. In tackling problems and effecting change, workers need to be open about their need for help. YFC also needs to work out how to share what is discovered.

It sometimes felt as if I had taken on an impossible task. If I had realised at the beginning of this process the problems that were to be faced by the local projects I wanted to work with, I am not sure that I would have chosen this avenue to explore. While what happened does reflect the problems that YFC has in the area of incarnational urban youth ministry, it was disappointing to see the disintegration of one project and the structural problems in another. It is very interesting to note that the 'successful' project (at least in terms of structure and worker stability) was All Saints, which is part of a strong church with a supportive leadership, although also in the inner-city as Forgreen was. This is an issue that YFC need to take note of when planning the location of other incarnational urban youth ministry projects.

While these three goals were being pursued I was also undertaking some biblical and theological research to help develop an understanding of incarnational urban youth ministry beyond that reported by workers. The hope at this stage was to develop a theological rationale for incarnational urban youth ministry that arose out of workers' experience but that was informed by appropriate biblical and theological material. The results of this research are contained in the next chapter.

Chapter 5

Reflection on Workers' Experience in the Light of the Example of Jesus Christ

> The starting point [of theological reflection] is experience – a full, deep, meaningful embrace of life. Reflection as a method involves recognizing what is in an event, naming it, relating it to other experiences and reflections, letting it shape the future (Kinast 1996: xiii).

Theological reflection is a discipline used in ministerial training or on practical theology courses. The titles and subtitles of two books on the subject highlight this: *Let Ministry Teach: A Guide to Theological Reflection* (Kinast 1996) and *Method in Ministry: Theological Reflection and Christian Ministry* (Whitehead and Whitehead 1995). There has also been a book in the, *What are they saying about...* series that explores biblical and contemporary theological themes (Kinast 2000).[1] In this book Kinast identifies five main styles of theological reflection: these are: ministerial, spiritual

---

[1] A helpful book giving a comprehensive overview of the topic and a variety of approaches to using theological reflection in practice is *The Art of Theological Reflection* (Killen and de Beer 1994).

wisdom, feminist, inculturation, and practical (2000: v).[2] Each style has three main elements, beginning with experience, correlating the experience with sources of Christian tradition, and identifying implications and action for the Christian life (2000: 1). The work of key practitioners for each style is identified and described.

Three of the styles of theological reflection are particularly helpful in understanding the theological reflection of this research project. In presenting a *ministerial* style of theological reflection, Kinast draws on the work of the Whiteheads. Their model uses three sources that they believe are important for pastoral decision making: 'Christian tradition, personal experience, and the resources of culture' (Whitehead and Whitehead 1995: x). They go on to describe the method that they encourage. They identify three stages:

> The initial stage (attending) involves seeking out the diverse information residing, often in a partly-hidden fashion, in personal experiences, the religious tradition and the culture. An intermediate stage (assertion) instigates a dialogue among these sources of information in order to clarify, challenge, and purify the insights and limits of each. The final stage (pastoral response) moves the reflection from insight toward personal and communal action (1995: x).

The situation analysis that began my research encompasses the attending stage, the action research project relates to the assertion stage as I used information gained in the situation analysis to put together the goals of the research project. The pieces of work arising out of the action research project such as the training policy, the paper on fruitfulness, and the final chapter, the manifesto for incarnational youth ministry will be the pastoral response stage. A difference between this model and some others is the inclusion of attending to culture as well as experience and tradition. This has been incorporated in two ways: a brief examination of youth culture and an exploration of the culture of YFC. Both of these will have an influence on the shape of the pastoral response.

The approach of Killen and de Beer is classified by Kinast as a *spiritual wisdom* style of theological reflection (2000: 15). They see the need for theological reflection as connected to the human drive for meaning (1994:x-xi). They analyze the way that humans naturally reflect and describe a five-part 'movement toward insight' (1994: 20). They describe this movement thus: 'When we enter our experience, we encounter our feelings. When we pay attention to those feelings, images

---

[2] These are the titles of the five main chapters of the book.

arise. Considering and questioning those images may spark insight. Insight leads, if we are willing and ready, to action' (1994: 21). What is helpful in this method is the focus on feelings and images. This puts words around what I experienced as a partly intuitive process in identifying kenosis as a concept to explore in relation to incarnational youth ministry. It is also an approach that would resonate well with incarnational youth workers who find feelings and images are an easier point of entry to theological reflection than other aspects of tradition. Using the image of fruitfulness was one way I sought to utilize a mode of communication to which incarnational youth workers could relate.

Kinast describes the *practical* style category of theological reflection as 'a critical reflection on current praxis rather than an application of theory to practice, and it concentrates on the community of faith and its relationship to the larger society' (2000:52). An example, in a British context, is the work of Ballard and Pritchard (1996). Their book *Practical Theology in Action* is subtitled *Christian Thinking in the Service of Church and Society*, which is relevant for the community focus of incarnational youth ministry. They regard theological reflection on practice as 'one of the indispensable tools of ministry. With it we will learn from experience and grow in ministerial maturity. Without it we run the risk either of pastoral ineffectiveness or of great error' (1996: 134). They take as a basic model the pastoral cycle, which they describe as usually having a four-fold action of experience, exploration, reflection, and action (1996:77-78). Their chapter called theological reflection specifically refers to the third phase of the cycle, but a broader understanding, as related in other passages, sees the whole process as theological reflection. What is helpful about the pastoral cycle is that it develops into a spiral, because each time you go through the cycle you begin again in a new place. This helpful insight lies behind the shaping of the manifesto. It could not have been written as it has been until the research had been completed; because each new area of study that opened up brought the understanding of incarnational youth ministry to a new place.

In the rest of this chapter, and those that follow, I do not adopt any one of these particular styles of theological reflection but seek to work with the core ideas of starting with experience, drawing in tradition, reflecting on the dialogue, and proposing action. In this chapter the tradition is that of the biblical narrative concerning Jesus.

Being 'Incarnational' Youth Workers – What are the Lessons to Learn from Jesus?

This is the question that I attempt to answer in this chapter. I began by thinking through what I had heard from incarnational youth workers, the way they had talked about their experiences and their understanding of their role (stage one). I then used this material and sought to relate it to the biblical research that was being undertaken (stage two) to try and draw out implications of what it meant to be an 'incarnational' youth worker (stage three). These implications will relate both to the workers and to the supporting agencies. The implications of being an incarnational youth worker seem to fall into two main categories which dominate the structure of this chapter:

♦ particular challenges and problems faced by incarnational youth workers
♦ principles for incarnational youth ministry.

Various issues relating to these two categories will be explored in more detail below as the experience of workers is taken as a starting point for reflection.

Main Biblical Sources
Throughout this research an understanding of the culture and tradition of YFC has been considered as an integral element in identifying material as part of the theological reflection process towards a pastoral response. This is why the main focus of reflection in this chapter is biblical, since that is the aspect of tradition most respected in YFC. Two main sources were selected for biblical reflection on the life and ministry of Jesus. The first was Philippians 2:5-11 because it had been highlighted as an important text in defining incarnational youth work from the perspective of the workers themselves. Furthermore, it was a key text used by YFC in a major promotional tool.[3] As the research developed it became clear that this was a text that merited deeper exploration and this is to be found in Chapter Seven.

The second biblical source was the gospel of Luke. In seeking to explore the life and ministry of Jesus it appeared most straightforward to focus on one of the gospel accounts. Luke was selected for three main reasons. The first was that his spirituality seemed helpful when considering long-term incarnational urban youth ministry. According to Stephen Barton, 'It is appropriate…to interpret the Lucan teaching as intending to foster a strong sense of the life of faith as a journey with the Lord Jesus in the context of which he makes known the qualities of character he requires of his followers' (1992: 100). He elaborates Luke's spirituality for 'the long haul' (1992: 100-104). Such a spirituality would be very applicable to incarnational workers.

---

[3] An international video in the 1980s.

The second reason for choosing Luke is the way that women are treated in the gospel. From a personal perspective, and in an organization committed to women's full participation in ministry, it is appropriate to reflect on a gospel that gives a more significant place to stories about women. Seim writes, 'It has been one of the common truths of Christian Testament scholarship that Luke shows a particular interest in women' (1994: 728). This was highlighted by several of the commentators I consulted. Prior comments that 'His portrayal of Jesus' concern for women is striking, when one remembers the patriarchal nature of the society' (1995: 50). Fitzmyer in summarising some of the themes in Luke's gospel that should be noted mentions 'the prominence of women in various episodes of Jesus' ministry; the pairing off of parables of men and women' (1981: 258). Cassidy argues that his reading of Luke suggests 'that Jesus had adopted a pattern of behaviour that implicitly opened the way to a new personal identity and social standing for women. By implication, their social roles were to be broadened appreciably, and they were to be participants in community life as independent persons' (1978: 37). However, some argue that Luke should not be interpreted as depicting a Jesus who liberates women. Seim summarizes the two sides of the argument:

> This difference between the two volumes [Luke and Acts] corresponds to a remarkable divergence in the present perception regarding the treatment of women by Luke: Is Luke within the Christian Testament corpus a rare friend of women reflecting equality and a radical revision of the role of women in the early church? Or is his major contribution to impose 'the Lukan silence', representing a programmatic androcentrism that pleads the subordination of women in a more subtle and indirect manner than the direct parenetic enforcement of the letters? (1994: 728).

After reviewing the material. Seim concludes that there is an ambiguity in Luke's gospel; she suggests that Luke 'transmits a double message...The women are brought to silence, but at the same time they continue to speak through the story' (1994: 761). In my own reading of the gospel the prominence of women, and particularly their involvement in the passion narrative, has been a liberating experience; they 'speak to me through the story'. Despite the ambiguity of possible interpretations about the role of women, I shall focus on Luke's gospel because women are more prominent than in the other gospels and it holds out the possibility of reading the text in terms of a more equal role for women. This is important to some of the incarnational youth workers I have spoken to who are committed to challenging discrimination in all its forms.

The third reason for drawing upon Luke is the emphasis on the poor and marginalized, which is shared by incarnational urban youth workers. Caird suggests that the whole of Luke's gospel is a commentary on the theme of the Kingdom of God. He writes:

> All his tenderness of heart and mastery of description are called into play as he presents to us the cavalcade of witnesses who can testify to the presence of the kingdom because they have discovered in Jesus the friend and champion of the sick, the poor, the penitent, the outcast, of women, Samaritans, and Gentiles (1963: 37).

This emphasis resonates strongly with incarnational urban youth workers who feel called to work amongst their contemporary counterparts.

Challenges and Problems Faced by Incarnational Youth Workers

Because this research arose out of a concern that YFC were not retaining incarnational urban youth workers, this section explores some of the difficulties workers have which may contribute to workers leaving this ministry prematurely. The focus on supporting workers may thus come across a little negatively. However, it should be read in conjunction with the material in Chapter 3 on fruitfulness, which considered many of the positive aspects of the ministry. Because of this danger of seeming negative it is important to emphasise the exciting and rewarding nature of incarnational youth ministry. It is a privilege to live and minister among those who are some of the most disadvantaged, and workers believed and communicated this to me. I have certainly experienced it myself over the last five years in inner city Birmingham.

When exploring the challenges and problems faced by incarnational youth workers, issues around management were the greatest concern. A number of other issues were raised, the major ones being the temptations faced by workers, meeting workers' needs, and the likelihood of being misunderstood. These are dealt with below.

Temptations

The synoptic gospels all recount that Jesus faced temptation at the beginning of his ministry. Nolland suggests that although there may be some doubt as to whether the temptation account is a literal one, 'there seems to be no particular reason for doubting that in some form or other the opening of Jesus' ministry was marked by such Satanic attack, probably in the context of a period of seclusion in the wilderness' (1989: 177). The temptations in Luke come in a different order to those in Matthew. There is no clear agreement about what the original order in Q[4] was or why they are presented differently. Fitzmyer provides a plausible argument in suggesting that 'Luke is said to have reversed the order of the last two scenes because of his geographical perspective – the climactic scene takes place in Jerusalem' (1981: 507)[5]. An interesting point is made by Evans who comments that 'Luke saw the whole life of Jesus as one of temptation, which comes to a head in the passion' (1990: 255). This highlights an important issue, that it is not only at the beginning of ministry that one is vulnerable to temptation. As circumstances change then a worker may become prey to new or different temptations. It is important for workers and those who support them to be aware of both the potential and actual pressures and problems to be faced in such ministry, so as to avoid them bringing a premature end to the ministry of the worker. This may need a culture of honesty and openness rather than the triumphalism or martyrdom that is sometimes a feature of evangelicalism.

In considering the temptations faced by Jesus it is helpful to note, as Fitzmyer does, that: 'The unifying link in the three is the series of quotations from Deuteronomy [chs. 6-8], derived from passages that recall three events of the Exodus in which the Israelites in the desert were put to the test and failed' (1981: 510). Green elaborates this:

> According to Deuteronomy, (1) Israel was allowed to hunger in order to learn that one does not live by bread alone (8:3); (2) Israel was instructed to worship the one and only God, and not to follow after any other god (6:4-15); and (3) Israel was commanded not to put the Lord God to the test (6:16). In each case Israel failed in their obedience to God (1997: 192).

Part of the significance of the temptation narrative is this parallel between Israel and Jesus. Goulder concludes that 'It is widely agreed that the thrust of the story is a contrast between Israel's failures in the desert and Jesus' victories' (1989a: 295).

Caird brings a different emphasis and makes an important point about the temptation narratives when he makes five observations about what is learnt about evil from the passage:

1. Evil is real and potent.
2. Evil is personal.
3. Evil is distorted good.

---

[4] Stanton writes that, 'Most recent writers assume 'Q' existed as a written document which disappeared shortly after it was incorporated by Matthew and Luke into their Gospels' (1992: 644). The rest of the article gives an overview of thinking on the topic.

[5] A view also held by Nolland (1989: 179).

4. Evil masquerades as good.
5. Evil is the enemy (1963: 79).

Those who are living and working in the inner city will be aware of the evil that exists; what they need to be particularly aware of is the way that this evil may trap them into betraying their original call and vision. Caird goes on to argue that:

> A man of fervent and dedicated spirit, feeling himself called to liberate the oppressed and to establish the reign of justice and peace, would be open to three types of temptation: to allow the good to usurp the place of the best, to seek God's ends by means alien to God's character, and to force God's hand by taking short cuts to success. And these are the three temptations of Jesus (1963: 79-80).

The focus on temptation came directly out of situations that had been perceived to go wrong, with a particular concern on the early stages of ministry. I sought to explore what some of those issues were and what might be learnt from the life and ministry of Jesus to help address them.

Sometimes incarnational urban youth workers come into ministry having experienced little testing. This lack of testing can potentially be dangerous, both for the person themselves and for the people they work with. If a worker succumbs to temptation and trust is broken, because a person has to leave prematurely, for example, it can negatively affect young people's perception of the church and Christianity. When we consider the gospel narrative of Jesus' life, Jesus did not begin his public ministry until he was about thirty,[6] and he was tested prior to his mission as the temptation narratives show.[7] This is a different experience to many in YFC. They can become involved in public ministry from age sixteen. A few will never have worked outside of a ministry context. This may be something YFC should reflect upon as they consider the recruitment of staff. Ever since I have been involved in YFC there has been a lot of talk about giving young people responsibility from an early age. Currently, the idea of peer leaders and younger leaders seems to be a trend in youth ministry. Is this an appropriate response to modern culture or is it part of that culture's veneration of youth and denigration of old age? It should be noted that the concept of 'young man' is a cultural one and Fitzmyer suggests that

---

[6] Luke 3:23. Nolland comments that, 'Luke uses the language of approximation for Jesus' age. The most that can be suggested is that such an age denotes an adequate measure of maturity (cf. Num 4:3)' (1989: 171).
[7] Lk. 4:1-13; Matt. 4:1-17; Mk. 1:12-13.

the reference to Saul as a young man[8] in Acts 7:58 could 'designate anyone from 24-40 years of age' (1998: 394). Perhaps a more important focus should be on the personal maturity of the individual, their self-awareness and understanding of their calling and role, rather than merely on age.

In reflecting on this idea that temptations relate to who a person is and how they see their role, I sought to identify the types of temptations faced by incarnational urban youth workers today. Rather than engaging in historical exegesis I have sought to use the narrative as a framework for exploring temptations faced by incarnational urban youth workers. I took as a starting point the areas of the flesh, idolatry, and power suggested by the temptation stories of Jesus. This will not be an exhaustive list of temptations but will indicate some of the key issues and pressures faced and raise awareness of the level of support, induction, training, and resources needed to help incarnational urban youth workers fulfil their mission.

Temptations of the Flesh[9]

In concluding his comments on the first temptation, Caird writes, 'To give priority to man's physical needs is to strip him of his dignity and make him one with the beasts that perish' (1963: 80). Caird has moved beyond looking solely at hunger for food as a temptation to generalizing about physical need. The question posed by Green could apply beyond bread to the satisfaction of other appetites: 'Will Jesus follow the leading of the Spirit and manifest unwavering trust in God to supply his needs; or will he relieve his hunger by exercising his power apart from God?' (1997: 194). The emphasis in Luke on Jesus being 'full of the Holy Spirit'[10] brings a recognition that workers need to trust the presence of the Spirit for the inner resources to stand against the temptations and testing that will certainly come their way.

In general terms, the first temptation relates to quick fix solutions to personal needs. The temptation for Jesus on a fast was related to food. For most workers it is not a physical hunger for food that causes them problems. Although there are a variety of physical

---

[8] Greek word *neanias*.

[9] I have deliberately chosen to use this term because it is one that has been used often in evangelical circles and gives a flavour of the sort of issues that are likely to be faced.

[10] Luke 4:1. Marshall writes, 'From the baptism onwards Jesus is continually filled with the Spirit…The role of the Spirit is primarily guidance, but there is no reason to exclude the thought of his powerful inspiration which (for Luke) enabled Jesus to overcome the tempter' (1978: 168-69).

needs or hungers that could be related to this temptation, the one most often talked about in youth ministry is sex. Despite an increasing willingness by workers today to talk about personal issues, such as sexual attraction, there can still be a hostility and readiness to judge amongst some. This can inhibit workers from talking easily about temptations in this realm. When a speaker at YFC Staff Training talked very honestly about sexual attraction towards a member of his church, some found it helpful and an opening for them to talk about their struggles. Others reacted less positively and were critical of the speaker and questioned whether he was an appropriate person to be invited.

YFC is aware of some of the issues and problems of sexual attraction and have had to face a range of difficult situations with both staff and volunteers. It has often been the case that frequent close contact between people over a period of time has resulted in sexual attraction developing, even when there was no initial attraction. With YFC's volunteers, there is a pastoral structure that seeks to provide people outside of the work environment to share with regularly. Some staff will have organised this for themselves. However, YFC should perhaps consider how personal accountability can be encouraged without it seeming as if the organization has a heavy 'shepherding' style of leadership.[11] Recent discussions have led to a suggestion that national YFC staff should have a day a term, that comes out of work time, to see someone for prayer, support, and so on. However, ultimately individuals are responsible for their own actions and there are likely to be continuing problems in this area, whatever support is provided, although appropriate support and a willingness on the worker's part to be open may enable some issues to be dealt with before the consequences get too serious.

YFC are aware of wider developments in this field and there

---

[11] A heavy 'shepherding' style of leadership may seek to put boundaries around a range of behaviour such as contact with the opposite sex or alcohol consumption, for example. This is done with volunteers in the form of an agreement that they sign, however, it is not made explicit with staff. Trying to make expectations of behaviour in an evangelical Christian organization clear while also treating people like mature adults can be a difficult tension. It is a complex issue that needs openness and honesty in debating it. The 'shepherding' movement arose in the 1960s and 70s and Barr suggests 'The motivation is clearly to bring moral accountability and spiritual maturity into the church in an age of immorality, irresponsibility and selfish individualism…There are dangers, however…Advice may be sought, community and support must be encouraged, but no single individual has an exclusive right to claim to know God's will for another believer' (1988: 639-40). See also Storr (1997).

has been considerable work done within the organization on child protection.[12] YFC have a child protection policy and compulsory training for all volunteers and workers. Generally, there is a high level of awareness of what is good and appropriate practice. However, little attention has been given beyond this to relationships with adults, colleagues, and volunteers, where most of the issues within YFC regarding temptations of the flesh have taken place. Developments outside of the organization need to be explored and best practice incorporated. One such development that may be helpful is the introduction of a policy by the Church of England relating to adults, not children.[13] In the Anglican theological college where I teach, the Principal has asked for it to be incorporated into modules. I have thus recently led a session on this with a group of youth work students where we looked at abuse, harassment, and bullying. An important point was that abuse could still take place even when there was consent because of the power dynamics involved. When someone is in leadership they have the responsibility not to break trust and to be accountable. Such training, along with being honest with potential workers about the temptations they may face would be a helpful contribution to supporting urban youth workers.

Although sex is an obvious issue to consider as a temptation of the flesh, there will be other issues that could be a problem to workers. It is important that there are mechanisms that help workers identify and address temptations of the flesh, which could range from excessive intake of alcohol to craving praise and affirmation in such a way that the ministry amongst young people is adversely affected. Some people find it hard to find their personal identity and affirmation in who they are in God and can be tempted to manipulate other workers or young people to meet their own emotional needs. It is also important spiritually for workers to realise that God makes provision for his people and is willing and able to meet the needs of those being tempted. This relates back to the need for people to maintain a good relationship with God and to have the space and time for this. If a worker is stressed and under pressure there is more danger of falling prey to temptations of the flesh and if God seems distant and remote there is less chance of accessing the spiritual resources needed to withstand temptation.

---

[12] See, for example the policy document on Child Protection from the House of Bishops (1999).
[13] "The Mistreatment of Adults by Those Authorised by Bishop's Licence To Leadership Positions in the Church." (House of Bishops: 2001)

Temptations of Idolatry

Nolland suggests that the second temptation faced by Jesus is 'a universal human temptation' (1989: 180). Fitzmyer describes it thus: 'This testing is not directed to him explicitly as Son, but it is challenging him to acknowledge someone other than the Father as his master and lord' (1981: 511). This is a form of idolatry. A recent paper called *Idolatry and spiritual parody: counterfeit faiths* looks back to the Church Fathers for a definition of idolatry:

> Idolatry, insists Tertullian, occurs when something is elevated 'in place of God, against God, and needs no physical idol. It matters not whether the 'something' is physical, or an abstract idea, or a lifestyle, or a political party, or even a conception of God originating purely in human imagination. For something originated has taken the place of the unoriginated (Ovey 2002: 2).[14]

In general terms, the second temptation relates to the way in which humans put something in the place which only God should fill. One of the saddest things I have seen in incarnational youth ministry is the pain and suffering caused when leaders who had become idols to those they worked amongst fell from that position. A danger in Christian ministry is the dominating charismatic personality who encourages people to follow them in such a way that people put more trust in them than they do in God. When something goes wrong it is devastating for those who are involved, as in the case of Chris Brain and the Nine O'Clock Service in Sheffield.[15] Storr, in a study of gurus called *Feet of Clay*, gives a warning about such people. He writes, 'many of those who are most obviously charismatic are, from the human point of view, deeply flawed characters who should be regarded with extreme caution' (1997: 220). He indicates some signs that give rise to concern: 'The gurus who should be regarded as potentially dangerous are those who are authoritarian and those who are paranoid. These two characteristics march hand in hand. I would like to add another; the capacity for oratory; perhaps the most dangerous weapon in a guru's armoury' (1997: 221). A particular cause for concern are gurus who seek to exercise control over different areas of their followers' lives or those who lead movements that cut themselves off geographically or socially. He believes that many gurus become sexually and financially corrupt because they are concerned with their own dominance (1997: 220-21). Storr also identifies some of the

---

[14] For further reading on idolatry as a problem in Christianity see *Harmful Religion* by Lawrence Osborn and Andrew Walker (1997).

[15] See *The Rise and Fall of the Nine O'Clock Service* (Howard 1996).

characteristics of leaders who can be trusted: they are non-authoritarian and seek to educate rather than dominate; they retain integrity; they influence others through their private behaviour (1997: 225-26). In considering human idols, Storr's work brings a sharp focus to the necessity of challenging or raising concerns if there are warning signs in the leadership of any project or ministry.

One of the difficulties in the whole mentoring/apprenticing approach to training and development is whether or not a dependence and trust on God is built rather than on the mentor. This perhaps relates back to the maturity of individuals involved in ministry, and the need for greater preparation and identification of appropriate support structures that seek to enable individuals to grow and develop in their faith. Safeguards also need to be put into place through appropriate training and supervision and the accessibility of someone whom an individual can approach to express concerns. A willingness of other workers to challenge what they see as inappropriate practice or behaviour should also be encouraged. Self-awareness sometimes only develops through a painful series of challenges where the impression that is being created is fed back to the individual initiating inappropriate behaviour.

Another temptation for workers is to make their own ministry into an idol. There can be a danger of believing that one is doing authentic ministry while others are just playing at it. If the type of ministry one is involved in is marginalized by the organization then this can exacerbate the problem. One manifestation of this can be adopting an exclusive or superior attitude. God calls people to different tasks in different contexts and it is not for Christians to judge the validity or otherwise of another's ministry based solely on the geographical location or people group one works with. I have observed the 'my area is worse than your area' type of conversation. This can be difficult for younger staff or volunteers who can perhaps make the wrong decision for future ministry based on a false hierarchy of values, or admiration for a particular worker or project. I have worked with several students who have been attracted by the 'glamorous' picture of urban ministry painted by those who have a calling and aptitude to it. The glamour quickly wears off when reality kicks in and students have changed their placement because they could not cope with the pressures they faced as an incarnational urban youth worker: they had been seduced by a false picture of what the ministry would be like.

One potential idol relates to the work and the desire to be a certain sort of worker. The wanting to 'be there' for young people, the desire to be available or needed, can quickly lead to burnout if boundaries are not put in place to limit availability. A further work related problem is being over confident and taking risks that are unnecessary. Empire building can be a problem for some, starting project after project without the infrastructure that justifies such expansion. Some goals may be good in and of themselves. An example might be the pursuit of justice or a good education for one's family. However, the pursuit of such goals can become more important than seeking God and pursuing his will. In Christian ministry, it can be quite easy for workers to find the time to pursue their own vision at the expense of the work they are paid to do or persuade others that their vision is actually God's vision for the project. Identifying aspects of the work where workers are prone to have idols can be helpful for those involved in supporting incarnational workers, because they may be able to identify danger signals before the worker is aware there is a problem. Each of us is vulnerable to different kinds of idolatry and it is helpful to have people alongside helping and supporting us. Workers need to identify and acknowledge what the potential idols are for them, individually, and work at dealing with them rather than letting them become stumbling blocks to effective ministry.[16]

Temptation to Misuse Power

In the third temptation, the devil encourages Jesus to demonstrate that he is God's Son by throwing himself from a great height and expecting God to protect him. It is a temptation to manipulate and misuse his position as Son of God; and Jesus resisted it. Fitzmyer describes it thus: 'Jesus is challenged again as Son to use his power to reveal himself...to his contemporaries and to conform to popular ideas of what a heaven-sent leader of the people would be' (1981: 511). Green describes the response of Jesus as recognizing 'the devil's strategy as an attempt to deflect him from his single-minded commitment to loyalty and obedience in God's service' (1997:196).

In general terms, the third temptation relates to the way in which humans exploit their position or power to achieve their ends. Misuse of power or position by incarnational urban youth workers could arise in several different ways. The first is in direct relation to young people. The sort of young people that incarnational urban youth workers are dealing with are often quite vulnerable, and there is a danger of spiritual abuse. An example of this is pressing a young person to make a commitment to Christ prematurely, so that they respond to please a worker rather than in response to the work of the Holy Spirit. There is also a danger of encouraging young people to be

---

[16] The material in this section comes from my own experience and that of a group of youth work trainers connected to the Centre for Youth Ministry.

too dependent on the worker. This can happen when instead of trying to empower a young person to make their own decisions the worker becomes a guru for the young person and provides the answers to all their questions. Again a discipling relationship, although sounding good in theory, can be a source of exploitation when a worker takes on a shepherding relationship holding the young person inappropriately accountable, rather than helping the young person grow in their relationship with God. This is to misuse the worker's position.

Another potential misuse of power reflects the danger of trying to put God or others on the spot in order to satisfy oneself that one is loved, affirmed or appreciated. Bock suggests that if Jesus responded positively to Satan in the third temptation he would be saying to God: 'I do not think you will take care of me as Son, to be sure I am going to place you in a situation where you must take care of me now and on my terms.' This demanding of miraculous protection, where it is not needed, is not faith or loyalty. It is sin' (1994: 381). When a worker is feeling low or discouraged there can be a temptation to fall into this sort of trap: to try and get God to do something, to give a sign or meet a need, for example, because the worker themselves needs more than their call to be able to continue trusting in God in that situation. As the Gideon story shows,[17] seeking a sign is not always wrong, but workers must be aware of the dangers of seeking to put God to the test.

A related idea is the danger of misusing scripture. In this third temptation it is suggested that the devil 'wants to recruit Jesus to participate in a test of the divine promises of Psalm 91' (Green 1997: 195). The devil uses scripture to try and get Jesus to conform to his will rather than the will of God. Workers may be tempted to do this with young people or with colleagues by using scripture to gain a measure of control over others. There is the related danger of a worker reading into Scripture what they want to hear God saying, so that it becomes an exercise in feeding their ego or their desires. Workers need to identify and acknowledge the ways in which they may be tempted to misuse their position *vis-a-vis* young people so that they can avoid a use of power which is controlling rather than enabling.

How Jesus Dealt with Temptation
The first point to note, and to communicate to workers, is that being tempted does not mean that a worker has necessarily done anything wrong. As Bock writes regarding Jesus: 'Such an emphasis [of the leading of the Holy Spirit] makes clear that Jesus' being exposed to temptation was not his fault in any way' (1994: 368-69). Workers can

---

[17] Judges 6:36-40.

take encouragement that Jesus has shared the kind of experiences they face: Hebrews 4:15-16 says: 'For we do not have a high priest who is unable to sympathize with our weaknesses, but we have one who in every respect has been tested as we are, yet without sin. Let us therefore approach the throne of grace with boldness, so that we may receive mercy and find grace to help in time of need'.

In the case of Jesus, as Marshall suggests, the temptations can be seen as attempts to deflect Jesus from his purpose (1978: 166). Obviously, temptations can deflect incarnational workers from their purpose. YFC need to consider how best they can help workers identify areas of temptation and also set up structures that enable such situations to be faced with support and encouragement, rather than privately and fearfully. This is particularly important in long-term incarnational urban youth ministry where it is easy for workers to identify with the despair that the young people are feeling. The temptation to become despairing and cynical is very real. It is often these more hidden pressures that are so hard to deal with. Saying no to drugs, or too much alcohol, is not difficult for many workers, but dealing with persistent negative attitudes, for example, can be very hard and can also damage the work.

The way Jesus lived his life and faced temptation can provide some help to workers when they are tempted. Bock suggests: 'The ultimate way to avoid falling into temptation is not to go one's own way. Faithfulness to God involves trusting him, worshiping him alone, and refusing to create a test of his goodness...Life is defined as doing God's will and walking in God's way, even if it entails suffering and self-denial' (1994: 383-84). Another aspect of this is described by Fitzmyer who describes how Jesus faced temptation. He writes 'He is portrayed as the conqueror because he is armed with 'the sword of the Spirit, the word of God,' to put it in non-Lucan, but nevertheless apt (Eph. 6:17) terminology' (1981: 512-13). So much seems to come back to maintaining a good relationship with God that the whole area of spiritual formation needs to be seriously considered and workers encouraged to find or develop a spirituality that nourishes and sustains them. There can be a danger sometimes of seeing people in ministry as superheroes. Having the right attitude to one's calling and ministry can help a worker withstand some of the temptations. The attitude towards ministry is discussed in depth in Chapter 7 on kenosis.

Meeting of Workers' Needs

A constant issue for workers engaged in long term incarnational youth ministry is about whether their needs, particularly material needs, will be met. At the beginning of both Luke 9 and 10, the sending out of the twelve and then the seventy, disciples are exhorted to take nothing with them on their journey. Others providing for the needs of those in ministry is assured in these passages. Marshall comments that the disciples can expect 'not opulence, but simply sustenance' (1978: 421). How far these instructions, relating to one incident, can be seen as relevant to mission today, is an interesting question. They refer to a specific short-term situation. A point made by commentators is that the instructions set the disciples apart and contrasted them with 'other peddlers of religion and philosophy. Modesty is the rule, ministry is the focus' (Bock 1994: 819). The latter phrase could well provide a principle to consider for those engaging in mission. Other passages such as 1 Corinthians 9 and 2 Corinthians 8-9, where in the former Paul argues for a right to support and in the latter the principle of generous giving to meet others' needs, suggest that ministers can expect support.

Theissen's categories of legitimacy for the missionary, based on the apostle Paul, have some relevance to understanding the position of incarnational youth workers. He describes 'a charismatic legitimation based on a style of life qualified in a special way'; 'a traditional legitimation based on origin (by means of commissions and traditions which have been received)'; a 'functional legitimation based on work which has been accomplished or is yet to be done' (1982: 42). How a worker understands their role in terms of these different categories may also affect perceptions of support, which has been a controversial issue in incarnational youth ministry within Youth for Christ. The second category is not so relevant in the discussion on incarnational youth workers except to the extent that a worker's call may be recognised as legitimate by a sending or home church and by the receiving church. Theissen's explanation of the first category involves trusting God's grace. A modern interpretation of this would be 'living by faith' which fits in with Theissen's explanation that it 'makes one dependent on others' generosity, which cannot be calculated in advance' (1982: 43). The style of life of an incarnational youth worker in this respect has been seen as following God's call to live in a specific place to work amongst young people there and to raise support from others to do this. This was the situation of some incarnational youth workers in Youth for Christ when the ministry first emerged, although others were given very low salaries and had to trust God for the rest. The situation now is more like the third category, with workers being paid a salary for a job to be done. Sometimes it is a professional level salary, particularly where government or trust funding has been raised, in other cases there is still an element of a vocational salary where workers are making a conscious choice to accept such a post.

Whether a worker is paid a salary in long-term incarnational urban youth ministry or raise their own support themselves, ultimately, the money often comes from other people's giving. This can lead to workers being very sensitive about how they use that money, despite the fact that one can make a biblical case for those involved in mission to be thus supported. The meaning of terms such as 'opulence' and 'sustenance' can vary from person to person; what is a luxury for one person is a necessity for another. To what extent does a worker take on definitions of the local community or their peers elsewhere, for example? In our current inner-city parish we would be perceived as rich: we have a dishwasher, DVD player and a computer and car each, for example. If we move three miles up the road the contents of our house would look modest, fifty year old curtains in the main living room probably not being the norm! Which standard is right or fair to expect people to live by if they bring with them the resources from a middle class home and lifestyle? When families and children are taken into account the discussion becomes even more difficult. Are the 'right' fashionable training shoes a necessity for a child or a luxury? That may depend on the individual child, but such decisions can cause conflict. When someone is in ministry, others seem to feel they have the right to question or criticize the use of resources. Accountability for use of resources is important, but so also is trusting the integrity of workers. The use of money is an issue that needs greater debate, and workers in these situations may need help to develop realistic expectations and to work out a budget. For example, where are the safe places for a woman to go on a day off, if they do not want to go shopping, and how much would this cost? It is agreed that breaks are necessary but how are they financed? Plummer makes an interesting point that provision is 'salary and not alms'[18] (1901: 274). On this basis, if a worker is paid a salary, allowance or stipend, they should have the right to decide how to spend it just as others earning a salary do.

One of the most frequently used passages in relation to meeting needs is Luke 12:22-34. 'God's Providential Care and the Duty of Trust in Him' (1901: 325) is how Plummer labels this passage. It is an important text for those in ministry. The passage suggests that disciples should not be anxious about where their food or clothing is going to come from because God will look after them. An appeal to nature is made, God cares for the birds and humanity is more important than birds. Marshall concludes that 'God has certainly promised them the kingdom. So let them sit lightly to material possessions and help the poor; let them seek heavenly treasure, which will not perish, and thereby set their affections in the right place'. (1978: 525)

---

[18] In his commentary on Luke 10:7.

The practical outworking of this passage can be difficult to identify for incarnational workers. Clothing, for example, is a particularly sensitive issue for those involved in youth ministry. Christians can be perceived stereotypically as being boring, socks and sandals, greasy hair . Many of us will have met youth workers who are extremely effective, who make no attempt to dress fashionably, just as they will have met 'trendy' youth workers wearing all the 'right' labels. Ultimately, workers will need to be themselves, as young people can tell when they are not being authentic. For some this will mean continuing to buy expensive clothes that others would consider luxuries. You do not see many unbranded training shoes at a gathering of youth workers! Relationships are the most important thing, but sometimes image can hinder their development. Christians need to be able to live with their conscience in terms of how much they spend on what. However, sometimes workers need to ask questions about what is necessary and what is a luxury, and whether the money may be more effectively used elsewhere. Caird suggests that some of these things may not be such an issue if the injunction of the passage is followed: 'the real cure for worry is to put first things first, to care more about God's kingdom than about personal needs. Those who do so, find that God provides for his servants, but they also find that the necessities of life are fewer and simpler than selfishness supposes' (1963: 163).

Evans makes some helpful points based on the biblical passage referred to above, that those involved in incarnational work need to think through in order to make sure that they have a right attitude towards meeting their needs. He summarises why we should not worry about such issues:

> Anxious preoccupation with the means of existence is condemned on four distinct grounds - i) that life is more than the means of life, vv.22-23; ii) that it is attempting the impossible, vv. 25-26; iii) that the God who provides for birds and flowers will much more provide for disciples, vv.24, 27-30; and iv) that such things will accrue anyway to those who seek the kingdom (1990: 525).

These arguments can be hard for people to accept fully. It is interesting to note here that I have probably had more feedback on a sermon on this passage than on any other I have preached, when I emphasised the message that we should not worry but trust God who is our loving father. It is difficult in our current culture with consumerism as a predominant value not to worry about material things.[19] Again, the issue of spiritual discipline may be relevant here. Encouraging workers

---

[19] This argument is made by Cray (1998).

to meditate on scripture such as this or to use Ignatian[20] exercises to engage with the text could be helpful. Outside of this, there may perhaps be some merit in looking at collective budgets and responsibilities for raising funds so that each person does what they can rather than each person having to raise the same amount regardless of circumstances. If I was in material need, a telephone call to my family would see that need being met, but not all workers have that option and concern about material needs can take an ever-increasing amount of time and energy. This can be disabling, to this type of ministry and young people will be affected if a worker is giving much of their time and energy to worrying about financial or related issues rather than having emotional energy for the work.

Being Misunderstood
The disciples of Jesus did not understand his mission.[21] Evans, commenting on Lk. 9:43b-45 writes: 'So for Luke a principal aspect of the passion, which made it difficult for men, including the disciples, to accept Jesus as messiah, was that it contradicted their natural expectation of a hero and saviour' (1990: 425). Incarnational workers also share Jesus' fate of being misunderstood or being on the receiving end of differing expectations of what their ministry should involve. One of the frustrating things for them is that it is often other Christians who have a negative attitude towards working with the poor and the marginalized. Ajith Fernando sums up the issues when he writes, 'But the call of God is often like this. It takes us to places which others regard as impossible, to do work which looks like utter folly' (1988: 26). Randy White records the reactions his family got when they told their friends they were going to move into an inner city neighbourhood: ''You're moving where?' they would ask, and behind the question would lie not only concern for our safety but something close to a threat. Sometimes it would come right out in the open. 'I could never do what you've done'' (1996: 48).

This experience would be shared by YFC's long-term incarnational workers. They have responded to a call, it is a call that is likely to lead to them being misunderstood. In this, they share the experience of Jesus. It may be true to say that those who respond to a prophetic call will be following a different direction to the majority of their peers and that, unfortunately, there will be consequences to this that may make responding to the call more painful. For those in

---

[20] A system of meditating on the Bible by imagining oneself as part of the story or event.
[21] See, for example, Luke 9:43b-45; 18:31-34.

incarnational ministry, it is sad and demoralizing that other Christians sometimes seem to believe that someone is not being used most effectively by God if they are working among the poor. Margaret Walsh, a member of a religious order, experienced this while working 'incarnationally' in Wolverhampton. She writes: 'Some of our church friends say that we are wasting our time and that we could better use our gifts and training in the more traditional forms of evangelisation. In discussing the issue, I have found negative attitudes towards those on the margins''(1997: 75). Such a response has no biblical or theological understanding of the gospel in terms of an imperative to minister amongst the poor. However, when looking at the ministry of Jesus, it is clear that he started his work amongst the marginalized and they were the ones who followed him. Leech describes it thus: 'Jesus in fact creates a community of riffraff, and he who was himself born in the outhouse of an inn, offers grace to those who had no hope of participation in the eschatological banquet' (1990: 30). To take the incarnation seriously means that workers need to see how in their lives and ministry they can reflect Jesus' concern for the poor and marginalized. That this may mean being misunderstood is one of the costs of the ministry and something that can be hard to accept and deal with. However, as Fernando says, 'Of course, with the call of God comes God's provision, but we don't always see that at the start' (1998: 26). Being misunderstood is a difficult area to address. There is always a balance to be maintained between alerting workers of potential problems but not encouraging them to expect the worst. YFC does provide training for workers who have to raise support towards their salaries. This training helps address the issue of how a worker presents their work to others. However, more input on how to communicate a call to incarnational youth ministry to friends and family who would not immediately be sympathetic may be an important feature of equipping workers. Nevertheless, workers need to be able to live with being misunderstood.

Principles for Incarnational Youth Ministry
Other topics that emerged for reflection, along with challenges and problems faced by workers, were several that could be described as principles that underpinned incarnational youth ministry. They were aspects of the way that incarnational youth workers approach the task that seemed to be important for any such project. Thus in this section, the topics of prayer, being an example, 'being among' as a key to 'doing with', teamwork, and socio-political action are explored. The approach to this section was to identify elements of incarnational youth ministry that did not relate to specific work undertaken with young

people (this will vary according to the context), but reflected some principles that apply to this kind of ministry generally.

Prayer

The first principle that will be considered is the need for a worker to pray. Of all the things that I have been exhorted to do as a YFC worker, maintaining a regular prayer life has proved the most difficult. In talking to other workers, I know I am not alone. There are two ways in which prayer needs to be considered with respect to long-term incarnational urban youth workers. The first is for the workers themselves, helping them to develop and have time for prayer. The second is for managers in their areas of responsibility.

Jesus in prayer is a theme that runs through Luke's gospel. Barton says: 'It is important to note also, that Jesus' entire public ministry is framed by depiction of him at prayer, from the baptism to the crucifixion' (1992: 90). Spending time in prayer was something Jesus did regularly. Evans comments on 5:16, "But he withdrew' is in the periphrastic tense 'he was (in the habit of) withdrawing', not to avoid the crowds, but to punctuate the healing and preaching ministry with retreat to the desert, and for prayer' (1990: 296). This withdrawing from those one ministers among is important because it gives time to recharge spiritually, emotionally, and physically, and perhaps gain fresh insight, perspective or direction.[22] Regular prayer is important but also some pattern of retreat which allows a more protracted time to be spent seeking God and to be away from work to have the time and space to be objective. These are strategies that most would say are vital but are often squeezed out by a busy diary. Here again, the example of ordained Anglican ministry is helpful. There is a daily office to be said, which helps root ministry in prayer and, at least, an annual retreat is seen as an essential part of the pattern for ministry. Using a daily office may not be what most incarnational youth workers would be drawn to, but publications such as the Franciscans *Celebrating Common Prayer* (1992) or *Celtic Daily Prayer* (2000) from the Northumbria Community are very popular.[23] Trying to find a lifestyle that facilitates this time with God and time away from the crowds is a key to maintaining fruitfulness in ministry. If Jesus could only sustain his

---

[22] Green suggests that there is a connection between these times of prayer and the growing reputation of Jesus' ministry. He says that Luke's summary statement in 5:16 holds together 'two related phenomena' of withdrawing and praying (1997: 238).

[23] This is also available in sung and spoken formats on a CD, as very user-friendly format for youth workers who may prefer not to use books.

ministry by a spirituality that included prayer and times apart how much more true this must be for his followers.

It could perhaps be argued that one can see Jesus the manager or team leader at prayer in Luke 6:12. Here he prayed all night before announcing who the disciples were to be. A reason for this is suggested by Evans: 'Reference to an all-night vigil of prayer, which is unique, marks the importance of the occasion, and perhaps implies that the decision to appoint twelve at all, as well as their selection, was communicated by God in prayer' (1990: 319).This suggests that important decisions should be made in the context of seeking God's will. This is paralleled by Acts 13:1-3 where it was decided after fasting and prayer to send Saul and Barnabas out. In both these situations it is implied that God's will was revealed through the process of prayer. For YFC, the latter example is probably more appropriate than the former: discerning the will of God corporately has more safeguards than an individual hearing God about issues that affect people's lives. Whatever structure is most appropriate, prayer needs to be a central part of a recruitment strategy that seeks to identify those God is calling to this work. Although it is understood that those involved in the selection of workers would be praying about this, it is hard to know how to incorporate this formally into the recruitment process. Clearly prayer is not merely a management tool to be used, but neither should it be excluded as selection processes get ever more 'professional' and compliant with legislation. This is perhaps a challenge for YFC's personnel department. I am not sure that 'God said we should appoint them' would be an adequate defence at an industrial tribunal! However, there needs to be some way of marrying the spiritual insights gained from discerning God's will alongside a realistic assessment of the capacity of an individual to do the job based on evidence gathered.

It is not only in matters relating to personnel that managers need insight, it is also in relation to the work. Green suggests that it is more than just the choice of the apostles that came through prayer, it was also the work that they did: 'Both...grow out of Jesus' nocturnal prayer' (1997: 258). Caird suggests that 'He [Jesus] emerged from solitude with his path clear and resolution strong' (1963: 100). Again, in a YFC context it would be better if this happened corporately. The concept of receiving vision and direction out of a time of prayer is the right starting place for a Christian organization. A development in recent years has been that the leadership team have called regular days of prayer and fasting for the work of YFC. So often it is working out how all the different parts of the jigsaw fit together and ensuring that the insights gained from prayer get a voice in the process of appointing staff or developing vision. The integration of prayer with decision-making is vital within a Christian organization such as YFC.

Being an Example[24]

Incarnational youth workers seek to be an example or model of what Jesus is like to the young people they are working with. That's why they choose to live where they are working. Given that the young people may well not read the Bible (or only know of Jesus as represented through stained glass or art, for example), it may be that youth workers are the only representation they see. Incarnational youth workers, following the example of Jesus, can thus become representatives of Jesus, incarnate in the environment where they are living and working. Their representation may be crucial in the process of an individual young person accepting or rejecting the gospel. An implication for incarnational workers is to act intentionally the way that Jesus would (or Jesus would, if he were you) in a particular situation. Of course, it may not always be easy to see what this might mean in practice. However, such an intention, based upon the prayer and meditation highlighted in the previous section, will be likely to have some impact over a period of time. Workers can model Jesus by the way they live. Also they will need to learn and understand the culture in order to communicate in a relevant way as Jesus did.

However, the whole idea of being an example or model of Jesus is one that could put pressure on people. In an evangelical setting, this is related to a set of ethical or moral behaviours as well. Depending on the context, this can include expectations about alcohol consumption, smoking, leisure activities, dress, sexual relationships, swearing, church attendance, and one's devotional life, to list just some of the issues I have had discussions about within YFC and in various evangelical churches where I have worshipped. This is particularly a pertinent issue with people who have not grown up in an evangelical culture or who join YFC from outside of this tradition. Unrealistic expectations of what is expected need to be avoided, and one implication for YFC could be to engage more explicitly in examining the realities of life in ministry. When people move out of other types of employment there can be an expectation that there is more time for such things as prayer, bible reading, and developing one's relationship with God in Christian ministry. The experience of many is that maintaining and developing a relationship with God actually becomes more difficult in ministry. Spending time with God may now feel like

---

[24] Philippians 2:5-11 is also an important passage in discussing 'being an example'.

something a worker has to do as part of their job, rather than choosing to do so freely. Seeking to ensure that there are other more experienced workers or mature Christians that workers can talk to, particularly when they first start in incarnational youth ministry, could be an important source of support and assist workers to be realistic. Sharing the attitude or approach of Jesus is a positive concept, unless it leaves the worker constrained and condemned because they cannot reconcile aspects of their life with being an example of Jesus. Perhaps this could be explored as part of a probation, or exploratory, period when the issues around staying long term in incarnational youth ministry are examined.

If Jesus is God made manifest in human life, then studying his life and behaviour should enable Christians to see how humanity, made in the image of God, should act. In this way, incarnational youth workers can seek to show what it is to be truly human. This way of thinking can encourage a worker to be themselves, in seeking to reflect the fact that they are made in the image of God through trying to live their lives in accordance with the example set by Jesus.

'Being Among' – a Key to 'Doing With'

Incarnational youth workers have often found that it is through just being there in an area that doors open to be involved in the doing. It is the accessibility and the growing familiarity that helps build trust and a willingness on the part of a young person to engage with the worker. Jesus lived, worked, and played amongst a specific cultural group in Galilee. Much of his ministry happened as he was going about his daily life. Very little of his life is recorded, possibly because it would make very dull reading! Incarnational workers need to be prepared to share the mundane aspects of the life of Jesus too. White shares his experience of long term incarnational urban ministry:

> I am amazed at how mundane and ordinary the essence of our ministry here is. It is based on availability and openness. As Steve Morris, a friend and long-time inner-city minister says, 'Ministry at its core is simple. It involves following the initiative of Jesus as he connects us to people he wants to serve'. Service, interest and involvement communicate love (1996: 60).

Sustaining fruitfulness may mean that a worker needs to put limits on their availability, but an incarnational approach suggests more than a nine to five commitment – it is 'being among'.

Being involved in a local area means discovering what is there and being prepared to be involved in the lives of the people who live there, on their terms. It is vital that the actions of an incarnational worker match their words. The way in which the gospel is communicated through incarnational ministry is of importance. Bausch recounts a story of an executive who was running to get a train and in his haste knocked over a fruit stall. He got on the train but felt guilty that he had not gone back to help. He decided to go back and discovered that the person looking after the stall was blind. He helped him pick up the fruit and offered him money for the damage caused. The boy looking after the stall asked him 'Are you Jesus?' (1994: 177-78). Workers could helpfully meditate on whether their actions would ever evoke a similar response. So often in the urban environment mere words are not enough, as people say, 'Words are cheap'.

In relating actions and words Jesus provides a good example of integrity. This moves beyond being an example of Jesus to living a holistic, integrated lifestyle where a worker's 'being' communicates as much as their 'doing'. Sider states that:

> Jesus modeled what he taught. He not only announced the arrival of the messianic time of justice and shalom for the poor and oppressed, he also fed the hungry and welcomed the socially ostracized into his new community. His diverse circle of men and women, rich and poor, crippled and well, was a visible demonstration of the kingdom that he announced (1993: 73).

This is one of the challenges to those involved in incarnational ministry. Do workers model the kingdom that they are proclaiming? Who are their companions, to whom do they offer hospitality, what do they do? Confronting these challenges is an integral part of their mission. One of the implications of this 'community as a model' that Sider describes is that incarnational workers should not be working alone. YFC need to explore the implications of this for the way that incarnational youth ministry is set up. Senior and Stuhlmueller argue that,

> The quality of the community's life was recognized as part of its mission. The bond of love and unity among Christians, the commitment to good citizenship, and the suffering endured for others were part of their testimony to the gospel and, as such, proclaimed the good news as effectively as any word (1993: 337).

In communities, actions will be at least as important as words and an incarnational worker will need to relate to other Christians in order to demonstrate the gospel. It is the 'new commandment' of John 13:34-45 again. There should be something different about the way that Christians live their lives that make them distinctive. This can mean that significant time needs to be given to team building. It can sometimes take a shift in one's mindset to realise that having a meal or going bowling together as a team can be as integral to the work as face-to-face contact with young people.

However, this is not always an easy process and workers need to be aware that tensions can arise within one's own household as well as between colleagues. A womanist interpretation of the Mary and Martha story[25] by Renita Weems puts Mary's view (see vv. 41-42):

> Imagine: Centuries of women's intellectual suppression was toppling before my eyes. But the pained expression on my sister's face soon turned my glee to remorse. Martha was not challenging my right to learn. She was simply challenging my right to do so at her expense. Nor was Jesus defending my learning at my sister's expense. Actually, it was the way he looked from my sister, standing in the door of the cooking area hurt and embarrassed, to me sitting at his feet uncomfortable and silent, that made me bow my head in shame. It was as though he was waiting for us to talk to one another, rather than talk to him about one another (1988: 47).

Incarnational urban youth ministry can be a stressful role and it can be easy to take out frustrations on those one is close to. This reading of the text by Weems helps emphasise the importance of accepting each other and trying to work things out rather than condemning or confronting inappropriately. It is unrealistic to expect that workers can live conflict free among one another and in their community, but the emphasis needs to be on demonstrating the gospel by the quality of relationships that others can observe. 'Being among' can lead to new relationships and new actions, to an expression of community life that speaks of God's Kingdom.

Teamwork

One of the clearest things that can be seen in the gospels is that Jesus did not carry out his ministry alone. In some ways, the story of the cross, in the synoptic gospels, is so stark because it shows Jesus being abandoned by those close to him. The rest of the time Jesus is surrounded by others including his disciples and the wider group, many of whom were women, who supported him.[26] In Luke 10, we read that

---

[25] Luke 10:38-42.

[26] Luke 8:1-4.

Jesus sends the seventy out, two by two.[27] This is an important point that has a particular relevance for youth workers today. Government legislation[28] has led to the need to draw up *Safe from Harm* or child protection policies. These suggest that working alone is no longer appropriate in most cases, and if one is alone with a young person then a great deal of care needs to be taken. One of the reasons suggested for the practice of sending out workers two by two in Luke is based on the principle in Deut. 19:15 of having two witnesses to increase the impact and weight of testimony.[29] I am not sure that this is the most convincing reason; it seems to be very good sense to send people out in pairs for practical support and encouragement, as well as safety. There will also be mutual learning and more effective ministry. While one is talking, the other can listen. While one is attending to an issue, the other is free to notice that which is more hidden.

This passage also tells us something about the nature of teamwork in the gospels. Marshall describes this passage as containing a commission ('The harvest is plentiful but the labourers are few; therefore ask the Lord of the harvest to send out labourers into his harvest.' v. 2), a warning about dangers ('See I am sending you out like lambs into the midst of wolves.' v. 3), and details of preparations to be made (verses 4-10) (1978: 417). This is a model YFC needs to consider. Staff are commissioned by YFC, but I do not think that in many instances they are warned of dangers. The issues discussed concerning temptations above would make useful material for such warnings. With volunteers there is a commissioning, some warning of potential dangers as well as preparation in a residential training programme, but this could be done more thoroughly. An induction policy is in place for staff that covers the main work areas. This policy could be developed to encompass some of the issues identified in this discussion on the ministry of Jesus.

Another aspect of teamwork that Jesus demonstrates as a leader, is holding his team accountable. In Luke 9 Jesus sends out the twelve. When they return they report back to him and they try and withdraw to spend some time together.[30] Interpreted in the language of today, what was happening was something like supervision. Thompson states that, 'supervision is, in principle at least, a process through which an organisation seeks to meet its objectives through empowering its

---

[27] Luke 10:1-20.

[28] 1989 Children Act.

[29] This is suggested by Jeremias and reported by Evans (1990: 446)

[30] Luke 9:10.

staff' (1996: 48). This is what Jesus is doing in the sending out of the seventy. This is a necessary part of any youth ministry today, particularly incarnational urban youth ministry where complex issues can arise in relationships with young people or new situations faced on which a worker needs advice. A supervision policy needs to be encouraged and implemented. This will involve following the example of Jesus by providing, in today's terms, education, support, and accountability. Working in a team is the appropriate model in the demanding context of urban areas today. Teams have the potential to provide mutual accountability, support and the capacity for good practice.

Socio-Political Action

It is very difficult to be involved in incarnational work in urban areas and avoid confronting wider political and social issues. These may include the benefits system, young people in the care of social services, housing, health, and education, for example.

The way Jesus announces his ministry in Luke 4:16-20, using verses from Isaiah 58 and 61, demonstrates a concern for people beyond the spiritual.[31] Green writes:

> It is thus evident that Jesus' mission is directed to the poor – defined not merely in subjective, spiritual or personal, economic terms, but in the holistic sense of those who are for any number of socio-religious reasons relegated to positions outside the boundaries of God's people. By directing his good news to these people, Jesus indicates his refusal to recognize those socially determined boundaries, asserting instead that even these 'outsiders' are the objects of divine grace (1997: 211).

The idea of a preferential option for the poor, or a bias to the poor, is one which would be taken seriously within YFC but what this means, in reality, in respect of ministry varies. The main imperative YFC would take from Jesus would be that of the Great Commission.[32] This means that socio-political action will generally have a lower priority than proclamation evangelism. In the evangelical tradition within which YFC operates there has, in the lifetime of the organization, been a perceived division between evangelism and social action, between the personal and corporate understanding of sin.[33] An example of this is

---

[31] See, for example, Fitzmyer (1981: 532) for an explanation of the construction of the text as recorded by Luke.

[32] Matthew 28:16-20.

[33] This argument is put forward by Ronald Sider (1993) among others.

that World Vision developed out of the work of Youth for Christ, but was later established as a separate charity because of divergent aims between the two organizations. It is interesting that in Britain at least, the two are moving closer together again, and YFC are working with World Vision on their 24-hour famine project.

Bakke sees this lack of emphasis on the socio-political dimension as a potential consequence of too great an emphasis on the incarnation. He suggests that:

> Most of us have a personal theology, a personal conversion. I would call it a Philippian theology – a theology of Christ who left the heavens and came down to live within us. A 'my God and I' relationship - and it is wonderful. It's pietism. Most of us lack, however, a Colossian theology of a transcendent Christ, who is Lord of the systems and structures of the world, including those gigantic macrostructures of the metroplace, the city. And without that Colossian perspective we have relief theology, but no theology of reform (1988: 74-5).

Bakke's view could be seen as a little simplistic in its analysis of Phil. 2:5-11.This passage begins with the incarnation and ends with Jesus clearly acknowledged as Lord of all in heaven and on earth, and thus of the structures and institutions of humanity. However, the main point that he is making about theological perspectives held is a criticism that would, in part, be a valid one of an organization such as YFC. When you consider the training that both volunteers and staff receive (and I have to take some responsibility for this) there is very little focus on structural analysis or social action. Major social issues are explored, but usually from a personal or pastoral perspective, and little emphasis is placed on understanding or changing the structures. YFC are still trying to fully understand what a holistic approach to evangelism is. It is here that accessing resources from other agencies or working in partnership together is useful. Organizations as diverse as Frontier Youth Trust and the Urban Theology Unit have publications that bring a broader perspective to issues that YFC face and can help the organization develop its theology.[34]

It is important that a holistic gospel is preached in church, that the social dimension of the gospel is not excluded, marginalized or spiritualized. One reason for this is derived from the results of research regarding urban churches amongst Southern Baptists in the United States. It was found that two types of churches failed in the city: 'The church that thinks their ministry is words only will leave the city

---

[34] For example, the Urban Theology Unit's British Liberation Theology Series edited by Rowland and Vincent, and Pettie (1993) from Frontier Youth Trust.

because they won't pay the price of incarnation. Also the church that thinks their ministry is deeds only will die or become spiritually impotent because they have no word about Jesus, as life and hope and peace' (Cross cited in Conn 1993: 102). For incarnational youth workers there is the challenge of bringing both these aspects together: being genuinely incarnational in the approach to ministry as reflected in the discussion above but also being evangelistic in the sense of responding to YFC's mission statement to 'take good news relevantly to every young person in Britain'. In this context, socio-political action needs to be accepted as part of a worker's role.

YFC and Incarnational Youth Ministry
This section will draw together some of the conclusions from previous sections and identify issues that YFC need to focus on in relation to incarnational urban youth ministry, particularly in trying to improve the retention of workers.

This focus on workers who engage with young people in the wider community is pertinent for evangelicals, because there has been some criticism about a failure on the part of evangelical churches to engage with unchurched young people. In *Growing up Evangelical*, Ward calls one of his chapters 'Safety: The function of evangelical youth work' (1996: 161-85), and discusses the fear of youth culture and the desire of parents and churches to protect young people from it. The problem with this desire is that few, if any, outside of the church get to hear the gospel message or, if they do, they find it hard to feel a part of the church or stay in it. Ward writes:

> The mere presence of a group who are perceived as being 'rough-looking' around a church group is enough to cause parents unease...Unchurched young people are often not allowed time to adapt their lifestyle and faced with the clear boundaries of the youth group they often fall away (1996: 185).

Groups such as YFC can complement the work of the church by working with those who are outside the existing structures. Perhaps, also, they can work alongside churches and try and help them overcome this problem. The Rock Solid programme is one way they have sought to do this as well as providing consultancy and setting up a Church Resources Department.

Incarnational youth workers are seeking to imitate Jesus in their approach to ministry. Jesus as a human being was male, Jewish, single, and around thirty when he began his public ministry. Obviously, incarnational ministry cannot be about a narrow identification with Jesus, otherwise most would be excluded. Jesus was born into a particular culture at a specific time in history. Because incarnational workers are part of a different culture, in a different century, they need to work out how the person and ministry of Jesus, that they are using as their model and example, applies today. The ministry of Jesus took place in his own culture. Most incarnational workers today are crossing cultures to work with young people, they are missionaries. Incarnational urban youth workers are usually moving from a middle class area to a working class one, sometimes from south to north, from 'comfortable' Britain to the inner-city.

If we took the example of Jesus in a pedantic fashion, it might suggest that incarnational ministry can only be done amongst one's own culture. However, Luke's gospel has an emphasis on cross-cultural mission. Prior writes, 'His interest in Samaritans is apparent (e.g. the Good Samaritan parable, the incident of the ten lepers, the reference to the Samaritan villages, all exclusive to Luke, at 10:30-37, 17:11-19 and 9:51-55 respectively). Luke also devotes space to the Gentiles (1995: 50).[35] The final words of Jesus that Luke records, talks about his disciples being witnesses to the ends of the earth.[36] It would appear that Jesus himself gave a mandate for cross-cultural mission, and it is clear that the early church practised such mission. By engaging in cross-cultural incarnational work, YFC are working within a model probably established by Jesus and certainly engaged in by his earliest followers according to Luke/Acts.

However, the example of Jesus in his life and teaching suggests that incarnational workers need to understand the culture they have entered before they can begin communicating their message. The challenge for YFC here is to allow workers to spend time getting immersed in the local culture before they begin to do what others would regard as 'work'. Bob Holman writes of the beginning of his work: 'So I began to linger in the shop, making contacts, picking up tips about the area.' (1981: 6) Another person who set up a successful incarnational project suggested to me that for the first twelve months workers should just seek to get involved with what is already going on in the

---

[35] This is referenced by Prior in detail: "Elijah and Sidon; Elisha and Naaman the Syrian, only in Luke, at 4:26-27; the cure of the possessed man in the Gerasene district, Lk. 8:26-29, shared with Mt. 8 and Mk. 5; 'Men will come from east and west and north and south, and sit at the table in the kingdom of God', Lk. 13:29 and Mt. 8:11; dealings with the Roman centurion, Lk. 7:1-10 and Mt. 8:5-13."

[36] Acts 1:7-9.

community.[37] This will involve workers spending a lot of time 'being' rather than 'doing'. I think this is an issue where YFC probably needs to re-examine its approach. YFC needs to be involved in educating funders, and others involved in establishing projects, of the importance of this process of workers becoming part of a community and seeking to understand and appreciate the local culture.

Jesus began his public ministry rather later than most YFC workers. It is interesting to consider to what extent the period of preparation for ministry, and the testing at the beginning contributed to Jesus fulfilling his mission. I have worked with volunteers for many years in YFC and have noticed a big difference between those who have had experience of full time employment and those who have not. Those who have previously been employed seem to have developed certain core skills, they were more able to manage themselves and their time, and to work the necessary hours.

YFC has a volunteer programme that gives an opportunity for young people to spend some time in ministry. This is helpful for them in clarifying their calling and developing gifts that can be used in their local churches. However, some want to continue with YFC rather than study further or work elsewhere; they believe that God has called them to Christian ministry and they want to continue to pursue that call. Sometimes this is not helpful to the individual in the long term, because they can end up in their mid or late twenties with no further qualifications or experience outside of that gained with YFC.[38] This is where a more rigorous examination of call may be helpful. A good model to consider is the process that all seeking ordination in the Church of England pursue. There are a series of interviews, meetings, a rigorous selection conference and now psychometric tests.[39] If YFC are seeking workers who will commit themselves long term in a difficult situation, then a more considered process of identifying calling is needed. Jesus selected his disciples on the basis of prayer and then spent three years working with them before they were involved in any

---

[37] Conversation with Margaret Walsh. She had been part of a religious order working on an estate in Wolverhampton. See Walsh 1997 for further details of her work.

[38] There is now an opportunity within YFC for young people to study for a degree in youth and community work and applied theology as part of the Centre for Youth Ministry of which YFC is a partner. This is the work that I am now involved in. There are other similar courses run by Moorlands, Oasis, and Chester College, for example but CYM maintains the link with YFC.

[39] For a discussion of some of the issue see, for example, ABM's *A Review of the Selection Procedures in the Church of England* (1995).

meaningful independent ministry. In many ways, he could be described as apprenticing them. To be true to the way that Jesus carried out his incarnational ministry we need to be wary of sending people into urban settings to begin new work with little careful preparation having taken place. YFC have done this in the past.

Some of the difficulties experienced by long-term incarnational urban youth ministry projects have been because of the inexperience of staff. They had not been in such a pressured environment before and issues arose that were destructive to team work. To reflect the way that Jesus trained his disciples, such workers should be apprenticed by someone with more experience. This happens in some instances but perhaps this could be more explicit or clearly structured. This would give the opportunity for workers to more readily admit to, address, and discuss difficulties. YFC with its staff has to tread a careful line between required employment practice and a way of relating as Christians that is appropriate for a ministry environment.

In responding to a call to be incarnational workers in YFC, staff are implicitly taking on a responsibility to be an example of Jesus. This means trying to live the sort of life that Jesus did, with an emphasis on serving and putting the needs of others first. Although this is what all Christians should be doing, it is still a great challenge if you are serious about the task. Jesus kept going in spite of adversity and suffering: this is part of the challenge. Jesus was able to do this because he knew who he was, had a deep understanding of the Scriptures and a clear perception of purpose; furthermore, this was rooted in his relationship with God. This could suggest that YFC needs to spell out clearly what it will mean to be an incarnational worker and facilitate potential staff in thinking through their calling and whether they are comfortable with all the implications of such a role. It may be that a different sort of ministry may be appropriate first, before the greater pressure of incarnational ministry is undertaken. YFC should not be afraid to say 'no' or 'wait', or to suggest an option that will prepare people for their long-term calling.

YFC have tried to develop a holistic concept of mission that involves demonstrating the gospel as well as declaring it, but this demonstration is still largely directed towards individuals. For YFC to be truly authentic in their incarnational ministry there may need to be greater attention paid to socio-political issues by workers. Some would argue that today other agencies are involved in these issues and YFC should concentrate on what it does best. However, it is important to demonstrate a holistic application of the gospel, particularly among those who are the victims of injustice. In many respects, one cannot offer true pastoral support by merely focusing on the personal and ignoring the structural, because structures influence and affect the personal realm.

Another important point to note about the incarnational ministry of Jesus is that he did not undertake it alone. He had a group of twelve disciples with him and a larger group that included women who supported his ministry and provided for his needs. In situations where funds are limited and it is hard to recruit workers, there have been YFC incarnational workers who are based in an area by themselves. This is a clear departure from the style of incarnational ministry demonstrated by Jesus. Further thought needs to be given as to how incarnational ministry can be established that is built around a wider group who share in the work and support it. All projects have some sort of management committee but they are not usually engaging with the work on a regular basis and a worker can feel isolated and unsupported. A strong community of faith that supports the work and the worker would be a helpful.

The final point I want to make about the authenticity of YFC's incarnational ministry has been mentioned briefly above. It relates to the way that Jesus 'managed his project', to use YFC language. He allowed those who worked with him access to the whole of his life. There was always someone with Jesus at key points in his ministry, until the disciples deserted him at Gethsemane. He was accessible much of the time, when not alone with his Father, and he modelled the qualities he wanted his disciples to have. I have recently been on several residentials at a Conference Centre run by the Sisters of St Paul. The person in charge was fully involved in serving in the kitchen as well as running the place. The sisters were available to people through everyday activities, you did not need an appointment to have a quiet word with them. They reflected Jesus to me in a way that very few of the heads of evangelical organizations I have met do. This is a real challenge to YFC: does the leadership, at all levels, model the leadership of Jesus? In incarnational ministry this will be more apparent, because a greater number of people may see how a team or project operates. It is also a challenge to the leadership of the national organization. How do workers on the ground have access to them and are they modelling the sort of leadership to them? Are they modelling the sort of leadership that should be demonstrated locally? Furthermore, Jesus treated people as individuals and helped them fulfil their potential. He seemed to know when to encourage, when to rebuke, when to release, when to hold back. Although YFC seeks to lead using Jesus as a model, we have developed on a hierarchical basis more in line with secular organizations. This means that we have tended to adopt secular approaches to management. This is not wrong in itself and there is much YFC can learn from secular organizations yet adopting a servant model of leadership as demonstrated by Jesus can be inspiring and encouraging to staff who see their leaders seeking to imitate Jesus as they are.

Many of the reflections above are based on my seventeen years of experience with YFC and my knowledge of a range of incarnational projects as well as the specific experience described in previous chapters. It is clear that in some respects, YFC is involved in authentic incarnational work, whereas in other respects, further development needs to take place. A range of issues that relate to both to the work and the workers has been highlighted. This material could be used to develop the preparation and support of workers involved in incarnational urban youth ministry, as well as providing some guidance for existing or new projects. However, nowhere in the original project was there a plan for this material to be collated and distributed to YFC outside the format of this thesis. At this point, the end of the action research phase of the project was reached. I than had the opportunity to reflect on what had been accomplished and what the next steps might be.

Limitations and Possibilities

Having got this far in the process, there was a frustration. We had investigated and explored incarnational youth ministry and identified a whole range of issues and recommendations, many of which could probably be the subject of a thesis in their own right. The main limitation was that there was no coherent, integrated framework that could be used to develop incarnational youth ministry that drew the different threads of the work together. Originally, the goals of the project were based around what was possible in my role as the Training Manager of YFC and what seemed realistic to accomplish at that time. In many ways, I had accomplished what I had hoped to, in identifying ways of supporting incarnational urban youth workers, through the papers on management and fruitfulness, for example. What had not happened was putting together something that could be used to establish new projects, or evaluate existing projects, that was rooted in theology as well as experience. There was also the feeling that I had looked in depth at what already happened but had not taken enough steps back to look at what could or should happen. There were two main options available at this point. One would be to develop the papers already written as part of the action research project into a guide for setting up incarnational youth ministry. This would have the merits of being based on workers' experience but would have a limited biblical and theological basis. A further option would be to develop the theological reflection that I had begun and add further dimensions that seemed pertinent to an in depth study of incarnational youth ministry. This would facilitate the development of a theological rationale for incarnational youth ministry that took both the workers' experience and the biblical and theological tradition seriously. However, a theological rationale on its own would not necessarily be an accessible document for all involved in incarnational youth ministry. Indeed the phrase 'theological rationale' would deter some workers from engaging with it. What seemed useful was to look at a way of presenting a theological rationale that would work in the YFC context. The idea of a manifesto for incarnational youth ministry seemed to be one worth pursuing. The term 'manifesto' is a familiar one, and although it may sound a little boring for anyone who finds politics dull, it does encapsulate the idea of important principles and proposals from a particular perspective. The manifesto would be short and easy to read, understand, and apply. For those who wanted to go deeper, a commentary identifying the different elements of the research that contributed to the conclusion presented in the manifesto would be written. Developing a manifesto would enable a more thorough process of theological reflection to take place and to provide a pastoral response that encapsulates the whole of the research, rather than just the different elements that were the outcomes of the original action research project.

Alongside this my role within YFC was changing and I was beginning to be involved in developing a professionally qualifying and academic degree course in youth and community work and applied theology. One of the aims of the course was to look at how theology, theory, and practice could all be integrated, rather than adding theology as a bolt on extra or leaving students to work out the theological implications of what was being taught for themselves. This challenged me as to what I had accomplished in my own research. I had looked at practice, theory, and theology, but what had not emerged thus far was a piece of work that integrated all the different elements of the research, that brought together the thinking that had developed through the different goals pursued. This was what students would be expected to do and I was motivated and challenged to seek to do this as part of my own research.

Another reason for wanting to pursue my study further was discovering that there was a lack of theologically based writing about youth work, particularly from a British perspective. In the bibliography for this book, the works of Pete Ward are the only British youth work texts that have a strong theological element to them. Through my research, I had been challenged to move beyond a simplistic application of the Bible to my work and I wanted to produce something that YFC workers could engage with to help incarnational workers develop a deeper biblical and theological understanding of their work.

A starting point would be to reflect on 'incarnation' as this had not been considered in depth, and in doing this identify an approach to the concept that could inform incarnational ministry beyond the 'dwelling among' of John 1:14 and the example of Phil. 2:5-11. Beyond this, identifying someone whose incarnational ministry could be an example and inspiration to workers would also be helpful because of the way that hearing stories encourages and motivates. I was seeking to be broader in my theological reflection and draw on tradition as well as biblical and theological material to inform and be informed by what I had discovered in the original research.

The next step was to explore what this contextual theological rationale for incarnational youth work should contain. The hope was to bring a new depth of research into YFC that would identify a rationale, in the form of a manifesto, that could be widely used and that would be able to be interpreted contextually.

Chapter 6

Developing a Contextual Approach Towards a Theological Rationale

> If your theological efforts are offered up to the Lord and then to the world, if they are informed by the Word of God and the community of faith, and if they are celebrated at the altar of God, then they will exceed intellectual exercise and produce more than self-serving defences. Such theology will lead to love and service, growth and maturity. It is the driving force of servant leaders...Our work together here is not an end in itself; it is all for the glory of God and for the benefit of the young people we serve (Borgman 1997: 233).

A Theological Rationale for Incarnational Youth Ministry

In an organization such as YFC, it is good to use theology to reflect on practice as a means of developing it, as well as learning from experience or by trial and error. The project phase of the research ended with the identification of a need for a theological rationale for long-term incarnational youth ministry within YFC. As Borgman so rightly points out above, theological endeavour should enhance the practice of ministry. However, the way that he talks about theological endeavour makes it clear that it is a holistic pursuit: it cannot be reduced to just academic knowledge, it is about what is brought from worship, from the reading of the word. It is a theology that motivates and inspires; and it is this understanding that I am trying to apply in developing a contextual theological rationale. I do not want dry words that give purely practical guidelines, I want a sense of vision, passion, and engagement to inform what is produced.

Within the original research project some significant biblical reflection had taken place. This highlighted the need for further theological reflection at greater depth to be able to present an integrated, contextual rationale for incarnational youth ministry. I had researched the workers' experience and begun to look at this in the light of the biblical tradition. But this did not complete the process of theological reflection. I have already identified several styles of theological reflection that were helpful when studying incarnational youth ministry. The model that lends itself best to this process of developing a contextual theological rationale is that of the Whiteheads (1995). To recap, their model involves three stages. The first stage (attending) involves discovering relevant information from culture, tradition and experience. The second stage (assertion) initiates dialogue between the different sources of information to clarify and develop insights and limitations in the sources. The third stage (pastoral response) seeks to identify action, both personal and communal, from the reflection (1995: x). Much of the first two stages are recorded in previous chapters. Some summary material will appear in this chapter along with new elements that merit inclusion in a contextual theological rationale for incarnational youth ministry. In all, five elements that contribute to a theological rationale will be considered. Two of them will be explored in greater depth in Chapters seven and eight as they are major new areas of research and little work has been done on them thus far. Stage three occurs in the final chapter.

Attending first involves taking account of the evangelical heritage, ethos, and culture of YFC. This is essential to ensure that other parts of the process would produce a response that would gain acceptance within YFC. It would be counter-productive to pursue areas of theological reflection that were outside of the YFC tradition to such an extent that the outcome of the research would be dismissed because of it. An aspect of that tradition that merited attention was to seek to place incarnational youth ministry within a missiological framework. Mission is the core activity of YFC. Incarnational youth ministry is described as 'demonstration' by YFC and I will seek to place this concept within a broader missiological framework. Having revisited the context of incarnational youth ministry in relation to both YFC and its mission, the next element is to draw in key issues from the workers' perspective that has been described in depth in earlier chapters. Because we are talking about 'incarnational' ministry, a deeper understanding of what it means to be 'incarnational' is sought. Some initial thoughts were explored in the previous chapter. These were largely based on biblical material, and it is now important to explore the concept more thoroughly to say how it can inform an understanding of incarnational ministry. Finally, I wanted to draw on historical tradition. To do this I wanted to look at a ministry that could bring new insights to the exploration of incarnational youth ministry. What emerged from this was that Dietrich Bonhoeffer might be an appropriate role model, in some respects, and that studying his life could be an inspiration to incarnational youth workers. This chapter summarises the main elements from these five sources and also engages in some of the assertion process, initiating a dialogue between these different elements.

Element One: Youth for Christ

The evangelical heritage, ethos, and culture of YFC have been explained in detail in previous chapters. Here, I want to give a brief background to the contemporary role of theology within the organization, as part of the wider context within which the theological rationale is being developed. With the aim of developing a theological underpinning for its ministry, YFC developed 'Position Papers'.[1] These papers seek to articulate a theological rationale for different aspects of the work, such as youth evangelism, and the role of women and men in ministry. Specifically, the essays focus on biblical reflection (Howell undated a: 1). Apart from one paper on youth homelessness, little attention has been given to a theological rationale for demonstration ministry within YFC. However, there is a Position Paper by Baker on enculturalising[2] the gospel within youth culture, which has some relevance to this research. In essence, this paper encourages the idea of

---

[1] Position papers are YFC's way of exploring theological issues that relate to the ministry of the organization and have usually been written by staff members. They are usually 3,000-5,000 words in length and are available from YFC's Head Office or in Centre for Youth Ministry libraries.

[2] I suggest that the correct term in the title should have been 'inculturating' rather than 'enculturalising...' Arbuckle provides a helpful distinction between the two terms. He describes enculturation as a sociological term that involves the learning of a culture from childhood and inculturation as "the dynamic relation between the Christian message and culture or cultures; an insertion of the Christian life into a culture; an ongoing process of reciprocal and critical interaction and assimilation between them" (1990: 17).

'doing what Jesus did'. Baker takes as a key text Phil. 2:6-8. He writes:

> The strongest argument for enculturalising the good news within the world of young people is the example of Jesus. When God chose to communicate with us he took the form of a human person. Jesus gave up all he had, became a human being like us, and entered our world because he wanted to communicate with us. This, the incarnation, is a central theme of the Christian faith and is beautifully summarised in Phil. 2:6-8 (Baker undated: 1).

Although this is the same theological starting point for some incarnational urban youth workers, there is a critical difference. Baker talks about incarnation as meaning taking the gospel in a relevant way to young people, whereas incarnational urban youth workers focus more on being the gospel to young people, communicating the gospel in a relevant way is just a part of this. This missiological divergence represents one of the main differences there is in YFC thinking about what it is to be an 'incarnational' worker, with people arguing for and against the need to live in the neighbourhood where someone is working. Although the paper by Baker on inculturating the gospel is a helpful starting point for exploring a theological rationale for YFC ministry, further work is necessary to understand what it might mean for specific forms of ministry. This is the task being engaged in here and elsewhere. YFC have started a series of theological forums where members of staff share their research. Incarnational youth work was one of the topics debated at the first of these forums, which included debate about whether or not it is necessary to live where you work, as mentioned above.[3]

In emphasising the need to live among the community where they are working, incarnational urban youth workers are adopting a similar missiological approach to that of other workers from different traditions. Margaret Walsh, in writing about her experience of incarnational urban ministry, says that:

> I believe that we should be [a] challenge to the world of comfort and materialism by our lifestyle and values which will be different from the norm. As it says in the *Evangelii*

---

[3] For example, Nick Shepherd, as Centre Director of Greenwich YFC, contributed an unpublished paper titled, 'The myths of incarnational youth work' to an internal YFC research forum in January 2000. Another member of staff is in dialogue with a colleague from Australia over the incarnation and youth work.

Nuntiandi: 'We should arouse a spirit of enquiry in those who see our way of life. Witness of this kind constitutes in itself a proclamation of the good news' (1997: 69).

This relates back to the idea of demonstrating the gospel as a way of declaring it, and some incarnational urban youth workers would argue that this can only be done authentically by living among the young people one serves. My experience as a Curate's wife has reinforced the benefits of doing this, in terms of one's accessibility to the community and the greater understanding and identification that is gained by living in an area rather than just working in it.

Element Two: A Missiology for Incarnational Youth Workers

YFC is an organization that is evangelistic; it has as its mission statement: 'Taking good news relevantly to every young person in Britain.' Because of this, a theological rationale will need to engage with an understanding of evangelism that resonates with incarnational urban youth ministry. YFC's 4D approach to evangelism was explained above. What is needed here is a missiology that explains what is meant by 'demonstration'.

Evangelicals have, in the past, struggled with issues of evangelism and social action. Although writing about the American scene, Pahl's comment that 'Youth for Christ continues to struggle with the issue of relating salvation to public concern' (2000: 108) would have been true in the mid 1990s when I began this research. However, incarnational youth workers have tended to have a broader understanding of their task. Swinton, although writing from a mental health perspective, summarises well an understanding of the mission of the church which would be shared by some of the incarnational youth workers within YFC, who have clearly thought through their understanding of who Christ is and what the implications of that are for their own calling and lifestyle.[4] Swinton writes: 'The church is called to image Christ in his boundary-breaking mission of liberation and to adopt a stance of solidarity with the poor and against injustice and oppression in all of its forms' (2000: 12). This definition picks up several of the strands that emerged in the project phase of the research. The idea of imaging Christ, being an example was noted, particularly in

---

[4] For example, the first Director of Birmingham YFC chose to buy a house in the inner city, establish an incarnational work in that area and live in an extended household with other workers. From a privileged background he chose to demonstrate a solidarity with the poor. This would not be the norm within YFC.

relation to Phil. 2:5-11. The concept of solidarity with the poor is expressed by the willingness to 'dwell among', that workers understand as their response to John 1:14. The commitment to work with those who are marginalized was also noted as a theme in Luke's gospel.

Salt and Light

What Biblical models might reflect and support such an understanding of the mission of incarnational youth workers? The metaphors of salt and light found in Mt. 5:13-16 seem to be a helpful starting point for several reasons. First, YFC introduced the terms into their definition of demonstration in a new corporate brochure that was introduced in 2000. It explained the terms thus:

> YFC are working in many cities, towns and villages, being 'salt and light' to those varied and challenging surroundings. We engage in community development as a means of meeting material need and/or building long term, unconditional relationships with young people demonstrating God's acceptance and love (undated: 1).[5]

Secondly, these images of salt and light, deriving from the Sermon on the Mount, would be familiar and acceptable to YFC workers, who would see them as ideas that can co-exist with the predominant idea of mission as proclamation evangelism. Thirdly, they are also terms that have historically been used within evangelicalism to denote a ministry oriented towards social action or engagement with the community; and the link to demonstration would be understood.[6] Fourthly, salt needs to be a part of something else to be effective and light needs to be uncovered and penetrate the environment to be useful. Both these factors resonate with the idea of 'being among', of being immersed, and not merely 'visiting'. Another advantage of these metaphors is that the way they can be interpreted in different contexts is left open. What can we learn, then, from these metaphors that might develop the understanding of incarnational youth ministry? The translation in *The Message* brings a fresh perspective to the passage and in many respects could be seen as describing incarnational youth

---

[5] The brochure itself has no date on it. It has the title YFC but no author or editor is named. It has a grey cover and is A5, in portrait format.

[6] See, for example, Roy Joslin's *Urban Harvest*. In a chapter entitled 'Salt where it counts' Joslin writes 'The subject which we have begun to examine here is usually described as the Christian's 'involvement' with society' (1982: 274). *Light in the City* is the title of a book telling stories of Church Urban Fund projects (Grundy 1990).

ministry:

> Let me tell you why you are here. You're here to be salt-seasoning that brings out the God-flavors of this earth. If you lose your saltiness, how will people taste godliness? You've lost your usefulness and will end up in the garbage. Here's another way to put it: You're here to be light, bringing out the God-colors in the world. If I make you light-bearers, you don't think I'm going to hide you under a bucket, do you? I'm putting you on a light stand. Now that I've put you there on a hilltop, on a light-stand – shine! Keep open house; be generous with your lives. By opening up to others, you'll prompt people to open up with God, this generous Father in heaven.

Salt had several different uses in ancient times and was seen as having great value. As Pliny said, 'Nothing is more useful than salt and sunshine' (cited in Carson 1984: 138). Amongst other things, it was used in sacrifices and could be regarded as a symbol associated with covenants between Yahweh and his people (Lev. 2:13); it was a seasoning for food (Job 6:6) and a preservative. Guelich suggests that the correct interpretation of the metaphor of salt, in Mt. 5:13, is that 'disciples are to the earth what salt is to everyday life' (1982: 121). When all these factors are read from a contextual perspective related to incarnational youth workers, this suggests that workers can function in three ways: as a symbol of God's covenant with humanity, as seasoning, and as a preservative. One way in which this is worked out in practice is described by Joslin when he suggests that functioning as salt and light means that people will notice our good deeds (Mt. 5:16). He argues that:

> Such is the potential of these deeds that not only will people have their ignorance, prejudice and other false notions of Christianity undermined, but they will go as far as to 'praise your Father in heaven'. The relevance of the Christian faith for seven days a week will be plain (1982: 277).

This is one of the ways in which incarnational urban youth workers can make a difference: the whole of their lives have potential to be effective in the community, not just the formal times of 'youth work'. In fact, it is just as likely to be the good deeds that are not done in the context of 'work' that will be a sign and a challenge to others, because work is seen as what someone is paid to do. It is the voluntary good deeds that are beyond the expected youth worker's role that may be the most effective. Obviously, there is much less scope for this to happen if the worker does not live locally.

The text says 'You [plural] are the salt of the earth'. It is addressed to a community, not to an individual, and the scope, as Davies and Allison suggest, presupposes the mission to the gentiles (1988: 472). It is thus an inclusive metaphor that works well for incarnational youth workers who are often based in ethnically diverse areas and have a concern for the whole community. Incarnational youth workers can demonstrate God's covenant through the way they live their lives and the way that they communicate Christ. As a missionary God, the sending of incarnational youth workers to communities reiterates that characteristic missionary move demonstrated when Christ became human.

In terms of seasoning, salt is often what makes food taste good, but only when it becomes part of the food to which it is added. This suggests that incarnational youth workers need to become part of their surroundings. As Gerali writes:

> When missionaries go to foreign fields, they learn the languages, customs, practices, traditions, and values of the people they are trying to reach. To fully understand the community, they must bring those practices into their home...youth ministry requires the same (2001: 288). [7]

Incarnational youth workers can bring a presence into an environment which makes it seem better to the young people – without the workers, life would not 'taste as good'. This will include declaration of the Christian message when appropriate, as Christ is the seasoning that will make life taste best. But they can only season if they truly become immersed within what they are trying to season. This is an integral part of being involved in missionary work with young people.

Salt is still used today as a preservative in places where refrigeration is not a practical option. Incarnational youth workers, in challenging the decay and rottenness in structures and institutions that oppress marginalized young people, can begin to act as a preservative. They can seek an environment which is conducive to the growth and well being of young people. There is an interesting link here with Borgman's view of the God-ordained functions of culture. He suggests that the expectations of a culture are:

1. to nurture children to the full human potential of adulthood;
2. to provide justice for all people and classes of society;
3. to protect, and act responsibly in regard to, the environment;

---

[7] Donovan's (1982) work amongst the Masai is an excellent example of this approach.

4. to seek individually and corporately for transcendent meaning in the Creator of all – to 'grope after God' (1997: 84).

The culture of urban priority areas does not always lend itself to these expectations being fulfilled. But the idea of a preservative suggests that something is worth preserving. In urban priority areas there are good things to preserve but sometimes people need help in seeing this and working towards it. Furthermore, incarnational youth workers can seek to preserve the original purposes of God for the young people with whom they work, by helping young people to understand who they are in Christ and what God's purposes for humanity are.

In order for salt to function it has to interact with something else. In food, as a seasoning, it often dissolves and becomes part of what is eaten. In preserving it may also surround or enclose what is being preserved. Salt cannot work from a distance and so is an effective metaphor for the role of incarnational youth workers who seek to be part of the community, among the community, within the community.

The gospel passage goes on to say that disciples are light as well as salt. Keener comments: 'A disciple whose life reveals none of the Father's works is like invisible light for vision: useless' (1999: 173). Incarnational youth workers are attempting to reveal the Father's works through being like Christ in the situation. In the same way that a light cannot be hidden, so incarnational youth workers seek to live lives that are not hidden away but can be seen by the community and can function as a guide or at least illuminate a path. Again, the term 'light' is an echo of Old Testament images. Both Isa. 42:6 and 49:6 speak of the servant who will be a light to the nations for the purposes of salvation. Jesus, also, is encouraging his disciples to see themselves as light to those who are in darkness. Incarnational youth workers can understand their role as bringing this element of hope into their communities; they bring light and with it the potential of salvation. Their good works may bring praise to God in a context where many feel that there is little to praise God about. God can be glorified through the work of incarnational youth workers going into areas where salt and light are much needed.

In the same way as salt has connotations of purity (for example, Elisha purifying water with salt in 2 Kings 2: 19-23), so does light. Carson writes: 'In the OT as in the NT, it [light] most frequently symbolizes purity as opposed to filth, truth or knowledge as opposed to error and ignorance, and divine revelation as opposed to reprobation and abandonment by God' (1984: 139). This again can be related to the way in which incarnational youth workers can bring light in the form of revelation into a situation, for example, bringing an understanding of forgiveness, honesty, truth, integrity, and redemption in a situation where young people may feel abandoned by God.

There is a scene in the film 'Dead Man Walking' (Robbins 1995)[8] where the nun says to the inmate on death row 'You are a son of God'; he replies that he has been called lots of things in his life but has never been told that before. Perhaps it would have made a difference in his life if he had heard that at an early age. Because young people no longer grow up with an understanding of who God and Jesus are, part of YFC's mission is that they should know this. A part of the way that incarnational youth workers undertake this mission is to be salt and light in the communities where they live and work. Incarnational youth work involves ideas of 'being', it also involves 'doing' and this 'doing' is in terms of engaging with the community and the issues that affect it. It reflects the properties of salt and light, as Jesus applies them to his followers. Morris comments that

> What is good in society his followers keep wholesome. What is corrupt they oppose; they penetrate society for good and act as a kind of moral antiseptic. And they give tang to life like salt to a dish of food...The very purpose of being a follower of Jesus is to give light. Giving light is not an option, so to speak, which the disciple may or may not choose...when people have received the light of the gospel they will shine in a dark world (1992: 104-105).

Social engagement is an integral part of the role of the incarnational youth worker. One cannot be salt and light in isolation, being salt and light involves permeating the whole of the community, and this means addressing structural as well as personal issues.

Bias to the Poor

In addition to a missiology for incarnational youth workers based on the biblical images of salt and light, there needs to be incorporated what David Sheppard (1983) calls a 'bias to the poor', or what Latin American liberation theology refers to as a 'preferential option for the poor'. It is the combination of elements that provide a socially relevant missiology for incarnational urban youth workers. Sheppard describes how he came to his understanding:

> Bias to the poor sounds like a statement of political preference. My experience has been that some of the most central teachings of orthodox Christianity have lead me to this position. I shall

---

[8] Based on the true story of the work of Sister Helen Prejean.

argue from Jesus's theme of the Kingdom of God, the calling to the Church to be Catholic, reaching across all human divisions and the doctrine of the Incarnation; they lead me to claim that there is a divine bias to the poor, which should be reflected both in the Church and in the secular world (1983: 10).

In a book of essays on liberation theology in this country, Chris Rowland concludes his study of the gospel, the poor, and the churches by saying that: 'in the Gospels and the Pauline epistles, the memory of a Christ who opted for the poor is kept alive as is the need to follow in his footsteps' (1995: 53). Incarnational urban youth workers see themselves as following in the footsteps of Christ in their ministry. Living and working among the poor is their interpretation of what that means, at least in respect of God's call to them.

From Latin America, Boff and Boff put forward five reasons for a preferential option for the poor (1987: 44-46). The first they describe as a theo-logical (sic) motivation, God's perspective. They cite as an example of this, God's response to the cries of his people when they were being oppressed by the Egyptians (Ex. 3:7, 9) (1987: 44). Incarnational youth workers can resonate with this as they are responding to the cries of young people who are being oppressed through a lack of opportunity, a lack of love or whatever. Along with this theo-logical motivation there is a Christological motivation which has been touched upon above. The ways Boff and Boff see this Christological motivation operating include the parable of the good Samaritan,[9] which they describe as endorsing approaching people who have fallen by the wayside, making neighbours of those who are distant, and making brothers and sisters out of neighbours. By moving into urban priority areas this is exactly what incarnational youth workers are doing (1987: 44-45).

The third motivation is eschatological. It is illustrated by the parable of the sheep and the goats, which they suggest implies that our eternal salvation or damnation will be affected by the way we have accepted or rejected the poor. Although incarnational youth workers believe that their calling is to work amongst the poor, they would not see this as something which determines their salvation, they have a different theological understanding, because evangelicals believe that salvation depends on faith in Christ This motivation, as described by Boff and Boff, is one that would not be relevant in the YFC context, therefore (1987: 45). The fourth motivation is apostolic which reflects

---

[9] Lk. 10:35-37.

the practice of the early church who initially had all things in common[10] and who saw looking after the poor as an integral part of the gospel.[11] Again, incarnational youth workers would see that they are sent, that they too are apostles who are following the example of the early apostles in looking after the poor (1987: 45).

The fifth motivation is ecclesiological. In the Latin American context this has been formalized at the Medellin (1968) and Puebla (1979) conferences where a 'preferential option for the poor' was agreed. (1987: 45). For workers in YFC, there is the 'demonstration' element of the organization's approach to mission, which gives them the formal validation of their work. Some workers will also have been influenced by the debate about urban ministry that has happened in some parts of the church in this country. The Church of England published *Faith in the City* (1985) in the 1980s and the Church Urban Fund continues to support work with the poor. Some of the incarnational youth work projects that have been established by YFC have been supported by the Church Urban Fund[12] The Methodists published a report *The Cities* (1997) in the 1990s which had recommendations for both churches and public policy. These reports and their recommendations provide a further ecclesiological mandate for incarnational youth workers.

From the foregoing, therefore, a missiological basis for incarnational urban youth ministry may be proposed that derives from two elements: an understanding of being salt and light in ways which are appropriate to the context and a belief that the gospel includes a bias to, or preferential option for, the poor.

Element Three: The Workers' Perspective

The experience of workers themselves and the context they work in are important contributions to the development of a contextual theological rationale. Much of what I learnt from workers has been elaborated in previous chapters and will not be repeated here. What I have sought to do is highlight the most important issues that need to be kept in mind in drawing up a manifesto for incarnational urban youth work relating to both the workers and the work context.

The first key issue relates to how the work is measured. There has been a frustration among incarnational youth workers in knowing how to assess the work, or communicate what has been achieved when

---

[10] Acts 2 and 4 are cited in support of this.

[11] See, for example, Gal. 2:10 'They asked only one thing, that we remember the poor, which was actually what I was eager to do.'

[12] For example, in Manchester.

numbers seem meaningless. Quantitative assessments provide too narrow a base for evaluation. The youth work world, certainly in terms of access to funding, is very oriented towards 'outcomes'. The government use the phrase 'best value' as part of their process for evaluating youth and community work and other provision. Workers need a broader, more theological framework in which to assess their work. The research around fruitfulness relates to this.

A second key issue is about support and management. Problems in these two aspects, which are related in youth work practice, were the most common cause of workers either leaving projects or thinking about leaving. The theme of fruitfulness also fits in here in terms of what sort of environment helps a worker to be fruitful.

A third issue relates to calling. Each person that I spoke to was in the work because they believed that was what God had called them to do. How one identifies and distinguishes a call from God is a complex issue, but it is one with which a theological rationale for incarnational urban youth work will need to engage.

A fourth issue is about personal experience where words like vulnerability and suffering were often shared. These themes will be taken up when considering a particular approach to the incarnation that resonates with incarnational urban youth workers (Element Four). They also reflect the experience of Dietrich Bonhoeffer whose life and works will be reflected on in Element Five.

Lastly, workers talk about the importance of 'being' as much as 'doing'. This has several elements that could be explored as part of a theological rationale. One is about being part of the community rather than working in the community. A second is about being where God is already present and at work, and joining in with what he is doing. A third is about who you are as a person rather than what you do.

For youth organizations such as YFC an integral part of the ministry is understanding the culture. For example, YFC's 1993 strategy document begins by highlighting key cultural trends that the strategy was designed to address (Sheppard 1993: 4).[13] In the latter half of the nineties, the discussion of culture has often centred around the current cultural context, often labelled postmodernism. In a guide for churches on how to be culturally relevant, Graham Cray identifies four main changes that have come with postmodernism. The one which probably most affects youth workers is the shift from producer to

---

[13] These were a loss of truth, loss of love and security, and loss of purpose. This section of the document concludes: 'It is to this society and to these youth cultures that we are called and where we need to be found' (Sheppard 1993: 4).

consumer. Cray writes, 'I am what I buy, wear, drive, live in' (Cray and Simmonds 2000: 12).[14] Youth workers I speak to accept that as one of the biggest challenges that they face: the consumerism that is prevalent amongst young people of all socio-economic backgrounds. In such a cultural context, incarnational urban youth workers are often seeking to be counter-cultural.

The elements that have been identified as helping to shape a theological rationale are not very consumer oriented. Being salt and light are not about status; kenosis, an approach to the incarnation outlined below, is about relinquishment; and Bonhoeffer's life, to be discussed, demonstrates sacrifice. However, Gallagher highlights different aspects of postmodernism from Cray. He suggests that there is a quest for a post-materialist quality of life and a disillusion with utopias that can be met by demonstrating that the Gospel is an alternative 'Way', and by compassion and social solidarity (1997: 142). These aspects of postmodernism would resonate much more strongly with incarnational youth workers and may be part of what motivated them to be involved in the work in the first place. Pahl summarises an approach to youth ministry that is based more on these latter elements of postmodernism rather than on consumer orientation. He writes:

> It [youth ministry] calls for rare vulnerability and courage, and it calls for refusing to get too attached to conventions of church and culture. The core of Christian teaching, according to the Gospels, is that 'those who want to save their life will lose it, and those who lose their life for the sake of the gospel will save it' (Luke 8:35). This spiritual truth – that true life is found not by grasping but by loving – calls youth ministers to the dangerous task of incarnating, each in his or her own partial way, the presence of God to youth (2000: 171).

He writes this as a result of a bleak answer to the common question asked among young people today: 'What would Jesus do?' One reply was, he died. The experience of incarnational urban youth workers is often one that has far more in common with the difficult journey faced by Jesus, as he pursued his mission, than with the pursuit of personal fulfilment pursued by many of their peers, often at the expense of the vulnerable.

These tensions in different understandings of postmodernism can be reconciled. Leonard Sweet argues that 'one of the characteristic features of postmodern culture is that opposite things happen at the

---

[14] The other three moves are from an industrial society to an electronic age; universal to global; realism to constructivism.

same time without being contradictory' (1999: 27). In some senses, this is true of the different approaches to incarnational youth work discussed above. Workers may need to hold in tension their desire to be counter-cultural and work to gospel values while at the same time needing to be culturally relevant in their mode of communication to young people.

Element Four: Understanding of, and Insights from, the Term 'Incarnation'

Any theological rationale for incarnational youth ministry has to seek to understand the incarnation. Unfortunately, this is a complex task and what began to emerge from a study of 'incarnation' was a sharing of Basil Hume's view that, 'None of us will ever be able to fathom completely the meaning of the Incarnation' (1999: 24). One of the reasons for this is the classic difficulty identified by Albert Schweitzer. He pointed out that 'it was not only each epoch that found its reflection in Jesus; each individual created Him in accordance with his own character' (cited in O'Collins 1995: 221). It is very difficult not to be influenced by one's own culture, background, and theological tradition, and thereby create an understanding of the incarnation that matches these rather than letting one's understanding of the incarnation challenge aspects of one's life. I was very aware of this when seeking to identify ways in which the term had been used and understood in Christian Theology.

What I am seeking to do here is to summarize the approaches to the incarnation that seemed most relevant to incarnational youth ministry. These provide insights that I hope will contribute to the shaping of a theological rationale for the ministry. I will begin by briefly looking at the term and the classical understanding of Chalcedon, but then draw on different aspects of the incarnation that have relevance to incarnational youth workers, not all necessarily adhering to this historical theological position.

The term incarnation, as Hick points out, is not a biblical one. He suggests that theologically, the term 'incarnation' began in the official language of the church and was prompted by John 1:14 which talks about the Word being made flesh. The Greek phrase '*sarx egeneto*' in Latin becomes '*incarnatus*'.[15] Hick argues that the term was not meant to be metaphorical but was a theological shorthand for the idea that Jesus was truly God and truly human (1993: 101). This is the classical view of the term that over the centuries has been explored and

---

[15] The literal meaning of "incarnation" is 'embodiment in the flesh' (Dunn 1998: 30).

challenged.[16] Dunn argues that the phrase developed out of a sense of the feeling that previous ways of talking about God's revelation did not fully express the significance of that revelation in Jesus (1998: 46).

Debate about the incarnation continued in the early years of the church. Much of this debate centred on the humanity and divinity of Jesus. Various official pronouncements were made in the fourth and fifth centuries,[17] the last of which was at Chalcedon in 451. Here the relationship between the humanity and divinity of Jesus was articulated in terms of two 'natures' combined in one 'person'. It says:

> Following, then the holy Fathers, we all with one voice teach that it should be confessed that our Lord Jesus Christ is one and the same Son, the Same perfect in Godhead, the Same perfect in manhood, truly God and truly man, the Same [consisting] of a rational soul and a body; *homoousios* with the Father as to his Godhead, and the Same *homoousios* with us as to his manhood; in all things like unto us, sin only excepted … One and the same Christ, Son, Lord, Only-begotten, made known in two natures [which exist] without confusion, without change, without division, without separation; the difference of the natures having been in no wise taken away by reason of the union, but rather the properties of each being preserved, and [both] concurring into one Person (*prosopon*) and one *hypostasis* – not parted or divided into two Persons (*prosopa*), but one and the same Son and Only-begotten, the divine Logos, the Lord Jesus Christ (Sellers 1953: 210-11).

What was agreed was a highly technical form of words. As McGrath, an evangelical theologian, suggests, 'The principle in question could be summarized like this: provided it is recognized that Jesus Christ is both truly divine and truly human, the precise manner in which this is articulated or explored is not of fundamental importance' (1994: 295). According to Macquarrie this view was generally accepted until the Enlightenment in the mid-eighteenth century when the debate was reopened and which continues today (1993: 269). Although the Christological debate continues, this focus on an orthodox understanding of the incarnation is strategically important in light of the evangelical ethos and heritage of YFC. With this as a given, I sought to identify those aspects of the incarnation that appeared to be of relevance to incarnational youth workers and which would shape their

---

[16] Hick himself being a prominent challenger of this classical understanding.

[17] For example, the Councils of Nicea (325), Constantinople (381), Ephesus (431).

understanding of 'incarnational' as an approach to ministry.

When God became human in the form of Jesus, it was God who took the initiative in establishing a new sort of relationship with humanity. Swinton describes its continuing relevance:

> The incarnation, death, and resurrection of Jesus provide continuing evidence that God has not forgotten human beings, and that God continues to desire relationship and justice. Jesus' presence with the poor and marginalized reminds the world of the nature and focus of God's actions in the world (2000: 125).

Here, Swinton begins to provide a good theological rationale (relating to friendship in a mental health context) that can be applied to incarnational urban youth ministry.

There are several ways in which this engagement by God directly with humanity in the incarnation can be a helpful model. The first is the demonstration of the potential of a relationship with God becoming clearer. Becoming a Christian will offer hope to young people in a world where there may be little hope. This is a powerful message for youth workers to share. They will all have testimonies of how God has changed their lives, and, hopefully, their lives too will be a testimony of the difference being a Christian makes.

Secondly, in understanding the incarnation as emblematic of God's involvement in ordinary lives and communities, and seeing the Holy Spirit as continuing this work, God can be seen as present and already at work in communities where workers are. This helps us to understand incarnational ministry as having a mutuality: God is already at work and one can see signs of God in the people among whom one is working. The onus is not solely on the worker bringing the presence of God into a situation.

Thirdly, the incarnation could encourage a model of taking the initiative in building relationships with a group of people. The story of several of the incarnational youth workers was that they prayed about where they should be and then took the initiative to move to the community where they sensed God's calling. Some would argue that this is not necessarily in line with best youth and community work practice where a greater degree of dialogue with the community would normally be expected before establishing some work. However, as Christian youth workers, it will sometimes be the case that there is a more pressing theological justification for what one is doing than that suggested by secular understandings of youth work. It should be noted that there are dangers in this approach of an authoritarian style where a project is imposed without consultation or agreement. Taking the initiative should not be at the expense of treating people with respect.

Fourthly, if a manifestation of the incarnation today can be understood as the church, the body of Christ, then the form of this church may be important in terms of providing the support and context necessary for incarnational urban youth ministry. Hoekendijk suggests a profile of a church that reflects who God is. He uses the term 'Messianic community' to describe it and suggests that the charter for such a church is found in Phil. 2:5ff. He writes:

> If someone asks where the church is, then we ought to be able to answer: there, where people are emptying themselves, making themselves as nothing; there, where people serve, not just a little, but in the total service which has been imitated from the Messiah-Servant and in which the cross comes into view; and there, where the solidarity with the fellowman is not merely preached but is actually demonstrated (1967: 69).

This is a good description of what incarnational youth workers are seeking to do in their ministry. To what extent they can be involved in helping shape the mission of the local church to this end will vary, indeed they may be shaped by the church of which they are a part. It will help combat the alienation sometimes felt by incarnational urban youth workers, if they are part of a body that shares a similar understanding of ministry. Also, in an ecclesial context where the emphasis is on others, then experimenting with different models of church for young people will be less of a problem. The challenge is to find such churches and the funding needed to sustain incarnational youth ministry. Partnerships between agencies such as YFC and churches that take a 'Messianic community' approach could provide the right kind of management and support for workers who are engaging as missionaries with young people and need the kind of back up, encouragement, and understanding given to missionaries in other contexts.

Liberation theology emphasises the humanity of Jesus in the incarnation bringing helpful insights to incarnational urban youth ministry. Vincent explains one of the implications in this way: 'From the common sense of human existence, from the dignity of every human being, from the long history of democracy, justice, equality and fraternity – from each arises the strong demand that oppression is not and should not be the fate of human beings anywhere' (1995: 20). What is attractive about liberation theology is that it starts with the experience of the poor and oppressed, the situation that urban young people are in that incarnational youth workers work with. This is an approach that would be very much in keeping with current secular youth work thinking which emphasises the importance of letting young people's voices be heard and encouraging their participation in their communities.[18]

It is this idea of acknowledging and starting with the experience of the young people, rather than the Bible, as a means of exploring theology that is attracting some YFC workers, as well as fully engaging with the human Christ. Bosch writes, 'In this model, one is not interested in a Christ who offers only eternal salvation, but in a Christ who agonizes and sweats and bleeds with the victims of oppression (1993: 512-13). Those who are oppressed examine their own experience and see how this is reflected in the life of Christ, for example. What is new for many YFC staff is that those who are poor and oppressed are able to formulate a theology that is rooted in their own experience and that resonates with them. Such an approach can make theology more meaningful. For some, it will make Jesus seem alive and relevant in a way that has not been true before, when previous writings and images may have come from the perspective of those who had power rather than the powerless. This is important for incarnational youth workers because it often brings a political dimension into understanding the incarnation, which is broader than the individualistic responses to Jesus that are so often encouraged in an evangelical organization like YFC. As well as considering the humanity of Jesus, a focus on the divinity of Jesus assists the development of a theological rationale. In a situation where people feel a lack of value and dignity, the fact that Jesus is God but chose to become human can be a powerful message. O'Collins suggests that 'By assuming a human existence, the second person of the Trinity showed what we mean and meant to God. The alternative, a Jesus who is not truly divine, means that God was really unwilling to become human and did not after all set such a value on us' (1995: 228). The young people that incarnational youth workers are involved with are often lacking in self-esteem. Therefore, communicating exactly who Jesus is and what he did for them can be part of the process of improving the way they see themselves. Although this may not be an integral part of a theological rationale for incarnational urban youth ministry, it does suggest that having a thorough awareness of what is meant in using the term 'incarnational' can affect the content as well as the style of ministry.

Finally, the concept of 'kenosis' began to emerge as one that seemed to be worthwhile studying in depth in order to develop an

[18] See, for example, this official statement: 'The purpose of youth work is to facilitate and support young people's growth through dependence to interdependence by encouraging their personal and social development and enabling them to have a voice, influence and place in their communities' (National Youth Agency 2001: 1).

understanding of what 'incarnational' ministry involved. Early on Phil. 2:5-11 emerged as a significant passage in seeking to understand the concept of the incarnation and its implications for youth work. Although not always associated with an orthodox Christological position, YFC internationally,[19] prominent youth work writers,[20] and current YFC workers[21] had used this passage to describe their approach to youth work. Studying this passage led to exploring the idea of kenosis. Two factors contributed to this. First, the concept of kenosis resonated with the way that incarnational youth workers spoke to me about their experience and, secondly, it resonated with my own call to youth work and incarnational ministry. Although it was a new concept to me, it appeared fruitful to explore its meaning as a resource for a theological rationale for incarnational urban youth workers. However, similar to incarnation, 'kenosis' is a term that has a range of different understandings and part of my study has been to identify the specific understanding of kenosis that is helpful in developing a theological rationale for incarnational urban youth ministry. This is developed in the next chapter but an initial introduction to kenosis is outlined below.

The Greek word means self-emptying, and is found in Phil. 2:7 where it is translated 'emptied himself' in the NRSV. The term is historically associated with a group of German theologians (Thomassius, von Frank, Gess) from the mid-nineteenth century and British theologians from the late nineteenth and early twentieth centuries (Gore, Mackintosh, Weston, Forsyth, Quick) (Ferguson and Wright 1988: 364). Although a kenotic understanding of the incarnation has been popular, it has been subjected to strong criticism because of the implications for the traditionally held view of Jesus being fully human and fully divine.[22] Taylor explores a history of kenotic views and summarises his findings by saying,

> I think we may claim that the modern reaction against kenoticism is of value mainly as a protest against the views of its first proponents, and further that the swing of the pendulum must not prevent us for esteeming its worth in the hands of its better advocates ... Some form of kenosis is essential to any worthy doctrine of the incarnation (1958: 270).

---

[19] In a promotional video, referred to earlier.

[20] Paul Borthwick (1997), for example, who had a regular column in *Youthwork* magazine for many years and Steve Gerali (2001) who uses the passage and the term kenosis in a recent American youth work textbook.

[21] Jonny Baker (undated) and Johnny Douglas (undated), for example.

[22] A summary of the different understandings of the term is provided in Chapter seven.

A current view of the concept is provided by Fergusson. He suggests that the term is no longer being used to describe how the divine could take human form but, on the basis of exegesis of Phil. 2:5-11, 'it understands the life of God, as constituted in Jesus, to be essentially kenotic or self-abasing. What we see in the incarnation is a self-giving of the divine which corresponds to the self-giving of the immanent Trinity' (2001: 78).

However, it was reading Foster's interpretation that helped me to identify kenosis as an approach to the incarnation that might be valuable to pursue in greater depth. Foster suggested that the British kenoticists were responding to a view that traditional Christologies had not done justice to the human life of Jesus and, as he writes:

> ... it should be noted that many of the major themes of the British kenoticists have been incorporated into modern evangelical Christologies. The reality of Jesus' temptations, his single (as opposed to double) consciousness, and the depth of pathos of the cry of dereliction from the cross are universally affirmed today. In the 19th century they were often considered part of kenoticist's heretical innovations (1988: 364).

This link to the way evangelical Christologies have developed was a helpful one, because I was beginning to realise that the idea of kenosis helpfully summarised many of the aspects of incarnational youth worker's experience in moving into this kind of ministry.

Furthermore, although the idea of kenosis is most often linked with Phil. 2:5-11 and v.7 in particular, it is a theme which occurs far more widely in scripture than in this one verse where the word is used. This served to make it a helpful theme to explore in developing a theological rationale, because within YFC a biblical mandate for ministry is the most important aspect of a theological rationale. Two examples serve to illustrate the sort of possibilities that exist to develop further an understanding of kenosis as a basis of ministry. The first is the link with the servant imagery in Isaiah, particularly Ch. 53, suggested, for example, by Bockmuehl in his commentary on Philippians (1997: 163). The second is from Cronin's book, titled *Kenosis*, (1992) where he uses Luke 9:23 which talks about denying self and taking up the cross as the basis of his understanding. A greater biblical exploration of the concept of kenosis is contained in the next chapter.

Although some I consulted have told me that kenoticism is out of fashion, it was the one aspect of my study of the incarnation that really seemed to begin to provide insight into the practice of incarnational ministry as I was experiencing and studying it. Starting with practical experience, and seeing what biblical and theological material informs and resonates with that experience is a relatively new undertaking for me. However, in this part of the process of developing a contextual theological rationale, my practical experience and that of others corresponded most closely with kenoticism. This impression has been reinforced in reading recent material from a YFC worker describes Phil. 2 as 'the benchmark is seeking to be like Jesus' (Douglas undated: 6). A recent exposition of incarnational youth work by Gerali also picks up on the passage, and even uses the term kenosis. He writes: 'An incarnational approach to youth ministry demands that we embrace the same servant attitude (v.5)' (2001: 290). Thus it became clear that there was validity in pursuing in depth a kenotic understanding for the christological basis for a theological rationale.

Element Five: Dietrich Bonhoeffer as an Inspiration and Role Model

In the development of a theological rationale, there is a need to reflect theologically on incarnational ministry, not just from a biblical or theological perspective but also from the tradition of incarnational ministry in the past. I sought to identify others who had been involved in incarnational ministry whose experiences may shape or bring insight into my study. Initially I had hoped to find material from a youth work context but little material emerged that would bring an added dimension to the study undertaken so far. However, the person who seemed to have much to commend them in this context was Dietrich Bonhoeffer.[23]

There were several reasons why it seemed right to study Bonhoeffer in more depth. The main reason is that Bonhoeffer is someone who would be highly regarded within YFC,[24] and thus seen as a positive source for developing a theological rationale for incarnational youth ministry. A second reason was that his writings make it clear that he held an orthodox view of the incarnation and, therefore, he fitted within one of the parameters within which I was working. Thirdly, with Bonhoeffer having what others describe as a kenotic christology, this could inform other work on kenosis being undertaken.[25] A fourth reason that emerged as I began to study

---

[23] Bonhoeffer first came to my attention in this context was while reading about the incarnation. It was suggested that he had a kenotic element in his christology (McGrath 1994: 226).

[24] Based on informal soundings of incarnational youth workers and a leadership team member.

[25] His need to be among his fellow Germans rather than remaining abroad as Hitler rose to power, for example.

Bonhoeffer was a link made by his former student, friend, and biographer Eberhard Bethge between Bonhoeffer's christology and Philippians 2 (1970: 793). Fifthly, again emerging out of further study was Bonhoeffer's commitment to social action illustrated, for example by these words:[26] 'The Church has an unconditional obligation towards the victims of any social order, even when those victims do not belong to the Christian community' (cited in Bethge 1970: 208). Lastly, my own previous knowledge of his work was through reading *Life Together* (Bonhoeffer 1954) and I realized that his understandings of community could add another dimension to the theological rationale. A potentially helpful aspect was in counteracting the possibilities of focusing in an individualistic way on what kenosis might mean to incarnational youth workers.

Bonhoeffer is increasingly being identified as someone whose life and works are worthy of study. For example, Leon Howell writing in *Sojourners* states: 'It is a great legacy that Bonhoeffer's life and death, his witness, offer much for those today trying to be faithful to the gifts and demands of the gospel. That means a critical engagement with a man whose influence continues and grows' (1995). In this respect, a selected study of Bonhoeffer's theology in relation to incarnational ministry may have something to offer those in other disciplines than youth work and extend the relevance of this part of the research. One or two other people whose writings and example might be helpful were explored but none appeared to be as useful and acceptable within the context of incarnational youth ministry as Bonhoeffer. Although, there are many others whose insights might be helpful, an in depth study of a theologian with a kenotic understanding of incarnation and an incarnational understanding of ministry seemed to complement the theological work on incarnation and kenosis.[27] For the reasons stated above, Bonhoeffer seemed to be the appropriate person on which to focus. The conclusions from this study are contained Chapter eight.

---

[26] From a collection of his writings in German called *Gesammelte Schriften II* (Munich: Kaiser Verlag 1966: 48).

[27] For example, the work of Dorothy Day proved interesting and she was certainly involved in incarnational ministry. However, from a YFC perspective she would be less attractive as a source for developing a theological rationale because of the divergence of some of her views and lifestyle with an evangelical approach. In terms of a contemporary example of someone living an incarnational ministry, Bob Holman's writings are helpful in relation to practice but are not always as explicit theologically. See his writings listed in the bibliography.

Conclusion

I have sought to identify the elements that need to inform a contextual theological rationale for incarnational urban youth workers. Much of the material for the elements about YFC and workers was covered in the first stage of the research. The material on kenosis and Bonhoeffer has been identified subsequent to the action research project stage. Thus the following chapters will report on the study of kenosis and Bonhoeffer. The final chapter will seek to draw together all of this material in developing a manifesto for incarnational youth ministry which will be followed by the related theological rationale.

Chapter 7

Kenosis and Incarnational Youth Ministry

Kenosis: a joyous, kind, and loving attitude that is willing to give up selfish desires and to make sacrifices on behalf of others for the common good and the glory of God, doing this in a generous and creative way, avoiding the pitfall of pride and inspired by the love of God and the gift of grace (Ellis 2001: 108).

Ellis's definition (cited as the heading to this chapter) makes the theological concept of kenosis particularly relevant to incarnational urban youth workers and their practice. It moves beyond a discussion of doctrine to an understanding of practice in everyday life. This chapter unfolds the journey made between becoming aware of the term and its theological significance, and coming to see it as descriptive of a valid approach to ministry.

The main context for my study of kenosis emerged when seeking to establish a biblical rationale for incarnational youth work. This identified Phil. 2:5-11 as a significant passage. As already stated earlier, this text is important to YFC, and authors prominent in the youth ministry field, such as Paul Borthwick, acknowledge its importance in exploring incarnational youth work.[1] In the previous chapter, I summarized other reasons why kenosis emerged as a concept to study in greater depth, as well as giving a brief introduction to the meaning of the term.

In my exploration of kenosis I have found that the term is currently being used in a range of different contexts, which possibly suggests that it is coming back into fashion as a useful concept. For example, M. Scott Peck, a popular writer on contemporary spirituality, uses it as a key theme in a book called *Golf and the Spirit*. He writes, 'In doing battle on the golf course...I am attempting to practice kenosis: getting myself out of my own way. It is what spiritual growth is all about' (1999: 5). Although the term 'kenosis' is not used, Jack Mahoney, in writing about what Christian love means in the context of pastoral care, talks about the need for 'self-giving to the point of impoverishment in imitation of Jesus' own self-emptying on our behalf' (2000: 6). This appears to be an application of Phil. 2:7, although the connection to the verse is not explicitly made. Another example is a collection of essays called *The Work of Love*, subtitled 'Creation as Kenosis'. It is claimed on the back of the book that 'The development of kenotic ideas was one of the most important advances in theological thinking in the late twentieth century' (Polkinghorne 2001). Kenosis has also been used as a theme in interfaith dialogue, for example in Christopher Ives' book *Divine Emptiness and Historical Fullness* (1995).[2] Perhaps the general notion of kenosis is attractive because it is a concept that is counter-cultural to the predominant consumerism that is facing society and young people in particular.[3] In modeling a kenotic approach to ministry among young people, such as described in the quotation at the head of this chapter, incarnational youth workers may well be demonstrating a counter-cultural lifestyle. This lifestyle can give a sense of identity and purpose to them as workers that they may not find in a more traditional Christian youth work setting where the influence of consumerism is greater. Incarnational youth workers that I have talked to have often been

---

[1] Borthwick writes, 'The incarnational model of Jesus Christ finds its greatest summary in Phil 2:5-11' (1997: 11).

[2] This is a three-way dialogue between Buddhism, Judaism, and Christianity.

[3] See, for example, Graham Cray (1998: Ch.2).

attracted to alternative forms of lifestyle, for example, living in community, alternative worship, and links with alternative ways of being church.

However, as with the term 'incarnation', there are a variety of approaches to understanding the term 'kenosis'. In this chapter I will seek to give an overview of the doctrine, explore the way that the term has been used and the concept developed in the Bible and by commentators, and then draw some conclusions about what kenosis contributes to a theological rationale for incarnational youth work.

The Doctrine of Kenosis

A kenotic christology is a christology 'from below': it emphasizes the humanity of Jesus. As Hebblethwaite writes, 'Kenotic Christology enables us to see that, by incarnation, the humanity of God is that of a particular human being, a first century Jewish man' (1987: 30). Historically, a kenotic christology has suggested that the incarnate Christ either did not use, or emptied himself of, some of his divine attributes, usually considered to be omniscience, omnipresence, and omnipotence. As already stated, the idea of a kenotic christology is associated historically with a group of German and British theologians from the nineteenth and early twentieth centuries. Focusing on Thomasius and Gore, as examples of these approaches I will consider some contemporary responses to their views. Thomasius developed a kenotic christology as a response to developments in theology in the nineteenth century particularly those, such as Schleiermacher's, that emphasised the humanity of Jesus as opposed to his divinity. Brown suggests that early kenotic formulations were attempts to maintain the orthodox two natures understanding of Christ, but what resulted was interpreted by others as a diminishing of the divinity of Jesus (1975: 548). However, Macquarrie suggests that we should not too quickly dismiss these formulations of kenotic christology. He suggests that it is 'essentially a mediating christology', attempting to mediate between old and new understandings of Christ, and that this may well have been its attraction to the British theologians towards the end of the nineteenth century (1974: 116). Macquarrie believes that Thomasius's version has the most to commend it of the early kenoticists (1974: 120). Thomasius writes, 'As the assumption of human nature, the incarnation is at the same time the self-limitation of God the Son; and conversely, the self-limitation of the Son of God mediates the assumption of flesh. Divesting himself, he appropriates human kind; imparting himself to it, he truly participates in it, and in such manner unites himself with it and it with him as one person.' He goes on to explain the incarnation in kenotic language: 'In the unity of the two the incarnation is itself the deepest mystery of self-denying love, a deed of love in which the eternal Son of the Father becomes like unto us, in order, in suffering and dying, to reconcile us with God' (1965: 49). This idea of self limitation would seem to be perfectly in keeping with an omnipotent God who could choose to do this in certain circumstances, in order to further God's own mission. However, there has been debate as to what extent such divine self limitation diminishes the divinity of Jesus so that the relationship between Jesus and the eternal Logos is not clear.[4]

The foremost British proponent of a kenotic christology was Charles Gore writing from the late nineteenth century to the early twentieth century. One example of his view is to be found in *Belief in Christ*, published in 1922: 'the Incarnation is the supreme act of self-sacrificing sympathy by which one whose nature is divine was enabled to enter into human experience. He emptied Himself of divine prerogatives so far as was involved in really becoming man and growing, feeling, thinking and suffering as man' (1922: 226). Gore was trying to use kenotic views, as Brown suggests, to 'reconcile liberal, critical views of the OT with the acceptance of Jesus' authority as a teacher...Gore saw kenosis as an expression of the divine humility in general in the way in which God deliberately limits himself in his dealings with mankind' (1975: 548). He was trying to defend an orthodox two natures christology but, ultimately, many have found the attempt unsatisfactory because of what Gore says about the limitation of the divine. This is perhaps unfair given what he goes on to say, in the context of a discussion of definitions of Councils. He discusses various views of what the self-emptying means in terms of the limitation of God and writes, 'If we are wise we shall not attempt to answer the question' (1922: 226). However, despite the strong criticisms of the first kenotic christologies, the kenoticists have contributed to a broader understanding of christology. As already noted, many of their key themes have influenced modern evangelical christologies (Foster 1988: 364), and some more recent theologians have articulated a kenotic christology more able to withstand the previous criticisms (Gunton 1997).

In reflecting on the doctrine of kenosis historically, Torrance summarises his perspective on the early debates about kenosis when he writes, 'Whereas the Christian witness is to the self-accommodation for humanity of the Eternal God in a humanly inconceivable and unanticipatable act of grace, kenotic christology all too easily found itself re-engaging the kind of metaphysical interpretation which it originally sought to counteract' (2001: 214). This is a very real concern

---

[4] See, for example, MacKinnon's discussion (1976: 95).

from our context, because metaphysical debates have little to offer incarnational youth ministry, and the interpretation of kenosis as meaning that God is limited, make the use of the term problematic. However, a more helpful perspective for incarnational youth work is put forward by Gunton. In his study of the classical tradition of theology in relation to christology, Gunton criticizes those who understand kenotic christology as limiting divinity. He puts forward his view that one can speak of the self-emptying of God, but as an expression of, not a retraction of his deity. He goes on to say:

> The self-emptying is part of God's fullness, for the heart of what it means to be God is that he is able to empty himself on behalf of that which he is not himself. In other words, it is part of his love, through which he comes among us in our time and history to transform our existence from within (1997: 172).

This perspective will be developed further in the discussions below on the biblical material relating to kenosis.

kenos and *kenoo* in the Septuagint

Brown argues that there is no specific Hebrew word equivalent to the Greek noun *kenos*: he states that nineteen different Hebrew words are translated thus in the Septuagint. The word literally means 'empty', and is to be found frequently in Greek writing from the time of Homer onwards (Brown 1975: 546). Examples of a literal use of the term include Jer. 14:3 where it refers to vessels and Exod. 3:21 and Deut. 15:13 in relation to being empty-handed. There are also metaphorical meanings of the word. With humans it can mean ineffectual, hollow, vain, shallow, empty in mind, and lacking judgement, as in Judges 9:4 (worthless). With things, it means lacking content or missing effect as in Isa. 30:7, where it refers to worthless and empty advice given by the Egyptians. It is found often in the book of Job, for example referring to the empty nothings that his friends were seeking to comfort him with (e.g. 21:34).

The verb *kenoo* is seen in Greek writing from Herodotus onwards and means 'to empty'. Various forms of the verb are found in the LXX. According to Decker (undated) there are four main occurrences of the verb: Gen. 24:20 (literal usage – Rachel emptying a jar); 2 Chron. 24:11 (literal usage – emptying a chest of money); Jer. 14:2 (metaphorical – Judah languishing); Jer. 15:9 (metaphorical - woman languishing). Kittel suggests that there are two further examples of the verb used in a passive sense meaning 'to be desolate' and these are Ezek. 12:20, and 26:2 where places, rather than people, are referred to (1966: 661). In exploring the literal meaning of *kenoo* found in Gen. 24:20, Martin notes that the Hebrew word is *pi'el*. This means 'to make bare', but also 'to pour out' and 'to humiliate'and is linked to Isa. 53:12 (referring to the servant being 'poured out' to death), which some have used as an interpretative tool for the Philippians passage (1967: 167-8). Martin makes the point that the two main uses of the simple verb (the references in Jeremiah) are metaphorical rather than literal and that this is important to note when interpreting the use of the term in the New Testament (1967: 165).

kenos and *kenoo* in the New Testament

Within the New Testament, *kenos* and *kenoo* are predominantly Pauline words. However, the literal sense of the noun is found in Mk. 12:3 and Lk. 20:10, 11: in each case the word is translated 'empty-handed' in the context of the 'parable of the wicked tenants'. Also, it is used figuratively in Jas. 2:20 in relation to a senseless person (Kittel 1966: 660). *Kenoo*, the verb, is only used by Paul and his use will be explored below.

The noun *kenos* is predominantly used figuratively by Paul to mean what Brown describes as 'fruitlessness and inefficacy'. He uses it in circumstances where something would be in vain; for example, in 2 Cor. 6:1 it refers to grace and in 1 Cor. 15:14 it refers to proclamation and faith (1975: 547). An example of the literal use of the word *kenos* to mean empty includes Eph. 5:6 where it used in the context of words which may deceive.

There are four Pauline examples of the use of the verb *kenoo*, excluding Phil. 2:7. They are Rom. 4:14; 1 Cor. 1:17; 1 Cor. 9:15 and 2 Cor. 9:3. These are all examples of a more metaphorical use of the verb. Romans 4:14 talks about faith being 'null' and the promise 'void'; 1 Cor. 1:17 refers to the cross not being emptied of power; 1 Cor. 9:15 talks about Paul not being deprived of ground for boasting, and 2 Cor. 9:3 refers to the grounds for Paul boasting about the Corinthians not being empty.

Philippians 2:7 has been translated both literally and metaphorically, with the Authorised Version taking a more figurative translation 'he made himself of no reputation' and the New Revised Standard Version,[5] for example, using the word 'emptied'. Some translations talk about 'giving up', such as 'gave up all he had' (Good News Bible), 'gave up everything' (Contemporary English Version), 'gave up his place with God' (New Century Version). Other

---

[5] Along with the New American Standard Bible and the Revised Standard Version.

translations include a variety of expressions: the idea of 'stripping himself' (J. B Phillips and the Amplified Version); 'laid aside' (Living Bible); and 'made himself nothing' (Revised English Bible, New International Version). This range of translations gives an indication as to the diversity of interpretations of this verse and, by extension, as to what was entailed when Jesus became human. This is the root of some of the problems faced when talking about a 'kenotic' christology; an assumption may be made that a particular perspective on the humanity or divinity of Jesus is being taken.

From this brief survey, there appear to be a range of ways the word is used in the Bible. First, in a literal way to mean 'empty'. Secondly, metaphorically in negative terms of 'making empty, in vain, foolish, worthless or to no effect'. Thirdly, metaphorically in terms of 'relinquishing, renouncing, laying aside'. This latter, more active and positive, usage derives mainly from Phil. 2:7. In seeking to explore this concept more fully the wider context of the letter to the Philippians and the particular passage Phil. 2:5-11 will be explored. Subsequently, kenosis as a biblical theme will be considered in contexts where the word is not explicitly used, but the idea is present.

The Context of the Letter to the Philippians

Philippi is in the north-eastern corner of Macedonia. It was originally established as Krenides ('Springs' or 'Fountains')[6] by an Athenian exile, Callistratus, but was seized by Phillip II of Macedon[7] who renamed it. In 42 BCE it was established as a Roman military colony by Octavian (later Caesar Augustus) and a number of Roman war veterans settled there. According to Acts, the church at Philippi was the first that emerged from Paul's ministry in Europe, circa 49 CE.[8] Paul was imprisoned at Philippi on his first visit, but continued to go to the city over the years and received support from them for his ministry. When the letter was written the believers at Philippi were experiencing opposition; the civil authorities expected citizens to give first place to Caesar, whereas Christians believed that this homage should be given to Christ.[9] Alongside this, the congregation was suffering, and manifesting behaviour that detracted from unity such as arguing, gossiping, and displaying selfish ambition. Paul was concerned that this would affect the witness of the church. A further issue was that some

---

[6] The former is suggested by O'Brien (1991: 3) and the latter by Bockmuehl (1997: 3).
[7] The father of Alexander the Great.
[8] Acts 16:11-40.
[9] See Oakes (2001) Chapter 5 for a discussion of "Christ and the Emperor".

Judaizers were seeking to influence Gentile members of the congregation to be circumcised.[10]

Paul's letter, written in the early 60s CE (Fee 1995: 1) from prison[11] was seeking to address some of these issues, as well as expressing gratitude for their support. Letter writing was an important means of communication in the culture and various conventions were adopted. According to Fee, the letter performs two functions, that of a letter of friendship and a moral exhortation. (1995: 14).

There has been a renewed interest in examining the political and social context of early writings about Christianity in order to understand them. From this perspective, the letter to the Philippians is written to a people who are suffering economically and who are in danger of fragmenting rather than coming together in unity.[12] This resonates with incarnational urban youth ministry, which is carried out in places where people are suffering economically, and where there is increasing fragmentation.[13] It may be useful to consider if an understanding of Philippians can contribute to the situation faced by incarnational youth workers in multi-cultural areas. Is part of a call to unity now a call to break down barriers between different racial and religious groups, focusing on a common humanity?

Oakes has produced a detailed analysis of the archaeology and social history of Philippi and used this information to gain an understanding of the letter, including an exploration of Phil. 2:5-11 in particular. He develops a model of the likely make-up of the church at Philippi and concludes that it is 'a town-centred church, and one slanted towards those most accessible to Paul and his early converts' (2001: 59). Agriculture was more important at Philippi than in most of the other places Paul wrote letters to. This meant that Philippi was more tied economically into the colonial system. Oakes suggests that 'In none of the other cities was the experience of everyday life so firmly under the control of local, visible Romans' (2001: 76). This issue will be discussed below in the context of Phil. 2:5-11.

Paul in his writings, as Meeks notes, is often concerned about 'the internal life of the Christian groups in each city' (1983: 74), and exhorts others to follow his example. Phil. 3:17 says 'Brothers and

---

[10] Bockmuehl provides a helpful introduction to the context of the letter to the Philippians (1997: 1-46).

[11] Bockmuehl states that apart from Philemon, it is Paul's only undisputed letter written in captivity. (1997: 1)

[12] Oakes 2001: Ch. 3.

[13] As demonstrated, for example, by the disturbances in July 2001 in urban areas such as Bradford, Burnley, and Stoke.

sisters, join in imitating me, and observe those who live according to the example you have in us'. Along with Christ's example of humble service (2:5-11), Paul also uses himself (2:17), Timothy (2:20-22), and Epaphroditus (2:30) as models that the Philippians should follow.[14] This call to imitate himself is found in Paul's writings elsewhere, and in commenting on this O'Brien links it back to Paul following the 'servant model of his Master (cf. Phil. 2:7)' (1995: 105). This use of a role model resonates with the practice of incarnational youth workers who can provide the same sort of role model as say, Timothy, to the young people (as well as other Christians) they are working among. In doing this they too will need to reflect upon whether their ministry is truly an imitation of Christ's.

Along with explorations of the historical and cultural context that Paul was writing in, the structure of Phil. 2:5-11 has been subject to much speculation. Indeed, according to Witherington: 'The literature on this hymn ... is so voluminous that it is impossible to survey or summarize it all' (1994b: 97). As well as the sheer volume of literature there is a great diversity of interpretation as O'Brien remarks:

> The paragraph is the most difficult in Philippians to interpret...Little scholarly consensus has emerged in relation to the origin and authorship of the passage (pre-Pauline, Pauline or post-Pauline?), its form and structure (hymnic? The number of stanzas), the conceptual background of the passage (OT, Gnostic myth, general Hellenism, wisdom speculation?), or key exegetical issues (O'Brien 1991: 188).

Martin, revisiting the passage he has written on extensively, believes that:

> There is a formidable list of reasons why this Pauline period should continue to be the focus of interest, even as we acknowledge that the text has not yielded its full secrets. First, Philippians 2:5-11 taxes the skill of the translator, as many of the key words, especially to do with the presentation of Christ's role in the text, baffle the lexicographer's mind and offer a wide, often puzzling, variety of choice and interpretation (1998: 2).

Some of the major issues relating to interpretation are outlined below.

The first verse in the passage is problematic, Marshall describes it as 'one of the most tricky in the letter' 1991: 48). As Bruce

---

[14] O'Brien (1995: 86-88) discusses Paul as a model to the Philippians.

explains, 'The clause 'which...also in Christ' lacks a verb, which has to be supplied' (1995: 64). Hawthorne see it as 'the link between the two sections. It is the transition from exhortation to illustration (1991: 80). O'Brien (1991: 253-262) provides a detailed summary of the two main interpretations of the hymn, ethical and kerygmatic, and seeks to interpret v.5 in the light of his conclusions of the validity of these approaches.[15] His conclusion (which is reached after providing arguments against Käsemann's view that the ethical interpretation option is weakened by the inclusion of vv. 9-11 in the hymn) is that 'the Christ-hymn presents Jesus as the supreme example of the humble, self-sacrificing, self-giving service that Paul has just been urging the Philippians to practice in their relations to one another (1991: 262). Having reached this conclusion he believes that the best translation of v.5 is 'adopt towards one another, in your mutual relations, the same attitude that was found in Christ Jesus' (1991: 262).

One of the common scholarly debates is whether or not the passage is an existing hymn that Paul is using. There is no general agreement about this.[16] Recent scholarship gives a range of views. Seeley's comment summarises a mediating approach. He writes: 'True, Paul may not have been the hymn's author, but he did live during the same time as its composition, work in the same general stream of early Christian tradition, and like it enough to put it in one of his letters' (Seeley 1994). In contrast, Fee asserts that whatever its pre-history, this is Paul's writing:

> Finally, it needs to be stressed (1) that Paul is the *author* in terms of its inclusion, including *all* the present words of 2:6-11, and (2) that although Paul often quotes, this passage does *not* come by way of a quotation. The alleged 'hymn' is a *grammatical piece* inextricably connected to the present context' (1995: 46).

Oakes concludes that it fits the Philippian situation so well that Paul at a minimum reformulated an existing hymn. More likely, however, he took his beliefs about Christ and 'carefully crafted a rhetorically powerful Christological enforcement to his call, in 1:27-2:4 to stand firm and united' (2001: 210). In the context of this piece of

---

[15] Hawthorne suggests that Hendrickson, Lightfoot, Moule, Muller, Plummer and Bruce favour the ethical example interpretation and Beare, Martin in *Carmen Christi*, and Käsemann prefer the kerygmatic option (1991: 80).

[16] Lohmeyer was among the first to suggest this view, now shared by many. O'Brien writes 'Lohmeyer's ground-breaking analysis was regarded as the fundamental starting point for all subsequent studies' (1991: 189-90).

work, it is less important who wrote the hymn than the role it plays in the letter and what it may have to say to incarnational youth workers today. A slightly different view is put forward by Meeks who describes Pauline Christianity as 'entirely urban' (1983: 8) and Paul as a city person. (1983: 9) He places the Christ hymn in Philippians as one of a number of hymns or pre-existing material that Paul uses in his writings as part of the ritual of the early church.[17] It is likely that such material was used regularly in meetings:

> By chanting psalms, hymns, and odes to God (or to the Lord), among other things, the congregation also 'taught' and 'admonished' themselves and 'built up' the community. One large role of ritual speech and music is thus to promote group cohesion (Meeks 1983: 145).

With specific reference to the Philippians hymn, the function this performs is described as follows: 'And the whole mythic pattern of Christ's descent from divine to human form, submission to death, and subsequent exaltation and enthronement can be introduced by quoting a hymn or liturgical poem familiar to the readers, as basis for an appeal for unity and mutual regard' (1983: 181).

For some, a valid approach to understanding the context of 2:5-11 is to see it in relation to the Roman political situation. Seeley puts forward the view that 'competition between nascent christology, on the one hand, and Roman and Jewish political ideology on the other, points toward an organizing principle for the entire hymn.'[18] (1994) He suggests that the hymn claims for Christ some of the things claimed both for the emperor and for the Lord God, the ruler of Israel. This idea of considering an alternative political structure was one that found favour with some groups such as the Stoics and Cynics and the community at Qumran.[19] According to Seeley: 'In the hymn...one wing of a fledgling communal movement offers its own religio-political warrant in competition with other communities already on the scene' (1994). Seeley suggests that the hymn draws on Isaiah 45, which speaks about how God uses Cyrus for his purposes, particularly verse 23 which is paralleled in Phil. 2:10-11. Further, Seeley argues that by using this familiar form of words (from the Septuagint) the hymn is

---

[17] Suggested examples of other hymns or similar writings include Col. 1:15-20; Eph. 1:3-14; 1 Tim. 3:16 (Meeks 1983: 145).

[18] A view he attributes to Helmut Koester in an article on 'Jesus the Victim' in *Journal of Biblical Literature* 1992: 3-15.

[19] Seeley (1994) discusses this.

claiming that Jesus is Lord, a title given to him by the God of Israel. The implications of this are that 'the community behind the hymn is claiming that it is the heir to the promises made to the nation of Israel. In effect, it is presenting itself as the true Israel' (Seeley 1994). Seeley discusses different aspects of the hymn and the possible origins or connections to the events at the time the hymn was written. He concludes that a pertinent issue was that of rule. Jews had not enjoyed the experience of Roman rule and wanted a state with a true monarch, God. He summarises the situation thus:

> Though the hymn proclaimed Jesus' lordship over all, it must have been painfully obvious that his realm could not yet match such reality. Even so, his rule was becoming manifest in small cells forming within the Empire...They looked forward to the day when their master would return to exercise real, worldly power. Until then, they could take comfort in his cosmic kingship and know that he, too, had had to suffer the abuses of tyranny (1994).

This eschatological perspective does not necessarily resonate with incarnational youth workers, as deferred gratification is not a value held by many young people! However, what may be attractive to some is pursuing a community based on different values to the dominant culture.

A major theme in Philippians is that of suffering. Oakes cites 1:27-30; 2:15-18; 3:20-21 as evidence of this (2001: 77). He sees 'a pervasive three-fold parallel drawn between Christ's suffering, Paul's suffering, and the Philippians' suffering' (2001: 103). He also sees the theme of unity as being intertwined with suffering and explains 2:5-11 in this dual context as follows. Those who are suffering less are of higher status and are not financially helping others who are suffering more who tend to be of lower status. Helping others could be seen as difficult for the wealthier Christians because this would affect their social status in the social system of Philippian society. However, they are given the example of Christ who refused to take advantage of his status and chose to lower it, through becoming human and even more so through the manner of his death (2001: 200). The second part of the passage gives a reason why Christ's example should be followed. Oakes describes it thus:

> A poor, suffering Philippian might be most aware of the promise implicit in Christ's authority making Christ a safe basis of confidence. A wealthier Philippian who had suffered little might be struck most by the way in which Christ's

imperatives ought to displace certain social imperatives which had, for them, been far too dominant (2001: 207).

For incarnational youth workers a kenotic approach to ministry is not necessarily about suffering but primarily about seeking to imitate Christ's approach to ministry in a way that is relevant to their own social context.

What has been considered above is both the wider political system and the particular local situation in relation to Phil. 2:5-11 in its original context. If a similar passage were to be written today to incarnational youth workers the pertinent issues would be those that are faced in the culture they work in. At a wider level this might well mean the individualism prevalent in a culture which emphasises personal fulfilment at the expense of a wider community perspective; a 'pick and mix' approach to spirituality and religion which may move away from a coherent understanding of who Christ is and what that means to a Christian youth worker today. At the local level it may mean divisions and barriers between different age groups, religious or social groups.

Kenosis and Philippians 2:5-7

Various writers have attempted to classify the different understandings of the kenosis of Christ in Phil. 2:5-7. As a consequence of my research, I have drawn together a range of different *theological* interpretations into a list that outlines the main options and gives an indication of the breadth of understandings of the term.[20] First, that he *temporarily* relinquished relative aspects of divine power such as omniscience. Secondly, that Christ *fully* relinquished divine powers as the Logos became, not assumed, Christ's human soul. Thirdly, that he *voluntarily* chose not to use his divine attributes. Fourthly, that he relinquished his deity and it was *restored* at the ascension. Fifthly, that the Logos imparted divinity *little by little* to Christ's human soul until he was fully divine. Sixthly, that Christ had *two independent life centres* and each was unaware of the other's existence. Seventhly, that Christ acted *as if* he had no divine attributes. Eighthly, he *gave up*

---

[20] For further information on the range of interpretations see the following: Martin (1967: 63-95) describes the main twentieth century interpretations, and the translation of v. 7 (165-96); Coakley (1996:89-96), whose work was particularly helpful in drawing up this list; Decker (undated) also offers a range of interpretations of kenosis; James (1983), Macquarrie (1974), and Thomas (1970) provide brief historical overviews of kenoticism in articles; Wright (1986: 342-3) offers a chart summarizing different interpretations of some of the key Greek words in the passage.

independent exercise of divine powers. Ninthly, he chose not to have *particular forms of power* that are false and worldly, that might wrongly be construed as divine.

This list makes it clear that there is little agreement about what kenosis means and that it is very easy to misunderstand what is being said when the term is being used. Torrance summarises a helpful response to the problem: 'The Christian faith lives from the perception of who Jesus is, not how God can become human – a question that is not ultimately our concern. Such a refusal to be distracted from the 'Who' question was arguably one of the strengths of the classic christological accounts' (2001: 213). This seemed to be the most appropriate way of exploring kenosis in relation to incarnational youth ministry; the focus was on how kenosis informed such ministry, not formalizing a doctrinal position.

In identifying an approach to kenosis as part of a theological rationale for incarnational youth ministry, a *metaphorical* understanding, closest to the eighth and ninth definitions above, seems most appropriate. This theological understanding can be summarized as involving Christ using his divine powers through his interaction with the Father and the Spirit. From this perspective, Jesus Christ demonstrated an understanding of his role and mission as a servant in a way that contrasted powerfully with traditional expectations about how both human and divine rulers would exercise their role. There are several reasons why this metaphorical approach is appropriate. First, it is compatible with a Chalcedonian understanding of Jesus Christ being fully human and fully divine, the danger is that in using a word like kenosis, it is assumed that this is talking about Christ in a way that is not compatible with the orthodox understanding. Secondly, a metaphorical interpretation is valid exegetically.[21] Thirdly, it is an approach that seems relevant to incarnational youth workers and their practice. Two approaches to understanding kenosis more metaphorically have been selected because of their potential relevance to workers and are described below.

Becoming Human and Taking on the Form of a Servant
Some of the foremost commentators on the passage see that an essential aspect of kenosis in Christ Jesus becoming human involved taking the form of a servant. Martin (1960), for example, in his first major work on the passage, suggests that, having dismissed the view of kenosis meaning giving up relative attributes of divinity, later authors took the

---

[21] Martin concludes that the verb *kenoun* carries a metaphorical rather than a metaphysical meaning (1967: 194).

view that it meant taking on the form of a servant (1960: 23). In a recent commentary on Philippians, Bockmuehl follows this thinking. He argues that it is the servanthood of Christ that is important, in this instance related to the idea of not taking advantage of his position as equal with God. He suggests that Christ demonstrated through the incarnation and crucifixion a renunciation of a selfish way of life that would have used his deity for himself, and thus Christ modeled a way of service (1997: 133).

Barth has an emphasis on kenosis involving becoming human. He writes 'There must be no turning and twisting of the *ekenose*...he emptied himself of the form of God in taking on our form' (1962: 63-64). Wright, in an influential article on the meaning of the term *harpagmos* in Phil. 2 5-11, critiques Barth's understanding of kenosis as over-subtle and not doing justice to the term, in seeing it more as Christ adding something new (the form of a human) rather than giving up anything. Nevertheless, he does commend Barth's desire to emphasise the divinity of the human Jesus (1986: 334-35). Herrick and Mann, in their study of Christian leadership that takes vulnerability as a framework, advocate Barth's interpretation of kenosis in Phil. 2:7. In the context of youth work, I can see the value of their approach, because it is a helpful way of introducing Jesus as a model of leadership that seems attainable and accessible, that is, Jesus as a vulnerable human (1998: 14-15).

Wright's own interpretation of the passage is one that strongly resonates with me and seems to have something to say to incarnational youth ministry. He writes:

> *ekenosen* does not refer to the loss of divine attributes, but – in good Pauline fashion – to making something [his equality with God] powerless, emptying it of apparent significance. The real humiliation of the incarnation and the cross is that one who was himself God, and who never during the whole process stopped being God, could embrace such a vocation...Underneath this is the conclusion, all important in present Christological debate: incarnation and even crucifixion are to be seen as appropriate vehicles for the dynamic self-revelation of God (1986: 345-46).

What is attractive about this interpretation is that it is in harmony with an evangelical interpretation of the life of Jesus and suggests that in incarnational youth ministry the dynamic self-revelation of God comes through Christians who model themselves on Jesus' servant ministry.[22] This is developed in the next section.

---

[22] Related to this perspective of seeing kenosis relating to servanthood is a

A Pattern to Follow

The next interpretation flows from a paraenetic understanding of Philippians, where Paul encourages the believers at Philippi to follow the example of Jesus. The first four verses of Phil. 2 supply the immediate context for what follows and this seems to help support a paraenetic view. However, not all adhere to a paraenetic interpretation. Martin describes the situation thus: 'The 'ethical example' view which sees the hymn as a call to follow Christ in His traits of humility has been challenged from the side of German scholarship which construes the hymn in terms of soteriology not Christology, as Käsemann puts it, Philippians ii tells us what Christ did, not what He was' (1967: 83).[23] Fowl reflects on the situation more than fifty years after Käsemann's influential analysis: 'Over the past twenty years there has been a shift away from these scholarly emphases. Form-critical and history of religions approaches to this text have been challenged in terms of both their methods and their results. In addition while Käsemann's work seemed for a time to have ruled out interpretations of this passage that read it as an ethical story, there has been a renewed interest in discussing how this story functions ethically' (1998: 140).

Wright clearly sees a paraenetic application of the passage, he argues, 'The implication is clear: as God endorsed Jesus' interpretation of what equality with God meant in practice, so he will recognize self-giving love in his people as the true mark of the life of the Spirit' (1986: 347). For Williams, imitating Jesus will be the consequence of what is within a person: 'When we do 'imitate' Jesus in our choices and actions, this is more an outflowing from the inner gift than the result of a systematic effort to conform our behaviour to his' (2001: 222).

The idea of a paraenetic approach to understanding the passage is also suggested by Hurtado. He argues that the language found in 2:6-8 can be found in that of early Christian paraenesis and that a possible source for this is the early Jesus tradition. He writes: 'Further, this evidence suggests strongly that Jesus' actions are so described as to present them as a pattern to which the readers are to conform their

---

view that there are parallels between Phil. 2:7 and Isa. 53:12, the suffering servant (Kreitzer 1998:120 discussed this). Exploring this does not seem to add to an understanding of kenosis for incarnational youth workers, particularly when noting the difference between the suffering servant and humanity in Isaiah with the identification with humanity expressed in Philippians. Martin discusses this issue, presenting a range of interpretations (1967: 190).

[23] A more detailed analysis of the 'ethical interpretation' is found in Martin (1967: 84-88).

behaviour' (1984: 126). The example of Jesus, and the response of God to it, is seen as an encouragement to the Philippians to follow this example. The passage could also be seen as strengthening Paul's call to imitate him that occurs in Phil. 3:17, 'Brothers and sisters, join in imitating me'. Kurz suggests that this aspect of the book is one that has been given little attention. He uses the phrase 'exaltation after self-abasement' (1985: 112) to describe Christ's experience in Phil. 2:9-11 and suggests it is echoed in Paul's experience in Phil. 3:10-11, 12-16, 21. He argues that pedagogical principles, familiar to the original readers of the book, would have understood the role of the teacher in this way; a teacher is an example themselves of what they teach, and Paul was trying to teach the early church what it meant to follow Christ (1985: 106).

Fowl put the idea of the passage providing an ethical example into a wider context and talks about a 'phronetic'[24] application. He writes:

> Paul is trying to form in the Philippians the intellectual and moral abilities to be able to deploy their knowledge of the gospel in the concrete situations in which they find themselves, so that they will be able to live faithfully (or 'work worthily' 1:27). Within this scheme the story of Christ narrated in 2:6-11 functions as an exemplar, a concrete expression of a shared norm from which Paul and the Philippians can make analogical judgments about how they should live (1998: 145-46).

This is what incarnational youth workers are seeking to do in developing a contextual understanding of their role, using the example of the incarnation of Christ to guide and inspire them.

In using Phil. 2:5-11 as a key text for understanding the 'incarnational' element of the ministry, interpreting the passage paraenetically follows from this. Incarnational youth workers see Jesus as an example to follow and seek to model their approach to people, and to their ministry on him.

These are the key metaphorical interpretations of kenosis that have something to offer an understanding of incarnational youth ministry. I will now seek to draw some conclusions about the interpretation of the passage in respect of my research.

A Kenotic Interpretation of Philippians 2:5-11

A helpful comment is made by Taylor who writes, 'How much is to be

---

[24] From the Greek *phronesis*, one of the four cardinal virtues, meaning wisdom, good sense, good judgement, prudence (Mautner 1997: 424).

read into *ekenosen* is the theologian's problem...St. Paul says nothing about the abandonment of the attributes of God. We must distinguish between the kenosis he describes and kenosis as a Christological hypothesis' (1958: 77-8) With regard to Phil. 2:5-11 Martin, amongst others, suggests that one can no longer use this passage as a basis for a kenotic christology, as traditionally understood. He argues, for example, that modern scholars generally agree that a two natures christology is not part of the passage (1967: 171), and that the verb *kenoo* is used metaphorically not literally (1967: 70). Consequently, it is not appropriate to ask what Christ emptied himself of, because that is not the way the word is being used. Thus we are talking about a metaphorical self-emptying. Such an interpretation does not seem to be at odds with other ways the word is used in the Bible.

The shift in understanding of what kenosis means is evident through a reshaping of the question that is being asked. It is suggested by Sturch that the question 'How is it that the Word could become flesh?', which is where many elements of the debate on kenosis around Phil. 2:5-11 are located, is the wrong question (1977: 65). Richard frames it more specifically when he suggests that what is needed is a reformulation of the question 'What is kenosis in the light of the immutability of God?' to 'Who is God in the light of kenosis?' He writes: 'What is needed is a reevaluation of our understanding of God so that kenosis will appear not as a process of de-divination but rather as an attribute of God's love disclosed in the compassionate existence of Jesus (1997: 84).

The idea of starting with human experience in explorations of the appeal of kenotic christology is proposed by James. It is an approach that he believes still has something to offer today. He argues that most people will understand the concept of self-emptying and perhaps see this as the route by which we become more human, and that an authentic humanity is one where kenosis leads to plerosis, a sense of fulfillment (1983: 13). He talks about self-emptying in terms of a forgetting of self and a self-giving that is liberating, and sees this as a starting point for a transformed kenoticism. He believes strongly that what is needed is a christology that is both intellectually coherent and that inspires one to live the Christian life. He suggests that there is a danger that the two are often seen as mutually exclusive. James concludes his discussion by suggesting that

> Surely only in this way [a radically reformed kenoticism] might the gap between modern Christology and contemporary spirituality be bridged, for all theology only has a point because the faith is lived, and the point is to live the faith more

intelligently and with increased devotion. Might the kenoticists still have something to teach us? (1983: 14).

Richard is another who believes that a form of kenotic christology is one that has validity today. He approaches it from the same perspective as James in seeing it as having an intellectual and symbolic appeal that makes it attractive in our culture (1997: 8). It is perhaps attractive because it is counter-cultural and offers a response to many of the issues faced today. An example of this would be the potential destruction of humanity because of excess consumption in the pursuit of self-fulfillment, at the expense of those with little power. He suggests that there needs to be a move from being master of the earth to servant of the earth, a position in keeping with his understanding of kenosis (1997: 24-25).

In the light of the foregoing, there are valid grounds to interpret Phil. 2:5-11 with an emphasis on kenosis. In saying this I do not mean it as historically understood in terms of a diminution of the divinity of Christ. Rather kenosis may be understood as a self-emptying of someone who was fully divine and fully human and who through his humanity revealed something of who God is and provided an example of what humanity was intended to be. Although old ways of looking at kenoticism have been largely dismissed, I have sought to identify more recent examples in the development of thinking on kenosis and believe that this continued progression in the development of the concept has led to a kenotic approach to christology that is valid in YFC today.

The Usefulness of Philippians 2:5-11 to a Kenotic Understanding of Ministry

Phil. 2:5-11 is regarded as an important passage by many, and one that has been influential in shaping understandings of Christ and what it means to be a Christian. Ross provides an example when she introduces her book on power, priesthood and spiritual maturity with Phil. 2:5-10 and writes, 'The heart of Christianity is the self-emptying, kenotic humility God expressed in Jesus the Christ.' She goes on to suggest that this should be the beginning of any discussions of what priesthood or ministry should be (1988: xvi).

For the evangelical context of YFC, the passage is particularly useful now that a range of ways of interpreting the passage maintaining an orthodox christology have become acceptable. Martin, in his review of the passage under the title 'Where Christology Began', identifies Wright's article on the meaning of *harpagmos* as one of three landmark interpretations of this passage[25] (1998: 1). Wright's interpretation, noted above, lays an emphasis on Christ's actions as an aspect of the divine revelation of God. This gives a new understanding of what God is like and therefore what those who are made in the image of God should be like also. This suggests that Phil. 2:5-11 can make a good basis for developing an approach to different types of ministry such as that taken by Herrick and Mann (1998) regarding leadership and pastoral ministry.

Some translations of Phil. 2:5 help emphasize the corporate nature of the passage, which is a helpful emphasis when considering ministry. For example, the NEB's rendering of Phil. 2:5. 'Let your bearing towards one another arise out of your life in Christ Jesus' makes the corporate nature explicit. A difficulty in some translations is that 'you', (Let the same mind be in *you*) can be read individualistically, because the second person singular and plural are the same word in contemporary English. Hawthorne affirms the NEB translation of *en hymin* as 'towards one another'. He explains the context of v. 5 thus: 'This verse means that the hoped-for attitude outlined by Paul in vv 2-4 corresponds with that exhibited by Christ Jesus, especially in vv 6-9, and that the Philippians are bound to act in accordance with this attitude toward one another if they wish to imitate their Lord' (1991: 80-81). Witherington emphasizes the importance of this corporate understanding. He argues that the passage can be interpreted as saying that the Philippians can achieve unity by demonstrating that they share Christ's attitude in serving one another. Within a very hierarchical society this would have been a radical view (1994a: 64-65). It is very easy for the Bible to be read in an individualistic way and there is a danger that an emphasis on kenosis could lead to an unhealthy introspection unless the consequences of this kenosis in terms of those who are to be served is considered. This is particularly true in relation to youth work where false or excessive piety would be very off-putting to young people, whereas sacrificial emptying to be more effective in service would communicate something of the nature of Christ and Christianity that may be understood intuitively, if not in any other way.

Another way of looking at the consequences of kenosis in ministry terms, is to take Wright's suggestion that one can use verses 6-8 as a definition of what agape means. This is an interesting idea when put alongside a passage such as 1 Corinthians 13 (1986: 347). It gives a deeper understanding of what it means to be a servant and can be seen

---

[25] Others being Lohmeyer's interpretation of it as a hymn and Käsemann's repudiation of the passage as an ethical example.

as developing a strong role model as opposed to some of the images that come to mind on hearing the word 'servant' or 'slave'. Both these words have connotations of doing what someone else says and almost having no will of one's own. They can be oppressive words. To love effectively, as in 1 Cor. 13:4-8a, is more evocative of those who show great moral courage and leadership, and who are genuine examples of Christlikeness. Seeing Phil. 2:5-11 in terms of agape gives a more vivid understanding of both a kenotic christology underpinning a kenotic ministry.

A fascinating reading of the passage is that of Coakley. She responds to much of the feminist criticism of the concept of kenosis which argues that it is a means of oppressing women and reinforcing their subjugation.[26] The feminist argument is summarized by Papanikolaou:

> this definition of kenosis, especially the notion of kenosis as self-sacrificial love, emerged as an ethical imperative within the Christian tradition. Kenosis as obedience, humility, and self-sacrifice has a negative history as well. As feminists over the past century, and especially the last half-century have made clear, this understanding of kenosis has been used throughout the history of Christianity to maintain women in situations of oppression. Rather than offering a liberating salvation, the experience of kenosis, feminists would contend, has depersonalized women (2000).

One of the difficulties of this argument is how kenosis as a pattern for all Christians should be understood. Because a concept has been abused it should not be invalidated but rather reinterpreted and applied in a way that does not oppress any particular group. After considering a range of interpretations of Phil. 2:5-11, Coakley suggests that it can be expressed in the form of contemplative prayer, and roots this in an understanding of kenosis as avoiding snatching or grasping. She describes her understanding of contemplative prayer in this way:

> What I have elsewhere called the 'paradox of power and vulnerability' is I believe uniquely focused in this act of silent waiting on the divine in prayer. This is because we can only be properly 'empowered' here if we cease to set the agenda...this special 'self-emptying' is not a negation of self, but the place of self's transformation and expansion into God (1996: 107).

---

[26] See, for example, Frascati-Lochead 1998: 159f.

This fits well into an understanding of the ministry of Christ as reported in John's gospel where there is an emphasis on Christ's relationship with the Father and the inspiration for Jesus' ministry coming from the Father, for example, in John 5:19. In this sense it is an emptying of one's own will to follow God's will. This understanding of kenosis is helpful in that it can relate to everyday life, it is an approach to christology that shapes one's life and practice, and is not merely an intellectual position to defend.

The Theme of Kenosis in Paul's Writings Beyond Philippians

The theme of kenosis is not restricted to Philippians and can be found in some of Paul's other writings. Although the word itself may not be used, other passages have kenotic themes. One example is provided by Oepke who suggests that 2 Cor. 8:9 is the best commentary on Phil. 2:7 (1966: 661). This says: 'For you know the generous act of our Lord Jesus Christ, that though he was rich, yet for your sakes he became poor, so that by his poverty you might become rich'. Witherington also suggests a connection between the two passages: 'Here too Paul uses the language of changing one's social status to refer to Christ's condescension, not only in taking on human form, but also in dying the death of the disenfranchised in order to exhort his converts to similarly generous and selfless actions' (1994a: 70). The idea of kenosis as relinquishment of status for the sake of others comes across here.

Paul's language can be seen as having kenotic overtones through his use of the noun *doulos*, usually understood to mean 'slave'. The word is found in Phil. 2:5-11 and Martin points out that this is the only instance in the New Testament when the word is applied to Jesus (1967: 175). Paul uses the word to describe himself in Phil. 1:1; Gal. 1:10 and Rom. 1:1. In I Cor. 9:19 he says, 'For though I am free with respect to all, I have made myself a slave to all, so that I might win more of them'. Stanley describes this as a 'most revealing metaphor' and goes on to say that 'For Paul, such a total orientation of himself to the risen Lord was also the determining factor in his relationship to those Christian communities he founded' (1994: 131). Paul's writings indicate that it was not only himself that he expected to be a slave of Christ. In 2 Cor. 4:5 he uses the phrase 'ourselves as your slaves' and in Col. 4:12 he refers to Epaphras, using the word *doulos*. The verb is used in many instances in talking about the Christian life, for example in Rom. 6:16; 1 Cor. 7:22; Gal. 4:7. The phrase 'humble serving' is used by Wenham to describe this aspect of Paul's ministry and he argues that Paul was influenced by the teaching of Jesus on the subject, particularly the request of James and John to be prominent in the kingdom (Matt. 20:20-28; Mk. 10:35-45) (1995: 271). Being a slave, in this sense, involves relinquishing of rights to the person one is serving, for those in ministry it may be pertinent to debate to what extent this is the community one serves as well as Jesus; I would argue that Paul implies it is both. In our current culture where rights are demanded, to relinquish one's rights is clearly self-emptying, a kenosis.

The idea of weakness which has parallels with the kenosis of Christ is one that runs through Paul's writings. It is a particular theme in the first letter to the Corinthians where he talks about his own weakness and the responsibility the people of God have towards those who are weak.[27] An important verse is 1 Cor. 9:22 where he says: 'To the weak I became weak, so that I might win the weak. I have become all things to all people, that I might by all means save some.' This verse suggests that Paul was constantly in a process of self-emptying to take on the characteristics necessary to communicate Christ effectively. It was a kenotic approach to ministry: being ready to relinquish in order to serve others.

Paul sought to follow the example of Christ and encouraged others to follow him: 'Be imitators of me, as I am of Christ' (1 Cor. 11:1). It is interesting to consider what this might entail when one reads what could be seen as a summary of Paul's experience of ministry in 2 Cor. 6:4-10:

> but as servants of God we have commended ourselves in every way: through great endurance, in afflictions, hardships, calamities, beatings, imprisonment, riots, labors, sleepless nights, hunger; by purity, knowledge, patience, kindness, holiness of spirit, genuine love, truthful speech, and the power of God: with the weapons of righteousness for the right hand and for the left; in honour and dishonour, in ill repute and good repute. We are treated as imposters, and yet are true; as unknown, and yet are well known; as dying, and see – we are alive; as punished, and yet not killed: as sorrowful, yet always rejoicing: as poor, yet making many rich: as having nothing, and yet possessing everything.

Martin summarises the passage thus: 'To be sure, Paul had little to commend himself in terms of external credentials. But, inwardly and christologically he was the epitome of humble service and yet effectual ministry. His ministry called him to die both 'physically' and 'spiritually', yet the power of God enabled Paul to 'live' in triumph both now and in what the future might bring him' (1991: 182). There is an interesting contrast between the difficulties Paul faces in ministry

---

[27] See 1 Cor. 2:3-4.

and the way that he faces these difficulties, and it could be suggested that he responds to the difficulties in a way that imitates Christ's response to the challenges of his ministry. Could it be argued that there is a kenosis or relinquishment of what might be the usual human reaction to the difficulties and a plerosis or filling of a Christ-like reaction? The last part of the passage is a series of contrasts which suggest this emptiness and this fullness.

Paul's emphasis on the cross in his writings could be seen as an indication of a kenotic approach to ministry. According to Hays, in a study of Paul's writings to the Thessalonians, Philippians, Galatians and Philemon, a unifying theme or synthesis in Paul's writings is the idea of being crucified with Christ. He writes: 'For the most part, Paul regards this cruciform existence in the present time not as an ideal to be pursued but as a fact of experience' (1994: 241). In Gal. 5:19 Paul writes: 'I have been crucified with Christ', and in Phil. 3:10 'I want to know Christ and the power of his resurrection and the sharing of his sufferings by becoming like him in his death.' The idea of Jesus' crucifixion involves unmerited suffering. One could speculate that an aspect of kenosis could likewise involve such suffering as a consequence of decisions made to imitate Christ, which for Paul appears to be an everyday experience.

It is interesting to consider whether these parts of Paul's writings can be used to draw out a spirituality of ministry that turns upside down notions of 'worth' and 'fulness'. This spirituality would be based on both experience and the example of Christ, and is a way of looking at how kenosis can contribute towards a theological rationale for incarnational youth work.

A Kenotic Christology Beyond Paul

Not everyone who could be described as having a kenotic christology derives it solely from Phil. 2:5-11. Richard, for example, takes his kenotic christology from Mark's version of the passion and resurrection, as well the writings of Paul and the rest of the New Testament. He writes: 'The kenotic motif arises immediately out of the experience of the paschal mystery: the whole of the New Testament gives evidence of the kenotic motif' (1997: 41). He argues that the idea of kenosis does not originate with Paul, but is a recurring theme in the life of Christ and is an aspect of any christology that has its roots in the New Testament (1997: 61-62). He writes: 'The gospel of Mark is a parable about God's kenotic love for us, shown in and through the person of Jesus Christ (1997: 63). He suggests that a crucial text that informs this view is Mk. 10:45 which talks about Christ not coming to be served but to serve. He sees the image of the servant on a journey to

Jerusalem where the cross and suffering await him as an important one in the gospel. Bearing the cross is seen as the consequence of relinquishing power because the cross involves suffering, pain, and rejection. The account of Jesus in the garden of Gethsemane shows a kenosis with Jesus rejecting the power he has in his divinity and relinquishing his own will to follow the will of the Father. Richard argues that 'while Mark does not use the language of two natures, he uses two kinds of language with regard to Jesus: the language of suffering and powerlessness, and the language of omnipotence, of divine power. Jesus is simultaneously the Son of God possessing divine power and a victimized human being abandoned on the cross' (1997: 68).

Others also derive their understanding of kenotic christology from looking at Christ in the gospels rather than starting with Paul's writings. Cronin's definition of kenosis is based on Luke 9:23 which talks about denying self and taking up the cross. He says: 'Kenosis is a resolute divesting of all the person of every claim of self interest so as to be ready to live the Gospel of Christ in every aspect of living, freed from the dictates of personal preference' (1992: 1). This suggests a willingness to prefer the needs and interests of others.

Perhaps the most convincing argument for a kenotic theology outside of Phil. 2:5-11is found in the idea of creation by God. Macquarrie suggests that the kenosis seen in the incarnation, while it may be the climactic example of kenosis, is only part of the history of the idea. 'Creation too is kenosis, God limits himself by sharing the gift of existence with his creatures. Yet it is only so that he can be God, and this enables us to see more clearly the mysterious link between kenosis and plerosis' (1974: 124). Richard concurs with this view seeing creation as demanding a self-limitation or kenosis by God (1997: 149-50). Thus, Christ can be seen to be following a pattern established by God when in an act of self-limitation Christ becomes human; kenosis is not a new idea that started with the incarnation. Kenosis as a concept, whilst not being explicit in scripture outside of the instances cited above, is consistent with theological themes deeply rooted scripture, and a kenotic christology is one that makes sense of the incarnation within the biblical narrative.

Drawing the Threads Together – Proposing a Kenotic Framework for Ministry

There are at least three ways in which Phil. 2:5-11 can be utilized by Christians, elements of which have been discussed above. The first is *doctrinal*, seeing the text as a theological statement. This is generally an unhelpful one in the search for a theological rationale for incarnational youth work, because such discussion relates more to what voluntary self-limitation means in the context of the two natures doctrine. The second is the *paraenetic* view that sees the passage as having a moral appeal to imitate Christ. This is a way of reading the text that could relate to all Christians and thus does apply to incarnational youth workers; however, it does not provide specific insight to the ministry. The third approach is a *practical-spiritual* one that offers a way of approaching and understanding ministry. It would include a spirituality of voluntary self-surrender, of being nothing, being among those others may see as worthless, and having no regard for earthly status. All these are things I have heard incarnational youth workers talk about, they are part of their theology, even though this theology may not be clearly thought through or articulated. It moves beyond a simplistic idea of 'What would Jesus do', which is how a paraenetic approach could be interpreted, to seeking to have a coherent practical-spiritual framework that underpins the ministry. Thus a kenotic framework for ministry is being proposed based on this third perspective because it is one that resonates with the understanding of incarnational youth ministry being adopted in this research. It is not the only starting point for such a framework but is the one that has emerged from seeking to understand what is 'incarnational' about this youth ministry.

I see a kenotic framework for ministry as having three main components. In many respects the identification of these has been an intuitive process, as I have sought to identify strands or threads in the different discussions about kenosis that relate to incarnational youth work. These three strands are not necessarily specifically attributable to individual theologians or approaches to kenosis but are the result of the processing of all the material cited above in relation to the context of incarnational youth work.

The Attitude of Christ

The first thread involves the idea of having the same *attitude* or mind as Christ. The starting point for this is Phil. 2:5. The corporate nature of this verse was noted above and is an important starting point for a kenotic approach to ministry. For incarnational youth workers one of the difficulties is the attitude of other Christians, whether managers or family and friends. The original context of Phil. 2:5-11 included problems among the believers at Philippi that Paul was seeking to address. Incarnational youth workers will need to seek to maintain right attitudes towards people who perhaps do not understand their calling or ministry or who have a different perspective on the work. It needs to be remembered that, as Jn. 13:35, says, 'By this everyone will know that you are my disciples, if you have love for one another', maintaining right attitudes will add to the effectiveness of the mission of workers.

Phil. 2:6-8 then gives an indication of the sort of attitudes that Christ demonstrated in the incarnation. There was a willingness not to hold on to the position that he had, but to be the revelation of God in a way that was appropriate in the context. Incarnational youth workers aim to work in a way that is relevant to their context and seek God's will to enable them to do this. To do this requires time and space to be with God and with others who can help workers in this process. Seeking God needs to be done in a way that is appropriate for workers individually and corporately. Allowing time for this as part of a work schedule was highlighted in the work on fruitfulness. Church tradition offers many ways of doing this and having a spiritual director or soul friend, for example, may help workers identify how they can best pursue this.

An attitude that reflects Christ and what was involved in the incarnation is a willingness to relinquish what might be seen as rightfully one's own, in terms of such things as social status, power, possessions, and position. However, this relinquishment is not necessarily a negative thing. This kind of kenosis can lead to a plerosis, it is not an emptying for the sake of it, but an emptying that brings a filling that might be quite different in its nature but which brings with it a fulfilment and sense of sharing in Christ's ministry. This connects with the research on incarnational urban youth ministry both in terms of an approach to ministry and working through the challenges and costs of that ministry, also.

Being Servant-Like

Attitudes need to lead to *actions* and a second thread follows on from having the attitude of Christ, that of being servant-like, following the example of Christ who was and is God. This is counter-cultural in a consumerist society where the emphasis is on self-fulfilment. It brings with it a possibility of being misunderstood, persecuted, and enduring suffering. However, it brings too, the joy for the worker of knowing that they are being transformed into the likeness of Jesus as they minister in the way that he modelled. A worker's experience of being servant-like will come down to their attitude to this approach to ministry: if the first thread of this framework has been adopted then this second thread will be that much easier.

A servant seeks to do what is asked by the one who is served.

For those in ministry this can be seen as both God and the community one ministers among. An aspect of this will be the willingness to take on the appropriate form of ministry for the context or community one is in. As Paul says, in 1 Cor. 9:22, 'I have become all things to all people, that I might by all means save some.' This idea should be understood both individually and corporately, and has potentially interesting implications for those involved in youth work from a church perspective. What form of church best serves young people and reflects the kenotic action of Christ in being willing to take on the form necessary to fulfil his ministry?

It should be noted that there can be dangers in being servant-like through others trying to exploit the desire of the worker to serve God and their community or for the worker themselves to have a martyr-like attitude. Jesus served those he was among but from a place of security in who he was and what his mission was. Jesus was very clear that, first and foremost, he was God's servant, and that was the context in which he exercised his service to humanity.

Demonstrating Christ-like Love: Agape[28]

The third thread involves agape as the kind of love that can provide the *motivation* to work in a kenotic way. It is the love referred to in Phil. 2:1 and 1 Corinthians 13. It is one way that Wright (1986: 347) describes the kenosis of Christ. In terms of a practical-spiritual understanding, this is the love that Christ demonstrated through the incarnation and the crucifixion. I sometimes find it interesting to apply Jn. 3:16, 'For God so loved the world that he gave his only Son...', to 'Christ so loved the world that he gave his own life'. Ultimately, something must be motivating incarnational youth workers to be involved in the kind of work that they are doing, because it is a costly work. Loving others, preferring their needs, being willing to enter their world is what enables incarnational youth workers to pursue this ministry. It will usually be accompanied by a call from God, and workers will be motivated too by their love for God. But to stay long term and make the sacrifices that are entailed in this work speaks of a love for the people and the community one dwells among.

In the same way as for being servant-like, there may be danger in talking about agape as an element of a kenotic framework of

---

[28] One of the Greek words translated love. Vine describes it thus "Christian love, whether exercised toward the brethren, or toward men generally, is not an impulse from the feelings, it does not always run with the natural inclinations, nor does it spend itself only upon those for whom some affinity is discovered. Love seeks the welfare of all (1981: Vol. III: 21).

ministry. It could lead people to think that it is all right to allow oneself to be abused, and that they must blindly respond to the myriad of expectations that are put upon them, and so on. Jesus demonstrated a strong love that was willing to challenge both those close to him (as in his rebuke to Peter in Matt. 16:23) as well as the authorities (calling the Pharisees hypocrites in Matt. 15:7), that was angry (as in the cleansing of the temple in Jn. 2:15) and that went against social customs (as in the encounter with the woman of Samaria in Jn. 4). He was willing to relinquish his will to that of the Father (Matt. 26:42) but did not let others inappropriately dictate what he should do.[29]

An element of agape may be reconciliation. The kenosis of Christ was a way of reconciling humanity and God; it is an integral part of the ministry of Christ. Colossians 1:20 states 'and through him [Christ] God was pleased to reconcile to himself all things, whether on earth, or in heaven, by making peace through the blood of his cross.' In an increasingly fragmented world, young people need reconciliation in so many areas, often with adults, with those who are different to them, with a right perception of self, with authorities, with institutions including the church, and with Christ. Incarnational youth workers seek to both facilitate and model this reconciliation. Having the mind of Christ, sharing the attitude of Jesus and being servant-like will help workers demonstrate agape and hopefully, for some young people, reconcile them to Christ.

Conclusion

From an original starting point of trying to understand what the term 'incarnation' means I have identified a particular understanding of the incarnation that I believe resonates with incarnational youth workers to study in depth. In this chapter I have explored kenosis from a historical, biblical and ministry perspective. While kenosis can be seen as a theme that is integral to Phil. 2:5-11 there are many other parts of the Bible, particularly Paul's writings, where it is evident, if not explicit. It provides the basis for a theological understanding of incarnational youth ministry that contributes both to who a worker can be and to what a worker can do. It complements the work on fruitfulness undertaken previously by providing ingredients for a theological rationale for incarnational youth ministry. Finishing the study of kenosis with a kenotic framework for ministry will be of assistance in drawing up the manifesto for incarnational youth ministry as it provides

---

[29] Although it should be noted that the gospels record, 'For the Son of Man did not come to be served but to serve and give his life a ransom for many' (Mk. 10:45).

a way of interpreting 'incarnational' that is rooted in a biblical and theological understanding of the term. This is important because the original context the manifesto is being developed for is YFC who will value a manifesto that has a clear biblical rationale.

An unexpected development in exploring kenosis is a valid basis for ministry is that I have found the concept personally inspiring and relevant to the way that I approach my own ministry in higher education. It has provided a way of reconciling theological study and spirituality by providing a practical-spiritual understanding of kenosis, initially seen as a complex theological term. Studying the life and works of Bonhoeffer, the results of which are contained in the next chapter, adds to the way that the concept inspires and shapes ministry and kenosis is perhaps the most important concept to emerge in the development of a theological rationale for incarnational youth ministry.

Chapter 8

Dietrich Bonhoeffer – Inspiration and Role Model

> Even today, more than fifty years after his death in 1945, his life and thought continue to inspire and challenge Christians of many different denominations, as well as secular people with no religious commitment, throughout the world (de Gruchy 1999: 93).

This chapter will explore some ways in which Dietrich Bonhoeffer can be a role model and inspiration to incarnational youth workers. By role model I mean someone whose life is worthy of study and of imitation, someone to look up to and seek to learn from. His life and works will be explored in relation to three key elements of incarnational youth ministry. The first is how Bonhoeffer's understanding of the incarnation informs the concept of *'incarnational'* youth ministry. The second is the way in which Bonhoeffer's writings illuminate *community*, the context of incarnational youth ministry. This will be explored in two ways, working amongst the local community involved in social action, and working from within an expression of

Christian community. The third is to explore what can be learnt about a *kenotic* approach to ministry from Bonhoeffer. I will begin with a brief biography and introduction to Bonhoeffer as a theologian, to put his life and work in context.

Brief Biography

Dietrich was a twin, he and Sabine were born on 4th February 1906 in Breslau, Germany. They were the youngest of seven children born into a close, supportive upper middle class family. His father was head of a leading psychiatric institute in Berlin. The family were members of the Church of the Old Prussian Union (Lutheran and Reformed) but did not regularly attend. There was surprise at Bonhoeffer's decision to study theology. This can be seen as a desire to follow a different path to his siblings and to show his independence.[1] He went first to Tubingen University and then to Berlin University gaining a PhD by the age of 21; this was published in a revised form as *Sanctorum Communio* (1963). He completed a further doctoral thesis and then began training for the ordained ministry. He was involved in pastoral work in Barcelona before becoming a lecturer in Berlin in 1929. This was followed by time in North America at Union Theological Seminary in New York and a return to Germany in 1931 again as a lecturer but also as a pastor. It was during this time that his biographer Eberhard Bethge, a student, friend, colleague and later, member of the family, suggests that Bonhoeffer had a conversion experience in 1932.[2] Bethge writes 'Apart from outward signs that even his students noted in him, the later enquirer can detect some concealed references in Bonhoeffer's own hand that reveal a momentous change in him' (1970: 153). These changes in him included such things as going more frequently to church, systematic biblical meditation, and oral confession. He left Berlin in 1933 to work as a pastor in London but felt he should return to Germany to share in the struggle against Hitler, who had become Chancellor of Germany in 1933. On his return he became involved in training students for ordained ministry, including running a seminary at Finkenwalde. When this was closed by the authorities he continued to support the pastors he had trained. He travelled, renewing and developing ecumenical contacts and also began to be involved in political resistance to the Nazi regime, which led to him being involved in the conspiracy to kill Hitler that failed. Bonhoeffer was arrested in

---

[1] Bethge comes to this conclusion in his definitive biography of Bonhoeffer (1970: 20-27).
[2] Bethge has the title 'The Theologian becomes a Christian' to describe this period. (1970:153).

1943 for his part in this conspiracy. He was executed by the Gestapo on 9th April 1945 in a concentration camp at Flossenburg, shortly before the end of the war.

Bonhoeffer the Theologian

Some of the reasons for choosing to draw on Bonhoeffer as an inspiration and role model for incarnational youth workers were discussed in chapter six: his general acceptability within YFC, his kenotic christology with links to Phil. 2, a commitment to social action, his engagement with the concept of community, and his significance as a theologian. However, possibly the most compelling reason is provided by Godsey: 'Bonhoeffer might have said and written all of these deep thoughts and still have made little impact on the church and the world had he not practiced what he preached' (1981:161). He goes on to say how Bonhoeffer, in the conclusion to his outline for a book, developed while he was in prison, himself acknowledged the power of human example which derives from the humanity of Jesus and some of Paul's teachings.[3] Human example means that there are stories to tell. This is important in the current context of ministry where story telling has re-emerged as an important tool.[4] As Bausch writes: 'Doctrine is the material of texts; story is the stuff of life' (1984: 28). Through hearing stories of Bonhoeffer, incarnational youth workers can be inspired and challenged in a way that is rarely possible by just presenting the doctrine or the concept, in this case incarnation or kenosis.

Bonhoeffer is a significant person in twentieth century theology and one who is still deemed to have much to say to the contemporary context. de Gruchy, introducing the *Cambridge Companion to Dietrich Bonhoeffer*, says this of the scope of those attracted to his life and work: 'Numbered amongst them are people from different walks of life, different Christian and other religions traditions, different cultures and different academic disciplines' (1999: xvii). Howell (1995), in an article in the magazine *Sojourners*, calls Bonhoeffer a 'hero of conscience' and says that he should be viewed in the same light as Oscar Romero and Martin Luther King.

---

[3] The book was to consist of three sections: A Stocktaking of Christianity; The Real Meaning of Christian Faith; and Conclusions. Details are in the enlarged edition of *Letters and Papers from Prison* (1971: 380-88).

[4] For example, the Bible Society and Northumbria Society have an ongoing storytelling project; and John Drane in *The McDonaldization of the Church* (2000) talks about the importance of communicating the Christian message in story form.

One of the difficulties encountered in attempting to interpret his theology is the fragmented body of written work he left. He was only for short periods of time an academic theologian and most of his later writing was done while working for the church and whilst in prison. de Gruchy sees that this can be advantageous, '...the open-ended character of Bonhoeffer's legacy also means that we are not constricted by a closed system but are, rather, invited to become participants in a continuing quest which borders on our own horizons' (1999: 94). He goes on to comment that the challenge of Bonhoeffer is to work out what it means to follow Christ in one's own context and that one's reading of Bonhoeffer cannot helped but be shaped by the spectacles that context provides (1999: 96). I intend to try and identify what Bonhoeffer may have to say to incarnational youth workers about how they should follow Christ in their context.

A note of caution needs to be identified in relation to perceptions of Bonhoeffer and his theology. Some, such as John Robinson in *Honest to God* (1963), have sought to use Bonhoeffer's writings to pursue a liberal agenda that is not compatible with YFC's evangelical culture. My reading of Bonhoeffer across a range of his writing from the earliest in *Sanctorum Communio* (1963), to his writings from prison have left me with a belief that his Christology is compatible with the evangelical context of incarnational youth work in YFC. In fact, Robinson acknowledged himself that his book did not present the range of Bonhoeffer's theology: 'I have made no attempt to give a balanced picture of Bonhoeffer's theology as a whole, which cannot be done by concentrating, as I have done, on this final flowering of it'[5] (Robinson 1963: 36). It will be important in using Bonhoeffer within a YFC context to emphasize the orthodox christological understanding presented in the texts that are most significant in relation to incarnational youth ministry.[6]

Bonhoeffer has a very christocentric theology.[7] This

---

[5] Quotation from a footnote cited in Selby (1999: 228).

[6] *Christology* (1966), *Life Together* (1954) and, *The Cost of Discipleship* (1959b).

[7] This view is put forward by, among others, Richards who suggests that Bonhoeffer's Christology has an incarnational focus: "It could be said also that the clue to the understanding of his Christology is the incarnation because for him there is no God except the one incarnate in Christ." (1987:365) Bethge states this emphasis more strongly, 'Incarnation is thus at the heart of Bonhoeffer's theology.' (1961:34) Godsey argues that 'few Christians have allowed their thought to be shaped by Christ as consistently as did Dietrich Bonhoeffer' (1981: 162).

christology is presented in Bethge's writing up of his Berlin lectures of 1933, constructed from the notes of students, as *Christology* (1966).[8] Initially there were to be three parts to the lectures, the first two, the present Christ and the historical Christ were delivered, the last part, the eternal Christ was not completed. At the end of the introduction, Bonhoeffer summarises the basis for his further deliberations. He writes: 'For the christological question of its very nature, must be addressed to the whole Christ, the one Christ. This whole Christ is the historical Jesus who can never in any way be divorced from his work. He is asked and he replies as the one who is himself his work' (1966: 40). In the section on the present Christ Bonhoeffer explores Christ as word, sacrament, and community then discussed Christ as the centre of human existence, the centre of history and the mediator between God and nature. The second section, the historical Christ addresses some of the major heresies about Christ. He concludes this section by looking at a positive christology which incorporates Christ as the incarnate one, the humiliated one, and the exalted one.

The Relevance of Bonhoeffer's Understanding of the Incarnation
The incarnation is at the heart of Bonhoeffer's understanding of Christ. He writes in *Christology*: 'It must be observed that the incarnation is primarily a real revelation of the creator in the creature, and not a veiled revelation. Jesus Christ is the unveiled image of God' (1966: 109). Beyond this he believed that the incarnation resulted in a Christ who was both fully human and fully God. He argued that the Chalcedonian formula of one person and two natures left us with a mystery as to how Jesus was both human and God and that this mystery should be accepted by faith. He states that 'After Chalcedon, the question can no longer be 'How can the natures be thought of as different and the person as one?' but strictly, 'Who is this man of whom it is testified that he is God?'' (1966: 102). The answer to this Bonhoeffer believed could be found in the Bible. He asserts that the 'self-attestation of Jesus Christ is none other than that which is handed down to us by Scripture, and it comes to us in no other way than by the word of Scripture' (1966: 75). This emphasis on Christ, the revelation of God who is fully human and fully God and the importance of studying Scripture to understand Christ and the incarnation reinforces the relevance of Bonhoeffer's understanding to YFC's evangelical context.

If, as is suggested by the use of the term 'incarnational', youth workers are seeking to base their approach to ministry partly from

---

[8] The book was also published as *Christ the Center* (New York: Harper and Row, 1966).

looking at the incarnation, then Bonhoeffer's thoughts on this topic can add to the debate. In *Cost of Discipleship* he writes: 'The image of God has entered our midst, in the form of our fallen life, in the likeness of sinful flesh. In the teaching and acts of Christ, in his life and death, the image of God is revealed. In him the divine image has been re-created on earth' (1959b: 271). Through the incarnation God is revealed to humanity. There is an identification with humanity that Green, writing of Bonhoeffer's understanding of the incarnation, calls 'God with us, and God for us' (1999b: 114).[9] This is an important aspect of the incarnation for youth workers to replicate, they are there to be *with* the young people and to be *for* the young people. This involves two elements, the actual face to face work and advocacy on behalf of the young people demonstrating that they are for them. Added to this is the importance of the message that God is with us and for us. A youth worker can be present for young people in difficult situations and they can bring the message that God is there too, they are not alone. This message of God's presence comes through an understanding of what the incarnation involved in terms of the relationship between God and humanity. In his Christmas letter of 1939 to the students he trained at Finkenwalde, Bonhoeffer talks about this: 'The Christological formula, 'Two natures, one person', at the same time has supreme soteriological significance: Godhead and humanity separated from one another before Christ came, united with each other only in the incarnation of the Son of God' (1973: 28-33). Just as Christ was the agent of reconciliation so incarnational youth workers can themselves seek to act to reconcile young people to God by bringing the message of Jesus to them, through their words and actions. Thus one face of being incarnational is about seeking to bring unity in a fragmented society, unity between young people, within communities and within the church. This is clearly not an easy task but is a framework in which workers can seek to pursue their work with young people.

Bonhoeffer's understanding of the incarnation and the implications of that for Christian behaviour has relevance. That he himself was doing what he was writing about adds an extra dimension to the call for action. In an essay to fellow conspirators at New Year 1943, he wrote: 'Mere waiting and looking on is not Christian behaviour. The Christian is called to sympathy and action, not in the first place by his own sufferings, but by the sufferings of his brethren, for whose sake Christ suffered' (1971: 14). Obviously the context here is different in terms of the suffering of young people in urban priority

---

[9] Green comes to this conclusion as part of a discussion on Bonhoeffer's *Act and Being* (trans. M. Rumscheidt. Minneapolis: Fortress Press, 1996).

areas compared with what was happening in Germany during the Second World War. However, there is a principle of getting alongside those who are suffering because of Christ's willingness to suffer. Incarnational youth workers share this concern for those who suffer and are willing to respond to the suffering by living and working alongside them.

An important feature of Bonhoeffer's understanding of the incarnation that has profound consequence for workers trying to follow an 'incarnational' pattern is that he saw Christ as the humiliated one. He suggests in his Christology lectures that:

> In the humiliation, Christ enters the world of sin and death of his own free will. He enters it in such a way as to hide in it in weakness and not to be known as God-man. He does not enter in the royal clothes of a 'Form of God'. The claim which he raises as God-man in this form must provoke antagonism and hostility. He goes incognito as a beggar among beggars, as an outcast among the outcast, despairing among the despairing, dying among the dying. He also goes as sinner among the sinners, yet in that he is *peccator pessimus* (Luther), as sinless among the sinners (1966: 11)

He maintained this view of the importance of Christ being weak and it is still apparent in his later writings. In a letter dated 16th July 1944 he wrote: 'He is weak and powerless in the world, and that is precisely the way, the only way, in which he is with us and helps us' (1971: 360). If that is how Jesus ministered in the world, how should an incarnational youth worker minister, if seeking to follow the pattern of Jesus' ministry? For many youth workers there are similarities to the understanding of Christ in terms of a relinquishing of status gained from previous jobs or through academic qualifications and by being in a job that to some seems hard to define and little valued by others.[10] Williamson, in his study of Bonhoeffer in relation to theology and politics, sums up what it might mean to minister in a way based on the example of Jesus. He writes: 'If we keep our eyes glued to Jesus Christ, we shall see that the way in which God reveals himself to us is primarily through love, suffering, weakness, sacrifice, and surrender' (Williamson 1976: 91). This understanding of ministry is one that came out in discussions with incarnational youth workers such as Morag. She

---

[10] One person I worked with had a science doctorate and did not use his title as it would have been assumed he was a medical doctor. Workers may use the term 'youth worker' but a job where you hang out with young people where they are does not fit into many people's understanding of what 'work' is.

found that her understanding of calling evolved, she did not realise that this was what was being required of her when she began. It soon became clear, however, that to be 'incarnational', seeking to be like Christ, would mean she was going to share many of the aspects of Christ's ministry.

Linked to this is the idea of 'Jesus, the one for others' which emerged in Bonhoeffer's later writings. His thinking developed and he moved from talking about Christ pro me to Christ pro nobis, Christ for us. This thinking was apparent from the Christology lectures of 1933 onwards. As Feil writes:

> Toward the conclusion of the christology course Bonhoeffer introduced a significant variation of that [Christ pro me] assertion: 'Of this man, we say: 'This is God for us'. What is significant here is that Bonhoeffer quietly changed the pro me into pro nobis, 'for us', thereby laying the groundwork for his christological expression, 'Christ – the one for others', which emerged in his final letters (1985: 75).

This image underpins a rationale for being involved in society rather than seeing Christianity as a private religion. As Richards writes, 'It is because Christ is the 'man for others', the centre of human existence, that commitment to social action and involvement in human liberation is the inescapable task of the Christian. Discipleship, obedience and faith go hand in hand' (1987: 366).

Thus, Bonhoeffer's understanding of the incarnation is relevant to incarnational youth workers in several ways. The first is that in studying the Bible workers can know more of who Christ is and what this means for them as those trying to follow Christ's example in their ministry. The second is the implication of the incarnation in reconciling humanity and God and how workers can see reconciliation as part of their role. The third is the necessity of beliefs being worked out in actions through being alongside those who are suffering, for example. The fourth is an understanding of Christ as the weak one who workers identify with in his suffering and sacrifice. Finally, Jesus is the one for others whose example encourages workers to be committed to liberation beyond just that of personal salvation. This latter point is expanded below in relation to Bohoeffer's understanding of community.

In relation to Bonhoeffer's writings on community, I want to look at two aspects relevant to incarnational youth workers. First, what can be learnt about the Christian working within the community? Secondly, his understanding of Christian community, in relation to the seminary at Finkenwalde and his writings from this period.

Bonhoeffer and Society

Bonhoeffer understood that the church was Christ's body here on earth and, therefore, had a responsibility to act as Christ would have acted. These views would have long-term implications for Bonhoeffer. In 1933, the year that Hitler came to power in Germany, he identified three things that he believed were responsibilities for the church in relation to the state (cited in Bethge 1970: 208).[11] The first related to challenging the state: 'whether it could answer for its action as legitimate political action...In relation to the Jewish question, the Church must now put that question with utmost clarity'. If incarnational youth workers are to undertake this task, that will involve socio-political action and challenging government both locally and nationally. To deal holistically with the situation that young people they work with face this may be necessary on different occasions. Today the state is trying to address issues of social exclusion, particularly amongst young people. Paul Boateng, a home office minister, was appointed the first Minister for Youth in September 2000; a Children's Fund has been set up which will seek to work through community groups including faith based groups and seeks to target at risk children and young people. However, little impact seems to have been made regarding drugs, there is concern about the way asylum seekers and refugees are treated, a lack of jobs is still a serious issue in urban priority areas and racism is still a major issue in terms of police, justice, mental health and education services, for example. This leaves many areas for incarnational youth workers to continue to challenge and advocate on behalf of young people. The second task involved action on behalf of victims of the state: 'The Church has an unconditional obligation towards the victims of any social order, even where those victims do not belong to the Christian community.' Incarnational youth workers are already engaged in this task through their willingness to identify with, and work alongside the poor and marginalized who are often the victims in contemporary society. The term 'unconditional obligation' may need to be interpreted in the contemporary context but the concept of an obligation towards the victims of the social order is clearly part of what it means to have a 'bias to the poor'. The third element involved the church, putting a spoke in the wheel of the state if it went too far, as well as binding up the wounds of those beneath the wheel. This third task does not appear to have contemporary relevance in terms of incarnational youth ministry although some workers may engage in

---

[11] This material and the quotations are from the second volume of *Dietrich Bonhoeffer Gesammelte Schriften* Volumes I-V. Second edition. Edited by Eberhard Bethge. Munich: Kaiser Verlag, 1966.

such action in relation to pacifist beliefs, for example.

Bonhoeffer believed that the problems of the poor and the marginalized should be the responsibility of all Christians. He spoke strongly against those leaders who encouraged a dualistic approach where worship and issues of human rights were kept apart. Kelly writes, 'Bonhoeffer maintained that, in the reality of Jesus Christ's human solidarity with all peoples, including the hated Jew and the despised socialist, God invests the world with a unity in which one's faith and one's 'worldliness' must be reconciled' (1999: 248). Bonhoeffer encouraged churches and their leaders to engage with social action 'to care for the poor, to take risks for the cause of peace, to live daily the Sermon on the Mount, to profess solidarity with the Jews, and even to confront malice in government head-on' (Kelly 1999: 249). This concern for the poor and marginalized had been shown by Bonhoeffer from early in his career. Zerner writes, 'Bonhoeffer has already displayed sensitivity towards the struggles of marginal groups in society (blacks in New York City and poor, troubled teenagers in Berlin), revealing his unwillingness to retreat from reality' (1999: 190). This is a theological position that was more than just a concern for the marginalized, it was a willingness to work on their behalf and to see things from their points of view. As Richards states 'It follows that for Bonhoeffer as for Gutierrez salvation means the transformation of social structures, the liberation of man from political and social exploitation and his deliverance from injustice and oppression' (1987: 365). Indeed, his writings have echoes of liberation theology. In 'After Ten Years', a letter written at New Year 1943, to some of his fellow conspirators, he wrote: 'We have for once learnt to see the great events of world history from below, from the perspective of the outcast, the suspects, the maltreated, the powerless, the oppressed, the reviled – in short from the perspective of those who suffer' (1971: 17).

However, Bonhoeffer did not solely talk about social action, it was to be integrated with other aspects of life. In an exploration of the scope of responsibility of Christians in Bonhoeffer's thought Lovin writes, 'By intercession and proclamation, Christians make it clear that even in the most difficult times, they take responsibility for the life of the world in which Christ takes form in history' (1984: 145). In a letter to his godson as he was baptised, Bonhoeffer wrote 'Our being Christians today will be limited to two things: prayer and action for justice on behalf of all people. All Christian thinking, speaking, and organising must be born anew out of this prayer and action' (1971: 300). His life demonstrated an integration of spirituality and action that is helpful for incarnational youth workers to reflect on and seek to replicate in their own context.

For many incarnational youth workers there is a need to find a different theological framework from the one they had learnt early in their Christian life. The complexity of what they are faced with, the amount of suffering, and the injustice, for example, can challenge existing ways of understanding the Christian faith, particularly the individualistic evangelical version that many in YFC grew up with. Reading Bonhoeffer gives the opportunity to explore a range of pertinent issues and approaches but in the context of the writings of someone who clearly loves Christ and seeks to follow his example. His concern with working out what it really means to follow Christ in one's context is an inspiration to workers to have a clear theological rationale to what they do which can be applied to the changing context of youth work and the community. Otherwise there is a danger that when the situation becomes tough there is not the underpinning theologically and spirituality to sustain a worker and encourage them to continue. Bonhoeffer's strong statements about the importance of what would now be called socio-political action help workers who have a more holistic understanding of what youth ministry involves see that they are part of a long tradition of workers who have a broad understanding of the responsibilities of the Christian. Despite being in the minority in YFC in wanting to work with poor and marginalized young people in the community, Bonhoeffer provides an inspiration to help incarnational workers see that this is a valid calling.

Bonhoeffer and the Christian Community

The other major aspect to be explored in looking at the relevance of Bonhoeffer's understanding of community is how he saw the Christian community. Bonhoeffer's experiences at Finkenwalde where he set up what Bethge describes as an 'Evangelical House of Brethren' (1970: 385) shaped his notion of community, focussing on discipleship:

> There are two things the brethren have to learn during their short time in the seminary – first, how to lead a communal life in daily and strict obedience to the will of Christ Jesus, in the exercise of the humblest and highest service one Christian brother can perform for another; they must learn to recognize the strength and liberation to be found in brotherly service and communal life in a Christian community. This is something they are going to need. Secondly, they have to learn to serve the truth alone in the study of the Bible and its interpretation in their sermons and teaching (cited in Bethge 1970: 385).[12]

---

[12] From a letter by Bonhoeffer to W. Staemmler 27.6.1936.

This understanding of Christian community is found in *Life Together* (1954).[13] Here he writes: 'It means, first, that a Christian needs others because of Jesus Christ. It means, second, that a Christian comes to others only through Jesus Christ. It means, third, that in Jesus Christ we have been chosen from eternity, accepted in time, and united for eternity' (1954: 10-11). In this book he identified the basic elements of life at Finkenwalde: prayer, individual and corporate meditation, Bible study, solitude, fellowship, worship, the eucharist, confession, spiritual care, ministry and recreation. With all these elements there was a clear structure to life at the seminary. The spiritual practices that underpinned the training students received for ministry were intended to help sustain them after they finished this initial training. In relation to incarnational youth workers, it raises the question as to what place spiritual formation has in their training and whether people end up doing the job without having the spiritual resources to sustain them in this difficult and demanding work. Also, the seminary experience meant that people had to learn how to relate to one another and to accept and love those who were very different to them. Interpersonal conflict and lack of acceptance of others who are different can be a pressure in ministry, youth work as much as anything else. Sometimes it seems that people do not have the skills or tools that they need to deal with some of these problems and that there is a lack of willingness to deal with them in a thorough way. I have seen workers leave incarnational youth work situations because interpersonal difficulties were not resolved in a helpful and healthy way, and workers were left feeling vulnerable and isolated. It may not be possible to offer the intense seminary experience that Bonhoeffer instituted but there does need to be an awareness of what the skills and tools are that workers (and their managers) need to enable them to be equipped for their ministry.

Green helpfully summarizes the essentials of Bonhoeffer's community life: 'Being-with-each-other and being-for-each-other are spelt out in relation to intercessory prayer by the community members for each other; 'active helpfulness'; bearing the burdens of others; and mutual admonition. Being-for-each-other also involves personal confession and mutual forgiveness of sins' (Green 1999b: 125). This idea is a development of his first doctoral thesis and takes further the understanding of what church is. Again, these are helpful insights for incarnational youth workers. 'Being with' and 'being for' are very much elements of incarnational youth ministry and to see these as

---

[13] This book was written in four weeks in 1938 while Bonhoeffer was at his sister Sabine's house.

insights applied to the church and other Christians gives a holistic feel to the ministry. It also provides a structure for mutual support amongst a team and for the life of a team to reflect the life of Christ, which adds an extra dimension to the witness of the work.

There are warnings in Bonhoeffer's writings about community that it is important to identify. He talks about the dangers of Christian community that is based on human dreams rather than God's leading. He writes:

> He [the leader of the community] acts as if he is the creator of the Christian community, as if his dream binds men together. When things do not go his way, he calls the effort a failure. When his ideal picture is destroyed, he sees the community going to smash. So he becomes, first an accuser of his brethren, then an accuser of God, and finally the despairing accuser of himself' (1954: 16).

Some models of incarnational youth ministry are based on the concept of a community and the way that community is initiated and led is important. Incarnational youth ministry projects are not immune from the sorts of difficulty that Bonhoeffer describes. Understanding the right foundations of community, a focus on Christ and relationships based on Christ's example are important. Bonhoeffer has a helpful passage about the need to let others find their freedom in Christ and for us to see them as they are in Christ. He writes '...I must release the other person from every attempt of mine to regulate, coerce, and dominate him with my love. The other person needs to retain his independence of me; to be loved for what he is, as one for whom Christ became man, died, and rose again, for whom Christ brought forgiveness of sins and eternal life' (1954: 23). This again is two-fold, applying to both relationships with young people and with other Christians. Whether one fully agrees with Bonhoeffer's understanding of Christian community or not, what emerges is the importance of developing a communal life as a team or project that sustains and nurtures Christian workers in ministry.

Elements of a Kenotic Approach to Ministry in Bonhoeffer's Life and Writings

Anderson makes an interesting point when he states that 'The 'practice' of ministry...is not only the appropriate context for doing theological thinking, it is itself intrinsically a theological activity' (Anderson 1979: 7). In seeking to identify a kenotic approach in Bonhoeffer, I want to look at aspects of his life as well as his writings in the belief that his ministry was also part of his theology and may well reflect elements that he did not write about fully. In Chapter seven I described my understanding of a kenotic approach to ministry based on a broad understanding of the theme from the Bible as well as a more detailed examination of Phil. 2:5-11. In looking at identifying a kenotic approach to ministry in Bonhoeffer's life and writing it is this understanding of the term that I will be using.

Bonhoeffer in the Christology lectures criticizes the kenotic christology of German theologians of the nineteenth century, but this was largely with regard to an understanding of kenosis as being incompatible with the two natures, one person view that Bonhoeffer worked from (1966: 97-102). However, others have used the term kenosis or kenotic in describing aspects of Bonhoeffer's theology. It is interesting to note that, towards the end of his biography, Bethge uses this term to describe Bonhoeffer's Christology, when talking about some of his later writings from prison. He writes:

> The Christology was already there in *Act and Being*, as Lutheran kenotic Christology (the whole fullness precisely in the total condescension, Phil 2)...Bonhoeffer had preserved this Christology for fifteen years, continually making it more profound, in order to ground the present power of Christ even more clearly in the weakness of the human sufferings of Jesus (1970: 793).

Moltmann also sees Bonhoeffer's theology as being related to Phil. 2. He writes 'It is from his exegesis of Colossians 1, Ephesians 1, and Philippians 2 that he shapes his own peculiar view of the universal and ontological aspects of theocracy in Christ' (1967: 58-59).

A term that Bonhoeffer uses that has a kenotic feeling to it is that of *stellvertretung*. The literal meaning of the term is to stand in place of another. The word has been translated 'deputyship'. The phrase is used in connection with a discussion of what Bonhoeffer calls mandates, which are marriage, labour, government and the church in the world.[14] Moltmann explains it thus: 'Bonhoeffer is not talking of a purely external authority derived from an official position, but an authority which is existential and personal, resting upon self sacrifice and vicarious action for others' (1969: 86). Williamson offers his understanding of Bonhoeffer's term. He writes: 'A deputy is someone who is appointed to act for and on behalf of other people...He adheres to the Burkean idea whereby the deputy acts in accordance with his own conscience and judgment as to what the true welfare of the community, which includes his constituents, requires' (1976: 76).

---

[14] See *Ethics* p 254ff.

Green suggests, however, that the phrase is best expressed 'by speaking of people who personify their communities, and act vicariously on their behalf. People like Martin Luther King Jr., Nelson Mandela and Mahatma Gandhi illustrate what Bonhoeffer means' (1999b: 118-19). Bonhoeffer himself also belongs to this tradition. Obviously, Green's examples are of people who have come to public attention in this role. However, there are examples of people involved in incarnational youth ministry who have exercised 'deputyship'. Bob Holman's work in Bath being an example that has been written up.[15] Youth and community work practice has moved more towards workers facilitating people to act themselves on behalf of their community. However, an incarnational worker living within that community can work towards personifying their communities, at least in relation to local government and agencies that are involved in the community. The main point in relation to understanding this as a kenotic approach to ministry is the self-sacrifice that is involved here. A voluntary self-sacrifice and self emptying is involved in vicarious action on behalf of others.

A desire to imitate Christ was part of Bonhoeffer's motivation for studying Christ. This theme is found both in *The Cost of Discipleship* and in *Ethics*. The last chapter of the former book is about 'The Image of Christ' and in the draft for *Ethics* he talks about the principle of conformation to Christ. Bonhoeffer's understanding of conformation to Christ is that 'Formation comes only by being drawn into the form of Jesus Christ. It comes only as formation in His likeness, as conformation with the unique form of Him who was made man, was crucified and rose again' (1955: 18). It is interesting to consider the implications of incarnational youth ministry in the light of this imitation. Is suffering implicit in responding to the call? Bonhoeffer's ability to focus on Christ and follow him was rooted in a sense of God's call that required a total commitment as a response. Willmer argues that Bonhoeffer 'in himself, often felt weary, ready to give up...It was good therefore, to be called: the call of God took away the freedom to be temperamental. The command gave strength for living' (1999: 174-75).

In talking about responsibility, Lovin writes of Bonhoeffer's view: 'To say that God demands responsible action of us means that when we are confronted by a moral crisis, our basic commitment is not to save our own lives but to risk and if necessary to lose them on behalf of others' (1984: 141). This Bonhoeffer did when in a voluntary act, he moved from a comfortable life in the U.S.A. back to Germany. As

---

[15] In *Kids at the Door* (1981) and *Kids at the Door Revisited* (2000).

Nelson writes:

> In a deeply moving farewell letter to Reinhold Niebuhr, he etched his thoughts: 'I will have no right to participate in the reconstruction of Christian life in Germany after the war if I do not share the trials of this time with my people...Christians in Germany will face the terrible alternative of either willing the defeat of their nation in order that Christian civilisation my survive, or willing the victory of their nation and thereby destroying our civilisation. I know which of these alternatives I must choose; but I cannot make that choice in security (1999: 38-39).

He was sacrificing his comfort and safety to be alongside his people. He was also surrendering his nationalism in a way, in that he believed that defeat was the more Christian option. His identification was both incarnational and kenotic, it involved a being among and a relinquishing. It was an identification with individual others as well as the corporate other as expressed in his letter to Niebuhr. In a similar way, incarnational urban youth workers are often relinquishing a more comfortable lifestyle to identify with the people they feel called to minister among.

Bonhoeffer believed that freedom was bound up in relationship with others. This is very much in opposition to the current view of freedom in our culture as the pursuit of individual pleasure or fulfilment. He writes:

> In man God creates his image on earth. This means that man is like the Creator in that he is free. Actually he is free only by God's creation, by means of the Word of God; he is free for the worship of the Creator. In the language of the Bible, freedom is not something man has for himself but something he has for others. No man is free 'as such' that is, in a vacuum, in the way that he may be musical, intelligent, or blind as such...Being free means 'being free for the other', because the other has bound me to him. Only in relationship with the other am I free (1959a: 35).

This emphasises the voluntary self-surrender that is part of a kenotic approach to ministry. Hence, incarnational youth workers will find freedom through being free for others including the relinquishment of relationships. However, Bonhoeffer is very honest about the difficulties that following one's calling can lead to. In one of his letters from prison written on Christmas Eve, 1943 Bonhoeffer writes: 'It is nonsense to say that God fills the gap; he doesn't fill it, but on the contrary, he keeps it empty and so helps us keep alive our former communion with each other, even at the cost of pain' (1971: 176).

One of the ways in which Bonhoeffer was able to maintain this kenotic approach to ministry was again to follow the example of Jesus and take time to nurture his relationship with God. Anderson writes about the prayer life of Jesus in an essay with a title derived from Bonhoeffer's work, 'The Man who is for God'. He suggests that:

> One of the most fruitful insights into this relationship between Father and Son, even at the furthest extremity of self-emptying on the part of the Son, is the life of prayer which Jesus experienced. The prayers of Jesus exhibit two things: first, the intimate communion which he possessed with the Father in virtue of his sonship. The second thing which the prayers of Jesus reveal is that prayer is possible from the 'far side' of estrangement, as well as from the 'near side' of intimacy' (Anderson 1979b: 241-242).

This is an important point as all the workers I spoke to had experiences of estrangement. One does not always feel drawn to pray in such situations but sometimes it is the only thing that seems to be left to do. It is a strange paradox. That Jesus felt this estrangement and reached out to God in it, should be an encouragement that this is what is needed in the circumstances.

However, Bonhoeffer did not just pray at times when he felt estranged from God. It was an integral part of his life. In a letter to Bethge written while working on *Ethics*, Bonhoeffer wrote:

> I enjoy the daily morning prayers here very much. These prayers compel me to ponder the meaning of the biblical text...the regularly structured day for me means work and prayer. These make it easier for me in my relations with people and protect me from the emotional, physical and spiritual troubles which ensue from a lack of discipline (cited in Kelly 1999: 253).[16]

Rooting daily life in a pattern of prayer may well also be a source of spiritual sustenance, renewal and transformation to incarnational youth workers. Bonhoeffer believed that one encounters Christ in the Bible and this encounter was fundamental for him. Bethge comments on Bonhoeffer's use of the Bible: 'It should not be forgotten

---

[16] Translated by Kelly from *Kirkenkampf und Finkenwalde: Reolutionen Aufsatze Rundbriefe 1933-1943, in Gessamelte Schriften, vol. II* (Munich: Kaiser Verlag, 1959: 376).

how Bonhoeffer used his Bible for prayer. He thought that one should sit and listen prayerfully to the Bible, to hear whatever voice would speak' (1995: 64). It is likely that these spiritual disciplines enabled him to sustain his ministry, even at the great cost that he paid for following his beliefs. An observation about Bonhoeffer in prison written by a British Secret Service Officer[17] said that he 'always seemed to diffuse an atmosphere of happiness, of joy in every smallest event in life, and a deep gratitude for the mere fact that he was alive...He was one of the very few men I have ever met to whom his God was real and ever close to him' (cited in Nelson 1999: 44).

A reading of *The Cost of Discipleship* would also lend support to the idea that Bonhoeffer has a kenotic approach. He writes:

> If we would follow Jesus we must take certain definite steps. The first step, which follows the call, cuts the disciple off from his previous existence. The call to follow at once produces a new situation. To stay in the old situation makes discipleship impossible. The only right and proper way is quite literally to go with Jesus. The call to follow implies that there is only one way of believing in Jesus Christ, and that is by leaving all and going with the incarnate Son of God (1959b: 52).

Part of this following involves the idea of imitating Christ and becoming like Christ, it is very much a voluntary self surrender. An aspect of this is the importance of obedience, a voluntary, joyful obedience. He writes: 'For faith is only real when there is obedience, never without it, and faith only becomes faith in the act of obedience' (1959b: 54). Bonhoeffer is suggesting a radical faith, one that makes a genuine difference in life. The consequences of this obedience have also to be faced. As McFadyen suggests:

> For the invitation to share in Jesus' ministry and destiny was also an invitation to share in his poverty and suffering. Christ's call to repentance meant abandoning any absurd notion of isolated self-sufficiency and acknowledging instead one's poverty, one's need of God and others. Only those who become, like children, incapable of living alone and unaided can enter the kingdom (Mk. 10:15) (1990: 470).

Abandoning self-sufficiency and becoming interdependent speak very clearly of kenosis, a voluntary giving up of many of the attributes of a so-called 'normal adult existence' in our culture to

---

[17] Found in Captain Payne Best *The Venlo Incident* (London: Hutchinson, 1950: 200).

understand and participate fully in what faith entails.

Contributions to a Theological Rationale for Incarnational Youth Ministry

The main points that are contributed from studying Bonhoeffer's perspective on the incarnation are about who Christ is and what that means for incarnational youth workers who are seeking to imitate Christ. The incarnation is about God being with us and being for us. However, Christ is not with us as a King or Lord in the traditional senses of those words, he is with us as the humiliated one, the weak one, the one for others. The language and images that Bonhoeffer uses about the incarnation are very kenotic; they emphasise the voluntary self-surrender of Christ and his willingness to suffer on behalf of humanity. As Christians, Bonhoeffer suggests that we should be willing to suffer alongside our sisters and brothers who are suffering and share in this way in the suffering of Christ. It is not a glamorous calling, it is one rooted in an understanding derived from a study of the life of Christ as the Bible recounts it and in the living Christ as expressed in the word, sacrament and community that are the marks of Christ's presence in the world. The implications for a theological rationale based on the idea of following Christ in being incarnational are profound and this entails a kenotic approach to ministry as presented by Bonhoeffer, particularly in *The Cost of Discipleship*. He concludes this book with Eph. 5:1 'Be ye therefore imitators of God, as beloved children' (1959b: 275). In the final paragraph he explains what this means:

> It is only because he [Christ] became like us that we can become like him. It is only because we are identified with him that we can become like him. By being transformed into his image, we are enabled to model our lives on his. Now at last deeds are performed and life is lived in single-minded discipleship in the image of Christ and his words find unquestioning obedience (1959b: 274).

This could be seen as a mandate for being 'incarnational' in ministry – imitating Christ and being his disciple being the core elements of what it means to be like Christ.

There is an importance in seeing the two aspects of community, the community in which one works and the Christian community one is part of. This is not intended to be a dualistic statement and there are ways in which these communities overlap. However, it is important that attention is given to both of them in incarnational youth work. It is increasingly becoming clear that youth workers need a spirituality that sustains them. Part of that spirituality needs to have a corporate dimension because Christianity is not an individualistic faith, it is about being the body of Christ and a part of the body functioning in isolation is not really incarnating Christ in the most effective way.

The contribution of understanding Bonhoeffer's approach to ministry as kenotic contains many elements that were found in the areas of incarnation and community. In many ways this last section was a combination of the previous two: how an understanding of the incarnation is worked out in one's community. The points that need to be highlighted are the concept of deputyship, the idea that being free means being free for others and that we are called to be like Christ, not least in being dependent on a life of prayer to sustain one in one's calling and ministry. Each of these need to be considered in the search for a theological rationale for incarnational youth ministry.

Bonhoeffer is someone who sought to base his life on Christ, on identifying and doing the will of Christ. It is this, as Moltmann argues, that brings a unity to his theology. He writes: 'The key to the unity of Bonhoeffer's thought which underlies the various themes in his writings may be found in this statement: 'The more exclusively we acknowledge and confess Christ as Lord, the more freely the wide range of His dominion will be disclosed to us'' (1967: 56).[18] This is why Bonhoeffer is such an inspiration and a role model: his life and work is rooted in a desire to follow Christ, whatever the consequences. Echoing *The Message* paraphrase of John 1:14, Bonhoeffer moved into the neighbourhood of Nazi Germany and sought to live out his life there in obedience to Christ taking decisions that were costly and that ultimately led to his 'martyrdom'. He sought to be faithful to his calling and to his understanding of what the church should be in society. His story is challenging and gives an example of a life of ministry based on a kenotic understanding of the gospel, rooted in the desire to be faithful to what he thought Christ was calling him to. For me, he brings together the different threads that I have been exploring in developing a theological rationale for incarnational youth ministry.

---

[18] Quotation from *Ethics* (1955: 80).

Chapter 9

A Manifesto for Incarnational Youth Ministry

Being resident, the leaders soon became known to the locals. They met in the same shop, chatted on the same buses, Bob's children went to the same schools. These constant contacts meant that local people could evaluate the leaders. They also meant that the leaders could assess the needs of the area and identify those who might eventually get involved with the project (Holman 2000: 80).

A method of disseminating the findings of the research was needed. A manifesto was chosen as the best way of doing this because it would be an accessible document, easy to distribute and understand. It would communicate the key findings to workers, agencies and those involved in supporting incarnational youth ministry. A manifesto is a written declaration, a statement of principles. Webster's Dictionary (1993) defines it as: 'a public declaration of intentions, motives or views: a public statement of policy or opinion'.

The manifesto below emerges out of my research, my dialogue with incarnational youth workers, and my own experience of incarnational ministry. I have identified three themes or metaphors that are fundamental to this developed understanding of incarnational youth ministry and I have sought to build a theological rationale around them. The three themes or metaphors chosen all have biblical roots. As an evangelical organization, YFC values a biblical framework to understanding ministry and such biblical themes provide a helpful starting point for workers who want to develop their own theological rationale.

♦ The first theme is about *'Being fruitful'* and is primarily focused on the *worker*.

♦ The second theme, *'Being salt and light – incarnational mission'* focuses primarily on the *context* in which incarnational youth ministry is taking place.

♦ The third theme, *'Being kenotic – interpreting incarnational'*, focuses more on the *style and approach* to incarnational youth ministry.

In this chapter, the theological rationale will be presented in the form of a manifesto for incarnational youth ministry. It will be followed by a commentary that provides the background thinking and research from which the different elements of the manifesto emerged.

A Manifesto for Incarnational Youth Ministry

Introduction:
Living and working amongst the poor and marginalized, incarnational youth workers seek to: build relationships with young people; help them identify and make fruitful choices in their lives; encourage them to fulfil their potential; present the person and message of Jesus Christ, and journey with them as they explore what the future holds. It is a ministry that reflects God's bias to the poor. It is a committed, exciting, challenging, servant ministry that participates in Christ's self-giving.

Being Fruitful – a Vocation, a Context, a Challenge, and a Mandate
'You did not choose me, but I chose you. And I appointed you to go and bear fruit, fruit that will last' John 15:16a.

1. Called and Chosen for the Task – a Vocation
Incarnational youth ministry is a particular vocation; it is a ministry and role God calls people to and equips them for. Where there is a genuine

vocation there will be fruitfulness. The identification and encouragement of such vocations is important.

The model of Jesus is to root this process of identifying a call in prayer (Luke 6:12-13). Different spiritual traditions can inform and shape this process. An individual needs to experience a call to this distinctive ministry. However, uncritical or untested acceptance of what an individual says about their own calling is irresponsible. Fruitfulness is hindered if there is no genuine sense of call or there are unrealistic expectations of such ministry.

Preparation for ministry, often through some form of apprenticeship, is a pattern to be found in both the Old and New Testament (e.g. Jesus and his disciples; Eli and Samuel 1 Sam. 3; Paul and Timothy Acts 16:1-3). This pattern helps avoid mistakes and highlights support needs and other pertinent areas that may need to be addressed. It also helps to clarify the call.

2. The Context – Developing the Right Conditions for Growth
Fruitfulness is most likely if the conditions are right for the worker to flourish in that role and continue in it long term. Four parties contribute to this: the agency, the manager/management, the worker, and the wider Christian community.

Agencies need to have a sustainable infrastructure in place to enable incarnational youth workers to focus on the role they feel called to. The term encompasses the big picture of strategy and vision right down to the fine detail of a timetable that gives time for such things as networking and support. This is a necessity not an optional extra.

Resources to enable a worker to develop a viable spiritual support infrastructure are equally important to sustain long term work. Managers should release the time, resources and encouragement that are needed for workers to get the spiritual sustenance they need to do the job long term.

Fruitfulness is hampered if the worker becomes too stressed or overworks because of the demands of the work. Strategies to avoid burnout are necessary. Workers need space for themselves to be able to relax and rest. Daily, weekly, monthly, termly, and annual rhythms need to be explored and workers helped to identify and address sources of stress or pressure that stop them fulfilling their role. Workers need a life as well as a job.

The wider Christian community should be involved in legitimating the call of workers and in providing back-up support to enable them to do their role. As the body of Christ, each part should do its bit to help the rest of the body function; incarnational youth ministry needs more than face to face workers to be fruitful. It needs people who understand the task and are willing to play their part in achieving it.

3. The Importance and Challenge of Role Models

Role models can be sought whose experience helps develop the concept and practice of incarnational youth ministry, this should include the stories of the workers themselves. The experience of those who face the challenge of working on the edge, on the interface between church and world, amongst the poor and the marginalized are invaluable. For example, the story of Dietrich Bonhoeffer has partly inspired the understanding of incarnational ministry represented in this manifesto.

4. Fruitfulness – a Mandate

Christians have a mandate to be fruitful. Being fruitful in incarnational youth ministry will often involve a long-term commitment. Fruitfulness means different things in different contexts. The challenge for incarnational youth workers is to find appropriate ways to measure fruitfulness in their own context so they and others can be encouraged by the signs of growth and identify where seeds have been sown. Seeing fruit, however small, helps sustain a worker in their calling and ministry. This approach needs to be developed in contrast to a numerical definition of success that can damage an incarnational youth worker's self perception and the wider appreciation of this type of ministry.

Being Salt and Light – Incarnational Mission

Being salt and light will involve permeating the whole of a community in ways outlined below.

1. Moving Into the Neighbourhood (John 1:14)

This is the verse (from *The Message* translation preferred by some workers) that for many underpins their understanding of incarnational youth ministry, more traditionally it is rendered 'And the Word became flesh and lived among us' (NRSV). As Christ moved into the neighbourhood, so workers have literally moved into urban neighbourhoods. They 'dwell among' young people, are part of their lives, are there with them, are there for them and are salt and light in that community.

When workers move into the neighbourhood one of the strategies is to seek out 'people of peace' (Luke 10:6) in the neighbourhood and join in with what God is already doing in that community. This approach acknowledges that God is already at work in the neighbourhood and avoids the idea that it is only through the workers' arrival that God's work begins.

Another strategy for work in the neighbourhood is to be engaged in the whole of people's lives there. Youth work is concerned with the physical, social, emotional, psychological, intellectual, and spiritual needs of young people. As young people develop their potential in these dimensions incarnational youth workers get involved not only in the neighbourhood but also with the structures that create disadvantage and exclusion.

2. Being Salt

'You are the salt of the earth; but if salt has lost its taste, how can its saltiness be restored? It is no longer good for anything, but is thrown out and trampled under foot'
Matt. 5:13.

Salt is a seasoning and a preservative. Taking a metaphorical understanding, incarnational youth workers help young people's lives 'taste better' and they challenge decay and rottenness in the structures that oppress the young people they work with and help to fertilize new growth.

Salt has been seen as a symbol of the covenant between God and his people and priests (Lev. 2:13; Num. 18:19). Incarnational youth workers are a living witness to that covenant and by their lives mediate God's love in the community and to the young people, making real God's bias to the poor and marginalized (Luke 4:16-21).

3. Being Light

'You are the light of the world. A city built on a hill cannot be hid. No one after lighting a lamp puts it under the bushel basket, but on the lampstand, and it gives light to all in the house. In the same way, let your light shine before others, so that they may see your good works and give glory to your Father in heaven' Matt. 5:14-16.

Light that is hidden is useless. One of the benefits of incarnational youth ministry is that the light is there in the community, it can be seen as workers live out their everyday lives. In Isaiah (42:6 and 49:6) the prophet speaks of a servant who will be a light to the gentiles, who will bring salvation. One cannot be salt and light in isolation otherwise there is no one to 'taste' or 'see'.

Incarnational youth ministry is as much about who you are as what you do. The whole of life will be observed by others, the private/professional boundaries that other workers seek to maintain are much more blurred as workers live among the people they work alongside. Workers are encouraged to demonstrate the gospel, using words if they have to. That is what incarnational youth workers do in living amongst those they serve. It is part of a long tradition of Christian ministry of workers living out their calling, being there and doing good in whatever ways they can.

Paul exhorts the Corinthians to 'Be imitators of me as I am of Christ' (1 Cor. 11:1). Although it may be uncomfortable for incarnational youth workers, the reality is that they provide a role model to young people. Incarnational youth workers need to think about what young people need to see lived out and what sort of role model they can be.

The concept of light is also used in the context of understanding something - seeing the light. In contrast, for many young people, the Bible is a mystery. Incarnational urban youth workers need to develop theology relevant to the context and enable young people to see Christianity and the Bible in a way that empowers rather than constrains them. Liberation theology is one approach that helps the worker develop an approach to the Bible that starts with the actual experience of young people.

Being Kenotic – Interpreting 'Incarnational'

'Let your bearing towards one another arise out of your life in Christ Jesus. For the divine nature was his from the first; yet he did not think to snatch at equality with God, but made himself nothing, assuming the nature of a slave. Bearing the human likeness, revealed in human shape, he humbled himself, and in obedience accepted even death – death on a cross.' Phil. 2:5-8 NEB.

This passage expresses the essence of kenosis: following Jesus by putting aside self-interest because of a love for others and a desire to do God's will.

1. Being like Jesus – in Relationships and Actions

'Let your bearing towards one another arise out of your life in Christ' Phil. 2:5 NEB.

Jesus, through his incarnation, showed what it is to be truly human, he demonstrated God's love through his life and death. Seeking to be Christ-like in relationships is essential in incarnational ministry. The quality of relationships with other Christians is an integral part of mission and experience suggests that breakdown in relationships particularly between workers and managers is what most often brings incarnational youth ministry to a premature close.

There was a vocational intent in the action of Christ in becoming incarnate. He was willing to relinquish his previous position and become the revelation of God in the way that was appropriate at that time and in that context. The intention of incarnational youth workers to imitate Jesus can involve a similar loss of status, position, possessions or other consequence of their decision to be involved in this work, it involves demonstrating an active commitment to the 'bias to the poor' that can be seen as a focus of the ministry of Jesus.

In simplistic terms, being like Jesus could be seen as responding to the question 'What would Jesus do?' inscribed on the bracelets worn by many youth workers and young people. This may be better phrased as 'What would Jesus want me to do?' or 'How can I represent Jesus or truly be his representative in this situation?' Jesus sought to do His Father's will and encouraged his follower to do likewise. (Jn. 8:38; 12:49) Seeking God's will involves developing and maintaining a strong relationship with God and priority needs to be given to this part of the ministry.

2. Being a Servant

Incarnational youth workers want to serve the needs and aspirations of young people, to take seriously the agenda and culture of young people, and to serve them sacrificially. A question that flows from this is what form of church best serves young people and reflects the kenotic action of Christ in being willing to take on the form necessary to fulfil his ministry?

Incarnational youth workers will see themselves, however, as a servant of Jesus before they are servants of young people. One of the difficulties of being a servant of Jesus is that it is often a road that leads to suffering, workers need to be prepared for that. As Jesus was misunderstood and rejected, so those who follow him may suffer too.

Being a servant does not mean becoming a doormat or responding to the myriad of expectations that face incarnational youth workers from all sides. Jesus clearly demonstrated the role of servant to his disciples (Jn. 13:15, Mt. 20:28) but also demonstrated an assertiveness that was willing to challenge close associates (as in his rebuke to Peter in Matt. 16:23) the authorities (as in the cleansing of the temple in Jn. 2:15), and social customs (as in the encounter with the woman of Samaria in Jn. 4). He was willing to relinquish his will to that of the Father (Matt. 26:42) but did not let others inappropriately dictate what he should do.

3. Agape - the Love that Motivates

Being motivated by agape involves preferring their needs, being willing to enter their world is what enables incarnational youth workers to pursue this ministry. It is only possible to stay long term and make the sacrifices that are entailed in this work if there is a love, respect, and affection for the people and the community where workers have committed themselves.

Despite being motivated by agape, there will be times when life is hard. There will be a need to seek God and ask him to restore the first love that was felt in the early days or to share the compassion that Jesus so clearly felt and demonstrated to the poor and marginalized.

Reconciliation between God and humanity was part of Christ's mission. Part of loving young people involves seeking reconciliation. As well as incarnational youth workers seeking to see young people reconciled to God, there is an awareness that in the fragmented world in which they live these young people need reconciliation in many areas: with adults, with those who are different to them, with themselves, with the community, with authorities and institutions, including the church. This is part of the role of incarnational youth workers, seeking to make young people more whole. Kenosis, the non-assertion of status or of rights is crucial to this reconciling ministry.

Good youth work practice and true agape will mean allowing young people the freedom to accept or reject the message of Christ the worker brings. Incarnational youth workers will seek to preserve the freedom that God gave to humanity and be willing to continue long term in relationships that are not dependent on a young person making a commitment to follow Christ.

As a modern day 'exile' amongst the poor and marginalized, incarnational youth workers are fulfilling the words of Jeremiah in seeking the welfare of the city where God has sent them and where they will find their own welfare as they fulfil their calling (29:7). The manifesto has come full circle – beginning and ending with God's call and God's mission. Incarnational urban youth workers are seeking to follow the example of Jesus and many others throughout history who have put their own needs aside and sought to bring the salt and light of the gospel to those who may have few other opportunities to receive it. They are missionaries who need support and encouragement. Also, they are inspirations and role models to the communities where they live and to their contemporaries who may be searching for a more fulfilling life outside the individualism and consumerism of contemporary western society. They are building God's kingdom in some of the most difficult places in Britain, they deserve the respect and resourcing they need to be fruitful servants of God who are seeking to minister in a way that reflects the sacrificial, self-giving, kenotic example of Christ. This is incarnational urban youth ministry.

A Commentary on the Manifesto for Incarnational Youth Ministry

This manifesto is for incarnational youth workers, but many of the elements are transferable to other contexts. The framework may be taken and used as a basis to develop a rationale for other types of ministry.

A Being Fruitful – a Vocation, a Context, a Challenge, and a Mandate

The concept of fruitfulness was chosen as the first item in the manifesto because it underpins the understanding of incarnational youth ministry presented here. It is a positive theme, with biblical resonance that provides an alternative to numerical notions of 'success' in measuring youth ministry.

1. Called and Chosen for the Task – a Vocation

The workers I spoke to became incarnational youth workers because they felt that God had called them to that task. However, one of the original reasons for starting this whole research project was the relatively frequent turnover of people in a role that had initially been seen by workers as a long-term commitment. I was often told when I first started working with YFC that it was your call from God that would keep you going through the tough times. There is a deep spiritual truth in this: for example, Bonhoeffer often felt ready to give up but 'the call of God took away the freedom to be temperamental. The command gave strength for living' (Willmer 1999: 175). Thus workers leaving prematurely raises the question as to whether the call was initially discerned wrongly or the conditions to fulfil the calling were missing or, more generally, changes to personal circumstances meant that the initial call was no longer the main priority.

An emphasis on the importance of discerning a call came out of the original research project. The place of prayer and spiritual discernment in that process is one that YFC need to continue to consider. Some people are not convinced of using short term volunteers, e.g. gap year participants in incarnational youth ministry projects because of the potential disruption caused both to the local work and young people, as well as the time that is needed to help train volunteers. However, there is now a greater diversity in short term programmes and perhaps more of an option for projects to shape the nature of the commitment and the type of people taken. YFC have, for example, started a two year urban training programme because workers in these communities believed this was a more realistic time frame for both the individual being trained and the project where they were based.

Testing out a call is important, Jesus was tested at the beginning of his ministry (Lk. 4:1-13). The costs and benefits of providing individuals with opportunities to discover whether or not they are being called to long term incarnational youth ministry may well be an ongoing issue for workers and one where they need to work out what is right and appropriate for all those affected. However, it needs to be acknowledged that even with the most thought-through process of discerning a call, individuals have the freedom to choose how they interpret and respond to that call and see it unfolding in the future. Unexpected or unanticipated circumstances in family, health, faith or whatever may lead to an inability to fulfil the calling in the way originally hoped for. What would be good to avoid is workers leaving because of things that could have been anticipated at the beginning of the project and for which proper provision, in respect of support or supervision, for example, was not made.

2. The Context – Developing the Right Conditions for Growth

In talking to incarnational youth workers who had left this type of ministry, the most common reason for them leaving was issues around the management of the project they worked for. The responsibility of those who employ incarnational youth workers needs to be explored and good practice commended and used to help projects that have not yet developed effective management.

A phrase which sums up much of the responsibility of those managing the worker was identified by one of the interviewees as 'sustainable infrastructure'. It is universally agreed that effective management is vital. Someone interviewed commented that when everything around is unstable a worker needs that stability of structure at the core to enable them to be effective in carrying out their work. This sustainable infrastructure will involve such things as an appropriate strategy and vision; management and supervision; providing efficient administration, including that relating to the employment of the worker; adequate finance, ideally enabling a long term commitment both to the local community and to the workers; appropriate accommodation for work and personal use; pastoral care; induction, training, and development to be taken seriously; providing encouragement and affirmation in what are often difficult circumstances; prayer support; time for other integral parts of the role, such as networking and meeting with peers. A related issue to this is the need for people to help provide this sustainable infrastructure, the wider

Christian community are needed to support the face to face ministry that the workers undertake. Projects are more fragile if there is not a broad network of people helping to support and develop it.

Part of this sustainable infrastructure needs to be the opportunity for appropriate spiritual support and development. Ministry flows out of a relationship with God and finding a spiritual discipline that works is important for the incarnational youth worker. Kelly describes Bonhoeffer's approach to this:

> Discerning the rhythms of Bonhoeffer's 'spiritual strength'…brings us time and again to the intrinsic connection between prayer and action as expressed in his daily meditation on the biblical word, his efforts to form genuine Christian community, and his willingness to be led by God's grace to take Christlike risks to retrieve freedom and justice for a nation under the heel of a cruel dictatorship. (1999: 246).

Incarnational youth workers will have a range of approaches to being with God but whatever the nature of 'being with God' is for them it is a vital part of the work as it helps to sustain and enable a worker to cope with what arises. Time may well need to be set aside for this to happen within the working structure and it is one area where incarnational youth workers may well be able to learn from clergy who structure regular retreats and quiet days into their pattern of ministry. This will be an element of the balanced living that is necessary to sustain ministry long term. Along with this a pattern of life needs to be worked out that gives time for family, friends, recreation, study or whatever elements are necessary for the workers' wellbeing.

3. The Importance and Challenge of Role Models
Many of us remember a story in a way that a theological concept would not be recalled. Bausch writes: 'Doctrine is the material of texts; story is the stuff of life' (1984: 28). In considering a theological rationale for incarnational youth workers it seemed helpful to look at potential role models whose stories might illuminate their experience. I chose to consider Dietrich Bonhoeffer. Bonhoeffer was someone whose theology was matched by his life, he lived what he wrote about. Godsey writes: 'Bonhoeffer might have said and written all of these deep thoughts and still have made little impact on the church and the world had he not practised what he preached' (1981: 161). This is attractive to incarnational youth workers who are practitioners but who are often people attracted to exploring more deeply what their call and ministry means theologically. Reading a biography of Bonhoeffer and particularly his books *Life Together* and the *Cost of Discipleship*, which

were primarily written as a result of his time living in community training pastors at Finkenwalde, can help incarnational youth workers with their own understanding of the issues of community and discipleship. Different workers will be attracted by the life, ministry or works of different people, but drawing on Christian tradition as well as biblical and theological material can inform, challenge, and inspire. Consideration of different role models can help shape and sustain ministry in the present.

4. Fruitfulness – a Mandate

A mandate for fruitfulness comes from the verse that headed Section A. Morris comments on John 15:16 that 'The first function then of the disciples is that they are to be emissaries of Christ. The second thing is that they should 'bear fruit'' (1995: 600). Working out what 'fruit' is for incarnational youth ministry is a challenge to workers. Part of this involves finding appropriate ways to measure the work. This is often necessary for those funding it. However, it can also be important for the worker's own sense of well-being and self image as they reflect on how they are fulfilling their calling. Thus part of a theological rationale for a specific worker or project will entail working out what it means to be fruitful in that context and what is needed to enable the worker to be fruitful.

One of the dilemmas of incarnational youth ministry is how success is measured. Success is a prevalent concept in a society where consumerism and competition are so widespread. It is not a concept that is necessarily valid in ministry. The term 'fruitfulness' is preferred as one that has a biblical root and one that implies starting small and growing, an ongoing process. There is an implication that the conditions need to be right for fruit to be able to grow and ripen. There is also an element of acknowledging the possibility of a lack of fruit because seeds do not always grow as hoped.

Being Salt and Light – Incarnational Mission

As previously noted, in YFC there is a model of 4D evangelism. Incarnational youth ministry is regarded as primarily demonstration. In this context salt and light are appropriate biblical metaphors and a useful starting point for a missiology of incarnational youth ministry. These metaphors have been used in recent times to describe Christians working within communities or more widely in society.

1. Moving Into the Neighbourhood (John 1:14)

John 1:14 is seen as prompting the theological term 'incarnation' as the Greek term 'sarx egeneto' is 'incarnatus' in Latin. Hence, it is a key verse theologically and therefore, there is interest in what follows in that verse. Morris writes that the verb 'signifies 'to pitch one's tent'' (1995: 91). He goes on to argue that this should not be understood as limiting the incarnation. He argues that 'The term had come to be used in a conventional fashion of settling down permanently in a place (e.g. Rev. 12:12; there can be no more permanent dwelling than in heaven!) (1995: 91).

It is important to acknowledge that God is already at work in the community and amongst the people. Hence, a worker is seeing what God is doing and joins in with it rather than entering a community to do something to it. Being part of the community is often valued by the community who may not perhaps understand the reasons for the choices workers have made but appreciate that workers desire to be part of the community and are thus accessible at times of crisis, for example, when access to other more formal types of help are hard to come by.

The idea of 'people of peace' was raised in my visit to All Saints and through one of the ways of measuring fruitfulness that was discovered. It is partly an acknowledgement that ultimately mission is an activity of God and we are participating in it not initiating it.

2. Being Salt

'Being salt' can mean having a significant influence on young people. It can have a lasting impact on their lives. Evidence from an incarnational youth ministry project shows this as an outcome of the work. Nearly twenty years later Bob Holman talked to young people he had worked with in the Southdown Project. He reports: 'Interestingly, a number finished the interview with words like 'If it was not for the project, I don't know what would have happened to me'' (2000: 70). However, one of the criticisms was that the first leaders left too soon. This comment highlights the issue of how long term an incarnational youth workers commitment needs to be in order to maximise the effectiveness of the work.

Part of 'being light' is described by Margaret Walsh who writes about her experience in a small monastic urban community 'We should arouse a spirit of enquiry in those who see our way of life' (1997: 69). In this respect, the practice of some overseas mission agencies of sending at least two families out so that the relationships between Christians can be observed and show Christianity in action may be pertinent. How someone lives their everyday life with others and with the local community may have as much impact on what happens through their ministry as the actual work done. This is what it means to talk about the importance of 'being' as well as 'doing'.

The concept of a youth worker as a role model is not only a Christian one. It is to be found in secular youth and community textbooks also. In a recent text acknowledged as significant,[1] Kerry Young writes 'The idea of the youth worker as role model is, therefore, grounded in the necessity for workers to practise what they preach – to establish the 'moral authority' which underpins their integrity as people and gives credibility to their work as practitioners' (1999: 78). Because of the nature of the way that they work through living in the community incarnational youth workers are well placed to do this.

Liberation theology was identified as a helpful resource for workers in developing a new approach to the Bible. Vincent identifies the essential message of liberation theology. Writing in a British context, he says: 'From the common sense of human existence, from the dignity of every human being, from the long history of democracy, justice, equality and fraternity – from each arises the strong demand that oppression is not and should not be the fate of human beings anywhere' (1995: 20). Involving young people and/or the wider community in exploring the Bible in a new way helps them to see that this is the situation intended by God and that they are facing injustices that they can seek to address rather than merely accepting their situation.

Being Kenotic – Interpreting 'Incarnational'

The version of Phil. 2:5-11 at the head of this section is from the NEB as this translation is faithful to the original Greek and makes clear the corporate nature of the passage. In the earlier chapter on kenosis I used the NRSV (same mind) and NIV (attitude) in developing a kenotic approach to ministry. Having subsequently reflected further, this translation seems the more appropriate to use because of a desire to develop a manifesto that is read corporately as well as individually.

The approach taken in this section was to draw out the key points from the study undertaken on kenosis. An important passage in the study was Phil. 2:5-11. I had some reservations because of a feminist critique that the passage could be seen as reinforcing traditional patriarchal attitudes towards women and the behaviour that was expected of them. Coakley's (1996) writings helped me to gain a broader feminist perspective that interpreted the passage in a way that was not oppressive.

---

[1] Cited as 'A useful guide to understanding exactly what youth workers do. How do they make relationships with young people? How do they motivate and inspire them to reach their goals?' in Dixon (2001: 228).

1. Being like Jesus – in Relationships and Actions

Phil. 2:5 is addressed to the Philippians corporately, not individually. A translation that is close to the literal meaning of the Greek is that of the NEB which says 'Let your bearing towards one another arise out of your life in Christ'. One of Paul's concerns in the letter to the Philippians is the disunity amongst the believers. The earlier research demonstrated concerns that workers gave up incarnational youth ministry not because of problems with the face to face work with young people but often because of difficulties with the management of the project. This is not a problem solely faced by incarnational youth workers, it can be a difficulty in any employment situation. However, Scripture encourages good relationships with one another and, indeed, it can be seen as a very important part of the mission. In John 13:34-35 Jesus says 'I give you a new commandment, that you love one another, just as I have loved you; you also should love one another. By this everyone will know that you are my disciples, if you have love for one another'.

Being involved in incarnational youth ministry often involves a relinquishment of a worker's own preferences as they try to follow the will of God. The experience of some who have taken this path is that this relinquishment brings a greater fulfilment and a strong sense of sharing in the ministry of Christ among the poor and marginalized. It will often appear to be counter to the prevailing culture, which may only see the kenosis of the worker's actions.

One of the ways that incarnational youth workers share the attitude of Jesus is that of having a bias to the poor. David Sheppard popularised the term with his book *Bias to the Poor* published in 1983. He believed that a study of the Bible and the teachings of Christianity led to that conclusion. Liberation theologians use the term 'a preferential option for the poor' and argue that from a variety of perspectives.

Incarnational urban youth workers by the very nature of their role will have a bias to the poor but will not necessarily use this language. Some would talk about the need for justice or an imitation of Jesus who they would perceive as living and working among the poor and marginalized. A passage which would commonly be used to support this approach is Luke 4:16-21 where Jesus announces the nature of his ministry. Jesus here talks about being alongside the poor and needy which is what incarnational urban youth workers seek to do.

2. Being a Servant

For incarnational youth workers, young people are those they minister amongst, they could be described as servants of young people. This however, needs to be put into the context of Christian service where ultimately one is a servant of God and the priority is to serve in the way that He expects. One of the difficulties in talking about serving young people is the danger that this concept will be misuderstood to mean doing what young people want, regardless of the ethics or outcomes of that work. A worker will have to serve within their own ethical boundaries and Christian principles.

Considering the life of Bonhoeffer highlights the very real cost of being a follower of Jesus, of seeking to be his servant and following his example. A reading of the New Testament also suggests that suffering is often a consequence of faithfully following Jesus, seeking to have his mind, seeking to be a servant. Paul's writings make this clear.

Living a life that is different to that of the mainstream society will not always be easy. Evidence from incarnational youth workers suggests that some of the suffering that they face is because of the reactions of friends and family, often Christians, to the choices that they have made. Being misunderstood is often a consequence of this type of work and suffering will take a variety of forms. Workers will have different attitudes to the 'suffering' that may be involved in living in the inner city in terms of safety and security, standards of schools and other public services, for example. It is true that some incarnational youth workers have given up a comfortable, middle class lifestyle to follow their calling. Whether this is suffering depends on perceptions, there is often more joy and fulfilment in following one's calling and seeing God at work in places which seem to have little hope. What is often needed is a strategy to cope with the pressures that do exist.

A worker may well be living where there is much suffering amongst the community. Knowing how and when to respond to this suffering can be difficult. There are limits on what can be done practically and financially. One of the issues to be worked through is how a worker copes with feelings of powerlessness and frustration in situations where it seems that little is possible. This will often include the experience of dealing with authorities whose attitudes and services are not always what is needed by an individual or family in need. Another matter to be considered is a worker's own limitations. The boundaries that are necessary for the worker to remain in ministry long term will vary from person to person. These will be ongoing issues that will need to be worked out, particularly as family circumstances change.

3. Agape – the Love that Motivates
Tom Wright suggests that Phil. 2:6-8 is a definition of agape. (1986:

347). Agape, the love of 1 Corinthians 13, is the type of love that motivates and sustains engagement with a kenotic framework of ministry. In terms of a practical-spiritual understanding, this is the love that Christ demonstrated through the incarnation and the crucifixion. Ultimately, something must be motivating incarnational youth workers to be involved in the work that they are because it is a costly work.

Demonstrating agape means allowing young people to make their own decisions and seeing them reject Christ. However, it is important that the autonomy of the individual young person is respected. Bonhoeffer saw the dangers of trying to manipulate others through one's love for them. He writes 'I must release the other person from every attempt of mine to regulate, coerce and dominate him with my love. The other person needs to retain his independence of me; to be loved for what he is, as one for whom Christ became man, died and rose again, for whom Christ brought forgiveness of sins and eternal life' (1954: 23). Incarnational youth workers engage with this reality knowing that many of the young people they work with may choose to ignore these claims of who they are in Christ and what Christ did for them. Youth work is about voluntary association, the young person choosing to engage with the youth worker and what is being offered. Freedom is the gift that God gave humanity, however what incarnational youth workers are able to do is present the young person with an accessible image of God as they seek to imitate Christ by their words, action and lifestyle. An option that may not have been given to the young person through anyone else or any other means.

The manifesto ended with a return to the idea of calling. This was a deliberate decision to try and demonstrate the centrality of this concept but to also suggest that being involved in incarnational youth ministry is an ongoing process. The manifesto is more than a document to be consulted at the beginning of an incarnational youth ministry project. It will hopefully be something that will be returned to time and time again to the different elements, understanding what they mean and how they can shape the current context and how experience speaks into the manifesto.

Final Reflections

The manifesto contained in this chapter is the conclusion to the book. Reflecting on the process and the outcome there are several comments I wish to make. I have sought to develop a manifesto for incarnational youth ministry that comes from both my discussions with incarnational youth workers, and my academic research. It is also important to acknowledge that it is influenced by my own experiences of incarnational ministry in an extended household and being part of an inner-city clergy family. Schweitzer pointed out that, 'It was not only each epoch that found its reflection in Jesus; each individual created Him in accordance with his own character' (cited in O'Collins 1995: 221). The same is true of a manifesto or theological rationale. This manifesto is a starting point, each incarnational youth worker, or incarnational youth ministry project, will also need to contextualize a manifesto so it is relevant for their particular situation. I have sought to highlight key areas that need to be considered and offer some ways of looking at them that have been shaped by ongoing reflection and dialogue. In terms of my original aim of exploring how YFC can better support urban youth workers I hope this manifesto will provide food for thought and a theological basis for sustaining and developing established ministries, and initiating new ones. Incarnational urban youth ministry is a challenging, demanding, rewarding calling. With a clearer theological rationale for the work, it is to be hoped that long term incarnational youth ministry in urban priority areas will be sustained, that workers will flourish, that the work will be fruitful and through this the lives of many young people may be transformed.

Although incarnational youth ministry will have its own local flavour depending on the context, this thesis has sought to establish that incarnational youth ministry is essentially a kenotic ministry. This understanding flows from a distinctive understanding of the incarnation developed from exploring kenosis as an interpretation of Phil. 2:5-11 but also as a biblical and theological theme. Kenotic ministry was seen as a practical-spiritual response to understanding the incarnation and suggests a spirituality of self-surrender, sacrifice and relinquishment that is counter-cultural to much of the wider youth culture that workers encounter in their ministry. Dietrich Bonhoeffer models kenotic ministry in a way that can inspire and challenge and shape understanding of what incarnational ministry means today for youth workers. The manifesto and the materials developed as part of the original action research project are offered as tools to help initiate, sustain and develop such ministry in the future within and beyond YFC. Incarnational youth ministry has elements in common with other forms of incarnational ministry, working in an institution or a parish, for example or other types of youth work such as relational work. This framework for ministry can provide a starting point for further research in other contexts where this process would be helpful. Seeking to root a framework for ministry biblically and theologically, using theological reflection as a tool, contributes to the development of workers who have a spirituality that sustains them so that they are able to continue to respond to the call of God, challenges of culture and the exhortation to follow the example of Jesus.

Bibliography

ABM 1995. *A Review of the Selection Procedures in the Church of England: the Report of a Working Party.* ABM Policy Papers No. 6. London: Central Board of Finance of the Church of England.

Anderson, G. W. 1997. "The Problematic Translation of 'emptied himself' as found in Philippians 2:7."http://www.knight.org/advent/aaa.

Anderson, Ray S. 1979a. "A Theology for Ministry". In Ray S. Anderson, ed. *Theological Foundations for Ministry.* Edinburgh: T&T Clark.

--- 1979b. "The Man Who Is for God". In Ray S. Anderson, ed. *Theological Foundations for Ministry.* Edinburgh: T&T Clark.

--- 1979c. "Living in the World". In Ray S. Anderson, ed. *Theological Foundations for Ministry.* Edinburgh: T&T Clark.

Andrews, Dave 1989. *Can you hear the heartbeat?* London: Hodder and Stoughton

Arbuckle, Gerald 1990. *Earthing the Gospel.* London: Geoffrey Chapman

Archbishop of Canterbury's Commission on Urban Priority Areas 1985. *Faith in the City.* London: Church House Publishing.

Babcock Gove, Philip et al. ed., 1993. *Webster's 3rd New International Dictionary*. 1993. Unabridged. Springfield, MA: Merriam-Webster.

Baker, Jonny undated. *Enculturalising the Gospel within Youth Culture*. Halesowen: Youth for Christ

Bakke, Ray 1988. "Overcoming the real barriers to Urban Evangelization". In John E. Kyle, ed. *Urban Mission: God's Concern for the City*. Downers Grove, IL: IVP.

Ballard, Paul and Pritchard, John 1996. *Practical Theology in Action: Christian Thinking in the Service of Church and Society*. London: SPCK.

Banks, Robert 1980. *Paul's Idea of Community*. Grand Rapids: Eerdmans.

Barrett, C. K. 1962. *From First Adam to Last: A Study in Pauline Theology*. London: A & C Black.

Barrett, C. K. 1971. *The First Epistle to the Corinthians*. Black's New Testament Commentaries. Second edition. London: A & C Black.

Barrs, J. 1988. "Shepherding Movement". In Sinclair B. Ferguson, and David F. Wright eds. *New Dictionary of Theology*. Leicester: IVP.

Barth, Karl 1962. *The Epistle to the Philippians*. Translated by James W. Leitch. London: SCM Press.

Bartlett, David L. 1993. *Ministry in the New Testament*. Minneapolis: Fortress Press.

Bartlett, Karen 1996. *Jubilee*. Halesowen: Youth for Christ.

Barton, Stephen C. 1992. *The Spirituality of the Gospels*. London: SPCK.

Bassler, Jouette M., ed. 1994. *Pauline Theology* vol. 1. Minneapolis: Fortress Press.

Bausch, William J. 1984. *Storytelling Imagination and Faith*. Mystic, CT: Twenty-Third Publications.

Bell, Judith 1993. *Doing Your Research Project*. Buckingham: Open University Press.

Berger, Rose Marie 2000. "Saint Dorothy Day". *Sojourners* Vol. 29:4 (July/August 2000).

Bethge, Eberhard, 1967. "The Challenge of Dietrich Bonhoeffer's Life and Theology". In Ronald Gregor Smith, ed. *World Come of Age*. London: Collins.

--- 1970a. *Dietrich Bonhoeffer* Translated by Eric Mosbacher, Peter and Betty Ross, Frank Clarke and William Glen-Doepel. Edwin Robertson, ed. London: Collins.

--- 1970b. *Dietrich Bonhoeffer: Theologian, Christian, Contemporary.* New York: Harper Row.

--- 1979. *Prayer and Righteous Action.* Belfast: Christian Journals.

--- 1995. *Friendship and Resistance.* Geneva: World Council of Churches.

Bock, Darrell L. 1994. *Luke 1:1-9:50.* Grand Rapids: Baker Books.

--- 1996. Luke 9:51-24:53. Grand Rapids: Baker Books.

Bockmuehl, Markus 1997. *The Epistle to the Philippians.* Black's New Testament Commentaries. London: A & C Black.

Boff, Leonardo and Boff, Clodovis 1987. *Introducing Liberation Theology.* Tunbridge Wells: Burns and Oates.

Bolt, Peter and Thompson, Mark, eds. 2000. *The Gospel to the Nations.* Leicester: Apollos.

Bonhoeffer, Dietrich 1954. *Life Together.* Translated by John W. Doberstein. London: SCM Press.

--- 1955. *Ethics.* Translated by Neville Horton-Smith. London: SCM Press.

--- 1959a. *Creation and Fall.* Translated by John C. Fletcher. London: SCM Press.

--- 1959b. *The Cost of Discipleship.* Revised and unabridged edition. Translated by R. H. Fuller, revised by Irmgard Booth. London: SCM Press.

--- 1963. *Sanctorum Communio.* Translated by R. Gregor Smith. London: Collins.

--- 1966. *Christology.* Translated by John Bowden. London: Collins.

--- 1970. *No Rusty Swords.* Translated by John Bowden. Edwin H. Robertson, ed. London: Fontana.

--- 1971. *Letters and Papers from Prison.* The enlarged edition. Translated by Reginald Fuller, Frank Clarke, et al. Eberhard Bethge, ed. London: SCM Press.

--- 1973. *True Patriotism.* Translated and edited by Edwin H. Robertson. London: Collins.

--- 1979. "Christ, the Church, and the World". In Ray S. Anderson, ed. *Theological Foundations for Ministry.* Edinburgh: T&T Clark.

--- 1985. *Spiritual Care.* Translated and introduced by Jay C. Rochelle. Philadelphia: Fortress Press.

--- 1988. *Witness to Jesus Christ – selected writings.* John W. de Gruchy, ed. London: Collins.

Borgman, Dean 1997. *When Kumbaya Is Not Enough.* Peabody MA: Hendrickson.

Bornkamm, Gunther 1966. *Jesus of Nazareth.* London: Hodder and Stoughton.

Borthwick, Paul 1997. "Developing an international theology of youth ministry". Paper given to the Second International Conference on Youth Ministry, Oxford, 7.1.97.

Bosch, David J. 1993. *Transforming Mission*. Maryknoll, NY: Orbis Books.

Bowes, Lindsey 2001. *A Little Book of Evaluation*. Nottingham: DfES Publications.

Bradbury, Nicholas 1989. *City of God*. London: SPCK.

Bratcher, Dennis 1986. "The Poured–Out Life: The Kenosis Hymn in Context." http://www.cresource.org/kenosis.html.

Brierley, Peter 1993. *Reaching and Keeping Teenagers*. Bromley: Marc Europe.

Brierley, Peter, et al., eds. 1997. *Quadrant*. Autumn 1997. London: Christian Research Association.

Brierley, Peter, et al., eds. 1998. *CRA Fact File*. No. 5, Summer, 1998. London: Christian Research Association.

Brookfield, Stephen D. 1987. *Developing Critical Thinkers*. Buckingham: Open University.

Brown, Colin, ed. 1975. *The New International Dictionary of New Testament Theology* Vol.1. Exeter: Paternoster Press.

Brown, Colin, 1998. "Ernst Lohmeyer's *Kyrios Jesus*". In Ralph P. Martin and Brian J. Dodd, eds. *Where Christology Began*. Louisville: Westminster John Knox Press

Bruce, F. F. 1995. *Philippians*. New International Biblical Commentary. Carlisle: Paternoster.

Brueggemann, Walter 1993. *The Bible and Postmodern Imagination*. London: SCM Press.

Bryman, Alan 2001. *Social Research Methods*. Oxford: Oxford University Press.

Buxton, Graham 2001. *Dancing in the Dark*. Carlisle: Paternoster Press.

Caird, G. B. 1963. *The Gospel of Luke*. Pelican Gospel Commentary. Harmondsworth: Penguin.

Callahan, Annice 1992. *Spiritual Guides for Today*. London: Darton, Longman and Todd.

Cambell Ruth and Berry, Helen 2001. *Action Research Toolkit*. Edinburgh: Edinburgh Youth Social Inclusion Partnership.

Carson, D. A. 1984. "Matthew". In Frank E. Gabelein, ed. *The Expositor's Bible*. Grand Rapids: Zondervan.

Cassidy, Richard J. 1978. *Jesus, Politics and Society: A Study of Luke's Gospel*. Maryknoll, NY: Orbis Books.

Cashmore, Gwen and Puls, Joan 1990. *Clearing the Way*. Geneva: World Council of Churches.

Chalke, Steve with Relph, Penny 1995. *Making a Team Work*. Eastbourne: Kingsway.

Church of England 1996. *Youth A Part*. London: National Society/Church House Publishing.

Coakley, Sarah 1996. "Kenosis and Subversion: on the repression of 'vulnerability' in Christian Feminist writing". In Daphne Hampson, ed. *Swallowing a Fishbone?* London: SPCK.

Conn, Harvie, 1993. "A Contextual Theology of Mission for the City". In Charles Van Engen et al., eds. *The Good News of the Kingdom*. Maryknoll, NY: Orbis Books.

Copeland, Nelson Elwood Jnr 1997. "Ethical Heroism, Christian Empathy and Youth Empowerment". Paper given to the Second International Conference on Youth Ministry, Oxford, 8.1.97.

Coupland, Simon 2002. "Success: What Prosperity Teachers Miss". *Christianity and Renewal* (September 2002): 29-30.

Craig, Yvonne 1996. "What in the World is Happening?" In *Tomorrow is another Country*. London: Board of Education of the Church of England.

Cray, Graham 1998. *Postmodern Culture and Youth Discipleship*. Cambridge: Grove Pastoral 76.

Cray, Graham, et al. 1997. *The Post-Evangelical Debate*. London: Triangle.

Cray, Graham and Simmonds, Paul 2000. *Administry How to Guide – Being Culturally Relevant*. Sheffield: Administry.

Cronin, Kevin 1992. *Kenosis*. Shaftesbury: Element.

Croucher, Rowland 1986. *Recent Trends Among Evangelicals*. Bromley: MARC Europe.

Davies, W. D. and Allison, Dale C. 1988. *The Gospel According to St Matthew*. International Critical Commentary. Edinburgh: T & T Clark.

de Gruchy, John W. 1999. "The Reception of Bonhoeffer's Theology". In John W. de Gruchy, ed. *The Cambridge Companion to Dietrich Bonhoeffer*. Cambridge: Cambridge University Press.

de Gruchy, John W., ed. 1999. *The Cambridge Companion to Dietrich Bonhoeffer*. Cambridge: Cambridge University Press.

Dixon. Alison, ed. 2001. *The Careers and Personal Advisers' Handbook 2001/2*. Richmond: Trotman.

Dodd, Brian J. 1998. "The Story of Christ and the Imitation of Paul in Philippians 2-3". In Ralph P. Martin and Brian J. Dodd, eds. *Where Christology Began*. Louisville: Westminster John Knox Press.

Donovan, Vincent 1982. *Christianity Rediscovered*. London: SCM Press.

Douglas, Johnny undated. "The Incarnation and what it means for Youth Work today". Coursework for MA in Youth Ministry and Theology at King's College, London.

Douglas, Johnny and Brookes, John undated. "Incarnation and Youth Work". Unpublished paper.

Douglas, J. D., et al., eds. 1982. *New Bible Dictionary.* Leicester: IVP.

Drane, John 1997. *Faith in a Changing Culture.* London: Marshall Pickering.

--- 2000. *The McDonaldization of the Church.* London: Darton, Longman and Todd.

Driver, John 1993. "Messianic Evangelization". In Wilbert R. Shenk, ed. *The Transfiguration of Mission.* Scottdale, Ontario: Herald Press.

Duffield, Ian K. 1997. "Doing Urban Theology". In Ian K. Duffield, ed. *Urban Christ: Responses to John Vincent.* Sheffield: Urban Theology Unit.

Dunn, James D. G. 1996. *The Acts of the Apostles.* Peterborough: Epworth Press.

--- 1998a. *The Christ and the Spirit* Vol. 1 Christology. Edinburgh: T & T Clark.

--- 1998b. "Christ, Adam, and Pre-existence". In Ralph P. Martin and Brian J. Dodd, eds. *Where Christology Began.* Louisville: Westminster John Knox Press.

Elias, Jacob W. undated. "Lent Commentaries – Philippians background".

Ellis, George F. R. 2001. "Kenosis as a Unifying Theme for Life and Cosmology". In John Polkinghorne, ed. *The Work of Love.* London: SPCK.

Ellul, Jacques 1970. *The Meaning of the City.* Translated by Dennis Pardee. Grand Rapids: Eerdmans.

Evans, C. F. 1990. *Saint Luke.* London: SCM Press.

Fee, Gordon D. 1995. *Paul's Letter to the Philippians.* The New International Commentary on the New Testament. Grand Rapids: Eerdmans.

Feil, Ernest 1985. *The Theology of Dietrich Bonhoeffer.* Translated by Martin Rumscheidt. Philadelphia: Fortress Press.

Fergusson, David, 2001. "The Doctrine of the Incarnation". *Expository Times* Vol. 113:3 (December 2001): 75-79.

Ferguson, Sinclair B., and Wright, David F., eds. 1988. *New Dictionary of Theology.* Leicester: IVP.

Fernando, Ajith undated. "Youth for Christ International: Our Context Position Paper" http://www.gospelcom.net/yfc/yfci/yfc1.5.html

Fernando, Ajith, 1988. "Running away from God, Jonah 1:1-16". In John E. Kyle, ed. *Urban Mission: God's Concern for the City*. Downers Grove, IL: IVP.

Fitzmyer, Joseph A. 1981. *The Gospel according to Luke I-IX*. The Anchor Bible. New York: Doubleday.

--- 1985. *The Gospel according to Luke X-XXIV*. The Anchor Bible. New York: Doubleday.

Ford, David F. 1995. "Transformation". In Peter Sedgwick, ed. *God in the City*. London: Mowbray.

Ford, David F. and Green, Laurie 1995. "Distilling the wisdom". In Peter Sedgwick, ed. *God in the City*. London: Mowbray.

Foster, B. E. F. 1988. "Kenoticists". In Sinclair B. Ferguson and David F. Wright, eds. *New Dictionary of Theology*. Leicester: IVP.

Fowl, Stephen 1988. "Some Uses of Story in Moral Discourse: Reflections on Paul's Moral Discourse and our own". *Modern Theology* 4:4 (July 1988): 293-308.

Fowl, Stephen 1998. "Christology and Ethics in Philippians 2:5-11". In Ralph P. Martin and Brian J Dodd, eds. *Where Christology Began*. Louisville: Westminster John Knox Press.

Frascati-Lochead, Marta 1998. *Kenosis and Feminist Christology*. Albany: State University of New York Press.

Freire, Paulo 1996. *Pedagogy of the Oppressed*. Revised edition. London: Penguin.

Gallagher, Michael Paul 1997. *Clashing Symbols*. London: Darton, Longman and Todd.

Gauntlett, Caughey 1990. *Today in Darkest Britain*. Eastbourne: MARC.

Gerali, Steve 2001. "Seeing Clearly: Community Context". In Kenda Creasey Dean, Chap Clark and Dave Rahn, eds. *Starting Right*. Grand Rapids: Zondervan.

Godsey, John D. 1981. "The Legacy of Dietrich Bonhoeffer". In A. J. Klassen, ed. *A Bonhoeffer Legacy*. Grand Rapids: Eerdmans.

Goldingay, J. E. 1989. *Daniel*. Word Biblical Themes. Dallas: Word Books.

Gore, Charles 1922. *Belief in Christ*. London: John Murray.

--- 1926. *The Reconstruction of Belief*. London: John Murray.

Goulder, Michael D. 1989a. *Luke: A New Paradigm* Vol. 1. Luke 1-9:50. Sheffield: Sheffield Academic Press.

--- 1989b. *Luke: A New Paradigm* Vol. 2 Luke 9:50-24:53. Sheffield. Sheffield Academic Press.

Grant, Jacquelyn 1989. *White Women's Christ and Black Women's Jesus*. Atlanta: Scholars Press.

Green, Clifford J. 1999a. *Bonhoeffer: A Theology of Sociality*. Grand Rapids: Eerdmans.

--- 1999b. "Human Sociality and Christian Community". In John de Gruchy, ed. *The Cambridge Companion to Dietrich Bonhoeffer*. Cambridge: Cambridge University Press.

Green, Joel B., McKnight, Scot, and Marshall, I. Howard, eds 1992. *Dictionary of Jesus and the Gospels*. Leicester: IVP.

Green, Joel B. 1997. *The Gospel of Luke*. Grand Rapids: Eerdmans.

Green, Laurie 1993. *God in the Inner City*. Sheffield: Urban Theology Unit.

Grundy, Malcolm 1990. *Light in the City*. Norwich: Canterbury Press.

Guelich, Robert A. 1982. *The Sermon on the Mount*. Waco, TX: Word.

Gunton, Colin 1997. *Yesterday and Today*. Second edition. London: SPCK.

Hafeman, Scott, 2000. "'Because of weakness' (Galatians 4:13): the role of suffering in the mission of Paul". In Paul Barnett, et al., eds. *The Gospel to the Nations*. Leicester: Apollos.

Hamilton, William 1962. "A Secular Theology For A World Come Of Age". *Theology Today* Vol. 18 No. 1 (January): 435-459.

Harrison, Paul 1983. *Inside the Inner City*. Harmondsworth: Penguin.

Hawthorne, Gerald F. 1991. *Philippians*. Word Biblical Commentary. Milton Keynes: Word Books.

Hawthorne, Gerald F., Martin, Ralph P. and Reid, Daniel G., eds. 1993. *Dictionary of Paul and His Letters*. Downers Grove: IVP. accessed on the CD Rom IVP Essential Reference Collection.

Hays, Richard B. 1994. "Crucified with Christ – A Synthesis of the Theology of 1 and 2 Thessalonians, Philemon, Philippians, and Galatians". In Jouette M. Bassler, ed. *Pauline Theology* Vol 1. Minneapolis: Fortress Press.

Hebblethwaite, Brian 1983. "Incarnation". In Alan Richardson and John Bowden, eds. *A New Dictionary of Christian Theology*. London: SCM Press.

--- 1987. *The Incarnation*. Cambridge: Cambridge University Press.

Hebblethwaite, Margaret 1993. *Base Communities*. London: Geoffrey Chapman.

Herrick, Vanessa and Mann, Ivan 1998. *Jesus Wept*. London: Darton, Longman and Todd.

Hick, John 1989. "The Logic of God Incarnate". *Religious Studies* 25 No. 1 (March 1989): 409-423.

--- 1993. *The Metaphor of God Incarnate*. London: SCM Press.

Hock, Ronald F. 1980. *The Social Context of Paul's Ministry.* Philadelphia: Fortress Press.

Hodgson, Peter and King, Robert, eds. 1995. *Readings in Christian Theology.* London: SPCK.

Hoekendijk, J. C. 1967. *The Church Inside Out.* Translated by Isaac C. Rottenberg, L. A. Hoedemaker and Pieter Tijmes, eds. London: SCM Press.

Holden, Tony 1994. *Ways Through.* London: Epworth Press.

Holman, Bob 1981. *Kids at the Door.* Oxford: Basil Blackwell.

--- 1995. *Children and Crime.* Oxford: Lion.

--- 2000. *Kids at the Door Revisited.* Lyme Regis: Russell House.

House of Bishops 1999. *A Policy on Child Protection.* London: Church House Publishing.

House of Bishops 2001. "The Mistreatment of Adults by Those Authorised by Bishop's Licence to Leadership Positions in the Church". Unpublished paper from the House of Bishops.

Howard, George 1978. "Phil 2:60-11 and the Human Christ." *The Catholic Biblical Quarterly* Vol 40, No. 3 (July 1978): 368-387.

Howard, Roland 1996. *The Rise and Fall of the Nine O'Clock Service.* London: Mowbray.

Howell, David undated a. *Position Papers – What are they?* Halesowen: Youth for Christ.

--- undated b. *Youth Evangelism.* Halesowen: Youth for Christ.

--- 1995. "From parachurch to metachurch". In Pete Ward, ed. *The Church and Youth Ministry.* Oxford: Lynx.

Howell, Leon 1995. "The Tribulations of Dietrich Bonhoeffer". *Sojourners* May-June. Vol 24: 2. http://www.sojourners.com/soj9505/950531.html.

Hume, Basil 1999. *The Mystery of the Incarnation.* London: Darton, Longman and Todd.

Hurtado, L.W. 1984. "Jesus as Lordly Example in Philippians 2:5-11". In Peter Richardson and John C Hurd, eds. *From Jesus to Paul – Studies in Honour of Francis Wright Beare.* Waterloo, Ontario: Wilfred Laurier University Press.

Ives, Christopher 1995. *Divine Emptiness & Historical Fullness: a Buddhist–Jewish-Christian Conversation with Masao Abe.* Valley Forge PA: Trinity Press International.

Joslin, Roy 1982. *Urban Harvest.* Welwyn: Evangelical Press.

James, Graham 1983. "The Enduring Appeal of a Kenotic Christology". *Theology* Vol. LXXXVI, No. 709 (January): 7-14.

Keener, Craig S. 1993. *The IVP Bible Background Commentary*. Downers Grove: IVP.

Keener, Craig S. 1999. *A Commentary on the Gospel of Matthew*. Grand Rapids: Eerdmans.

Kelly, Geffrey B. 1994. "Sharing in the Pain of God: Dietrich Bonhoeffer's Reflections on Christian Vulnerability." *Weavings: A Journal of the Christian Spiritual Life* 8 (4) (July–August): 6-15.

--- 1999. "Prayer and Action for Justice: Bonhoeffer's Spirituality". In John de Gruchy, ed. *The Cambridge Companion to Dietrich Bonhoeffer*. Cambridge: Cambridge University Press

Kesler, Jay 1985. *The Mission of Youth for Christ International: Our Task*. Singapore: YFCI.

Killen, Patricia O' Connell and de Beer, John 1994. *The Art of Theological Reflection*. New York: Crossroad.

Kinast, Robert L. 1996. *Let Ministry Teach: A Guide to Theological Reflection*. Collegeville, MN: Liturgical Press.

--- 2000. *What Are They Saying About Theological Reflection?* New York: Paulist Press.

Kittel, Gerhard, ed. 1966. *Theological Dictionary of the New Testament*. Translated and edited by Geoffrey W. Bromily. Grand Rapids: Eerdmans.

Klassen A. J., ed. 1981. *A Bonhoeffer Legacy*. Grand Rapids: Eerdmans.

Kreitzer, Larry J. 1998. "When He at Last is First! Philippians 2:9-11 and the Exaltation of the Lord". In Ralph P. Martin and Brian J. Dodd, eds. *Where Christology Began*. Louisville: Westminster John Knox Press.

Kurz, William S. 1985. "Kenotic Imitation of Paul and of Christ in Philippians 2 and 3". In Fernando F. Segovia, ed. *Discipleship in the New Testament*. Philadelphia: Fortress Press.

Kyle, John E., ed. 1988. *Urban Mission: God's Concern for the City*. Downers Grove, IL: IVP.

Lacocque, André 1979. *The Book of Daniel*. Translated by David Pellauer and revised by the author. London: SPCK.

Leech, Kenneth 1990. *Care and Conflict*. London: Darton, Longman and Todd.

Lester, Landon 1998. "Dietrich Bonhoeffer". http://thesumners.com/bonhoeffer/essay02.html.

Lovin, Robin W. 1984. *Christian Faith and Public Choices*. Philadelphia: Fortress Press.

McFadyen, A. L. 1990. "The Call to Discipleship: Reflections on Bonhoeffer's Theme 50 years on". *Scottish Journal of Theology* Vol. 43: 461-483.

McGrath, Alister E. 1994. *Christian Theology*. Oxford: Blackwell.

MacKinnon, D. M. 1976. "The Relation of the Doctrines of the Incarnation and the Trinity". In Richard W. A. McKinney, ed. *In Creation, Christ and Culture – Studies in Honour of T. F. Torrance*. Edinburgh: T & T Clark.

Macquarrie, John 1974. "Kenoticism Reconsidered". *Theology* Vol. LXVII (March 1974):115-124.

--- 1993. "Incarnation". In Alister E. McGrath. *Modern Christian Thought*. Oxford: Blackwell.

Mahoney, Jack 2000. *The Moral Context of Pastoral Care*. Contact Pastoral Monograph Number 10. Edinburgh: Contact.

Marsh, Charles 1997. "Dietrich Bonhoeffer". In David Ford, ed. *Modern Theologians*. Oxford: Blackwell.

Marshall, I. Howard 1978. *The Gospel of Luke*. New International Greek Testament Commentary. Exeter: Paternoster Press.

--- 1991. *The Epistle to the Philippians*. Epworth Commentaries. London: Epworth Press.

Martin, Ralph P. 1960. *An Early Christian Confession: Philippains ii. 5-11 in Recent Interpretation*. London: Tyndale Press.

--- 1967. *Carmen Christi: Phillipians ii. 5-11 in recent Interpretation and in the Setting of Early Christian Worship*. Cambridge: Cambridge University Press.

--- 1980. *Philippians*. The New Century Bible Commentary. London: Marshall, Morgan & Scott.

--- 1987. *Philippians*. Tyndale New Testament Commentary. Second edition. Leicester: IVP.

--- 1991. *2 Corinthians*. Word Biblical Commentary. Waco, TX: Word Books.

--- 1998. "Carmen Christi Revisited". In Ralph P. Martin and Brian J Dodd, eds. *Where Christology Began*. Louisville: Westminster John Knox Press.

Martin, Ralph P. and Dodd, Brian J., eds. 1998. *Where Christology Began*. Louisville: Westminster John Knox Press.

Mautner, Thomas ed., 1997. *The Penguin Dictionary of Philosophy*. London: Penguin.

May, Tim 1997. *Social Research*. Buckingham: Open University Press.

Mayo, Bob 1996. *Gospel Exploded*. London: Triangle.

Meeks, Wayne A. 1983. *The First Urban Christians*. New Haven: Yale University Press.

Meggitt, Justin J. 1998. *Paul, Poverty and Survival*. Edinburgh: T & T Clark.

Merton, Thomas 1972. *Seeds of Contemplation*. Wheathampstead, Herts: Anthony Clarke Books.

Methodist Church 1997. *The Cities*. London: NCH, Action for Children.

Michaels, J. Ramsey 1989. *John*. New International Biblical Commentary. Peabody MA: Hendrickson.

Milgrom, Jacob 1991. *Leviticus 1-16*. The Anchor Bible. New York: Doubleday.

Milne, Bruce 1993. *The Message of John*. The Bible Speaks Today. Leicester: IVP.

Moeller, Martin F. 1995. "Remembering Dietrich Bonhoeffer: The Child, The Fool, The Sufferer". http://www.luther95.org/NECLA/internos/moeller.htm.

Moltmann, Jürgen and Weissbach, Jürgen 1967. *Two Studies in the Theology of Bonhoeffer*. Translated by Reginald H. Fuller and Ilse Fuller. New York: Charles Scribner's Sons.

Moltman, Jürgen 1974. *The Crucified God*. Translated by R. A. Wilson and John Bowden. London: SCM Press.

Morgan, Robert 1998. "Incarnation Myth and Theology – Ernst Käsemann's Interpretation of Philippians 2:5-11". In Ralph P. Martin and Brian J. Dodd, eds. *Where Christology Began*. Louisville: Westminster John Knox Press.

Morris, Leon 1992. *The Gospel According to Matthew*. Leicester: IVP.

--- 1995. *The Gospel According to St John*. New International Commentary. Revised edition. Grand Rapids: Eerdmans.

Motyer, Alec 1966. *The Richness of Christ*. London: IVF.

--- 1993. *The Prophecy of Isaiah*. Leicester: IVP.

Moule, C. F. D. 1997. *The Origin of Christology*. Cambridge: Cambridge University Press.

Musick, Erich 1997-9. "Kenosis Links". http://www.emusick.garagedoor.org.

National Youth Agency 2001. *Ethical Conduct in Youth Work*. Leicester: National Youth Agency.

Nazir-Ali, Michael 1993. *From Everywhere to Everywhere*. London: Collins Flame.

Nelson, F. Burton 1999. "The Life of Dietrich Bonhoeffer". In John de Gruchy, ed. *The Cambridge Companion to Dietrich Bonhoeffer*. Cambridge: Cambridge University Press.

Newlands, George 1983. "Christology". In Alan Richardson and John Bowden, eds. *A Dictionary of Theology*. London: SCM Press.

Nolland, John 1989. *Luke 1-9:20*. Word Biblical Commentary. Dallas: Word Books.

--- 1993a. *Luke 9:21-18:34*. Word Biblical Commentary. Dallas: Word Books.

--- 1993b. *Luke 18:35-24:53*. Word Biblical Commentary. Dallas: Word Books.

North, Gary 1994. *Leviticus: An Economic Commentary*. Tyler, TX: Institute for Christian Economics.

Northumbria Community 2000. *Celtic Daily Prayer*. London: Harper Collins.

Nouwen, Henri 1980. *Reaching Out*. London: Fount.

--- 1993. *Gracias*. Maryknoll, NY: Orbis Books.

--- 1996. *Bread for the Journey*. London: Darton, Longman and Todd.

Oakes, Peter 2001. *Philippians: From People to Letter*. Cambridge: Cambridge University Press.

O'Brien, Peter T. 1991. *The Epistle to the Philippians*. Grand Rapids: Eerdmans.

--- 1993. *Gospel and Mission in the Writings of Paul*. Grand Rapids: Baker Books.

O'Collins, Gerald 1995. *Christology*. Oxford: Oxford University Press.

Opepke, Albrecht 1966. "Kenosis". In Gerhard Kittel, ed. *Theological Dictionary of the New Testament*. Translated and edited by Geoffrey W. Bromily. Grand Rapids: Eerdmans.

Osborn, Lawrence and Walker, Andrew, eds. 1997. *Harmful Religion*. London: SPCK.

Ott, Heinrich 1971. *Reality and Faith*. Translated by Alex A. Morrison. London: Lutterworth.

Ovey, Michael 2002. "Idolatry and Spiritual Parody: Counterfeit Faiths". *Cambridge Papers* Vol. 11 No. 1 March 2002.

Pahl, Jon 2000. *Youth Ministry in Modern America*. Peabody MA: Hendrickson.

Pangritz, Andreas 1999. "Who is Jesus Christ, for us, today?" In John de Gruchy, ed. *The Cambridge Companion to Dietrich Bonhoeffer*. Cambridge: Cambridge University Press.

Papanikolaou, Aristotle 2000. "Person, kenosis and Abuse: Hans Urs von Balthasar and Feminist theologies in conversation." Paper presented to the Boston Theological Society 13 April 2000. http://www.bostontheological.org/colloquium/bts/btspapanikolaou.htm.

Peck, M. Scott 1999. *Golf and the Spirit*. New York: Harmony.

Pecota, D. B. 1988. "Young". In Geoffrey W. Bromiley, ed. *The International Standard Bible Encyclopedia*. Grand Rapids: Eerdmans.

Pelikan, Jaroslav 1981. "Bonhoeffer's *Christologie* of 1933". In Martin E. Marty, ed. *The Place of Bonhoeffer*. Westport, CN: Greenwood.

Perkins, Pheme 1994. "Philippians, 'Theology for Heavenly Politeuma'". In Jouette M. Bassler, ed. *Pauline Theology* Vol. 1. Minneapolis: Fortress Press.

Pettie, Allan 1993. *Towards a Theology of Frontier Youth Work*. Glasgow: Frontier Youth Trust.

Peterson, Eugene 1994. *The Message*. Colorado Springs: Navpress.

Phillips, John A. 1967. *The Form of Christ in the World: A Study of Bonhoeffer's Christology*. London: Collins.

Plummer, Alfred 1901. *Gospel According to St Luke. The International Critical Commentary*. Fourth edition. Edinburgh: T & T Clark.

Polkinghorne, John, ed. 2001. *The Work of Love: Creation as Kenosis*. London: SPCK.

Prior, Micahel 1995. *Jesus the Liberator: Nazareth Liberation Theology*. Sheffield: Sheffield Academic Press.

Pullinger, Jackie 2001. *Chasing the Dragon*. New edition. London: Hodder and Stoughton.

Puls, Joan 1989. *Hearts Set on the Pilgrimage*. London: Lamp Press.

--- 1993. *Seek Treasures in Small Fields*. London: Darton, Longman and Todd.

Punton, Jim undated. *Mission*. Frontier Focus Booklet. London: Frontier Youth Trust.

Quinn, Philip L. and Taliaferro, Charles, eds. 1997. *A Companion to Philosophy of Religion*. Oxford: Blackwell.

Rahner, Karl 1965. *Theological Investigations* Vol. 1. Second edition. Translated by Cornelius Ernst. London: Darton, Longman and Todd.

Reay, David G. 1994. *Evaluating Training*. London: Kogan Page.

Richard, Lucien 1997. *Christ The Self-Emptying of God*. Mahwah, NJ: Paulist Press.

Richards, Glyn 1987. "Faith and Praxis in Liberation Theology, Bonhoeffer and Gandhi". *Modern Theology* 3-4: 359-373.

Richardson, Alan and Bowden, John, eds. 1983. *A New Dictionary of Christian Theology*. London: SCM Press.

Richardson, Peter and Hurd, John C., eds. 1984. *From Jesus to Paul: Studies in Honour of Francis Wright Beare*. Waterloo, Ontario: Wilfred Laurier University Press.

Robbins, Tim 1995. *Dead Man Walking*. Polygram Filmed Entertainment.

Robinson, John 1963. *Honest to God*. London: SCM Press.

Ross, Maggie, 1988. *Pillars of Flame*. London: SCM Press.

Rowland, Chris and Vincent, John eds., 1995. *Liberation Theology UK.* British Liberation Theology 1. Sheffield: Urban Theology Unit.

Rowland, Chris 1995. "The Gospel, the Poor and the Churches". In Chris Rowland and John Vincent, eds. *Liberation Theology UK.* Sheffield: Urban Theology Unit.

Rowland, Chris and Vincent, John, eds., 1997. *Gospel from the City.* British Liberation Theology 2. Sheffield: Urban Theology Unit.

Rumscheidt, Martin 1999. "The Formation of Bonhoeffer's Theology". In John de Gruchy, ed. *The Cambridge Companion to Dietrich Bonhoeffer.* Cambridge: Cambridge University Press.

Sanders, James A. 1993. "Isaiah in Luke". In Craig A. Evans and James A. Sanders, eds. *Luke and Scripture.* Minneapolis: Fortress Press.

Sanford, John 1994. *Mystical Christianity: A Psychological Commentary on the Gospel of John.* New York: Crossroad.

Schottroff, Luise 1994. *Lydia's Impatient Sisters.* Translated by Barbara and Martin Rumscheidt. London: SCM Press.

Schüssler Fiorenza, Elisabeth, ed., 1994. *Searching the Scriptures* Vol. 2: A Feminist Commentary. London: SCM Press.

Scroggs, Robin 1988. *Christology in Paul and John.* Philadelphia: Fortress Press.

Sedgwick, Peter 1995. "Fear of the city?" In Peter Sedgwick, ed. *God in the City.* London: Mowbray.

Sedgwick, Peter, ed., 1995. *God in the City.* London: Mowbray.

Seeley, David 1994. "The Background of the Philippians Hymn (2:6-11)". http://www.depts.drew.edu/jhc/seelyphl.html. (Originally published *JHC* 1 (Fall 1994): 49-72)

Seim, Turid Karlsen 1994. "The Gospel of Luke". In Elisabeth Schüssler Fiorenza, ed. *Searching the Scriptures Vol. 2: A Feminist Commentary.* London: SCM Press.

Selby, Peter 1999. "Christianity in a World Come of Age". In John W. de Gruchy, ed. *The Cambridge Companion to Dietrich Bonhoeffer.* Cambridge: Cambridge University Press.

Sellers, R. V. 1953. *The Council of Chalcedon: A Historical and Doctrinal Survey.* London: SPCK.

Senior, Donald and Stuhlmueller, Carroll 1993. *The Biblical Foundations for Mission.* London: SCM Press.

Senter III, Mark H. 1997. "The Three Legged Stool of Youth Ministry". Paper presented to the Second International Conference on Youth Ministry. Oxford: 7.1.97.

Shenk, Wilbert R. 1993. "The Relevance of a Messianic Missiology for Mission Today". In *The Transfiguration of Mission*. Edited by Wilbert R. Shenk. Scottdale, Ontario: Herald Press.

Shepherd, Nick undated. "The Myths of Incarnational Youth Work". Unpublished paper.

Sheppard, David 1983. *Bias to the Poor*. London: Hodder and Stoughton.

Sheppard, Lowell 1993. *Where Faith and Strategy Meet*. Cleobury Mortimer: YFC.

Sider, Ronald 1993. *Evangelism and Social Action*. London: Hodder and Stoughton.

Silva, Moises 1988. *Philippians*. The Wycliffe Exegetical Commentary. Chicago: Moody Press.

Sloan, R. B. 1992. "Jubilee". In Joel B. Green, Scot McKnight, and I. Howard Marshall, eds. *Dictionary of Jesus and the Gospels*. Leicester: IVP.

Smalley, Stephen 1998. *John – Evangelist and Interpreter*. Second edition. Carlisle: Paternoster Press.

Society of St Francis 1992. *Celebrating Common Prayer*. London: Mowbray.

Soskice, Janet Martin 1985. *Metaphor and Religious Language*. Oxford: Clarendon Press.

Stanley, David, 1984. "Imitation in Paul's letters: Its Significance for His Relationship to Jesus and His Own Christian Foundations". In Peter Richardson and John C Hurd, eds. *From Jesus to Paul – Studies in Honour of Francis Wright Beare*. Waterloo, Ontario. Wilfred Laurier University Press.

Stanton, G. N. 1992. "Q". In Joel B. Green, Scot McKnight, and I. Howard Marshall, eds. *Dictionary of Jesus and the Gospels*. Leicester: IVP.

Storr, Anthony 1997. *Feet of Clay*. London: Harper Collins.

Stow, Peter with Fearon, Mike 1987. *Youth in the City*. London: Hodder and Stoughton.

Sturch, R. L., 1977. "The Metaphysics of the Incarnation". *Vox Evangelica*, Vol X: 66-76.

Swinton, John 2000. *Resurrecting the Person: Friendship and the Care of People with Mental Health Problems*. Nashville: Abingdon.

Surin, Kenneth 1989. "Some aspects of the 'grammar' of 'incarnation' and 'kenosis': reflections prompted by the writings of Donald MacKinnon". In Kenneth Surin, ed. *Christ, Ethics and Tragedy – Essays in Honour of Donald MacKinnon*. Cambridge: Cambridge University Press.

Sweet, Leonard 1999. *Soul Tsunami*. Grand Rapids: Zondervan.

Taylor, Vincent 1958. *The Person of Christ in New Testament Teaching*. London: Macmillan.

Theissen, Gerd 1982. *The Social Setting of Pauline Christianity*. Translated by John H. Schultz. Edinburgh: T & T Clark

Thomas, Thomas A. 1970. "The Kenosis Question". *Evangelical Quarterly* Vol. XLII No. 3 (Jul-Sep): 142-151.

Thomasius, Gottfried 1965. "Christ's Person and Work". In Claude Welch, ed. and translator. *God and Incarnation in Mid-Nineteenth Century German Theology*. New York: Oxford University Press.

Thompson, Neil 1996. *People Skills*. Basingstoke: Macmillan.

Tinsley, E. J. 1983. "Kenosis". In Gordon S. Wakefield, ed. *A Dictionary of Christian Spirituality*. London: SCM Press.

Tomlinson, Dave 1995. *The Post-Evangelical*. London: Triangle.

Torrance, Alan 2001. "Jesus in Christian Doctrine". In Markus Bockmuehl, ed. *The Cambridge Companion to Jesus*. Cambridge: Cambridge University Press.

Vanstone, W. H. 1977. *Love's Endeavour, Love's Expense*. London: Darton, Longman and Todd.

Vawter, Bruce and Hoppe, Leslie J. 1991. *Ezekiel*. International Theological Commentary. Grand Rapids: Eerdmans.

Vine, W. E. 1981. *An Expository Dictionary of New Testament Words*. London: Marshall, Morgan and Scott.

Vincent, John 1995 "Liberation Theology in Britain 1975-1995". In Chris Rowland and John Vincent, eds. *Liberation Theology UK*. British Liberation Theology 1. Sheffield: Urban Theology Unit.

Wakefield, Gordon S. ed., 1992. *A Dictionary of Christian Spirituality*. London: SCM Press.

Walker, Michael, 1988. "The Atonement and Justice". *Theology* Vol. XCI No. 741 (May): 180-187.

Walsh, Margaret, 1997. "Still Hoping!" In Chris Rowland and John Vincent, eds. *Gospel from the City*. British Liberation Theology 2. Sheffield: Urban Theology Unit.

Ward, Pete ed. 1995. *The Church and Youth Ministry*. Oxford: Lynx.

Ward, Pete 1996. *Growing up Evangelical*. London: SPCK.

--- 1997a. "The Theology of Youth Ministry". Notes given out at a Youth for Christ Training Event in February 1997.

--- 1997b. "The Tribes of Evangelicalism". In Graham Cray, et al. *The Post Evangelical Debate*. London: Triangle.

--- 1997c. *Youthwork and the Mission of God*. London: SPCK.

Welch, Claude, ed. and translator 1965. *God and Incarnation in Mid-Nineteenth Century German Theology*. New York: Oxford University Press.

Wenham, David, 1995. *Paul Follower of Jesus or Founder of Christianity?* Grand Rapids: Eerdmans.

Weems, Renita, J. 1988. *Just a Sister Away.* San Diego: Luramedia.

White, Randy 1996. *Journey to the Center of the City.* Downers Grove, IL: IVP.

Whitehead, James D. and Whitehead, Evelyn Eaton 1995. *Method in Ministry: Theological Reflection and Christian Ministry.* Revised edition. Franklin: Sheed and Ward.

Williams, Rowan 2001. "A History of Faith in Jesus". In Markus Bockmuehl, ed. *The Cambridge Companion to Jesus.* Cambridge: Cambridge University Press.

Williamson, Rene de Visme 1976. *Politics and Protestant Theology.* Baton Rouge: Louisiana State University Press.

Willmer, Haddon 1999. "Costly Discipleship". In John de Gruchy, ed. *The Cambridge Companion to Dietrich Bonhoeffer.* Cambridge: Cambridge University Press.

Wilson, Pip 1985. *Gutter Feelings.* Basingstoke: Marshalls.

Wink, Walter 1990. *Transforming Bible Study.* Revised edition. London: Mowbray.

Winter, R. 1996. "Some Principles and Procedures for the Conduct of Action Research". In O. Zuber-Skerrit, ed. *New Directions in Action Research.* London: Falmer Press.

Witherington III, Ben 1994a. *Friendship and Finances in Philippi.* Valley Forge, PA: Trinity Press International.

--- 1994b. *Paul's Narrative Thought World.* Louisville: John Knox Press.

Wright, N. T. 1986. "*Harpagmos* and the Meaning of Philippians 2: 5-11". *Journal of Theological Studies* N:S Vol. 37 Pt. 2 (October 1986): 321-352.

--- 1991. *The Climax of the Covenant.* Edinburgh: T & T Clark.

--- 1994. "Putting Paul Together Again – Toward a Synthesis of Pauline Theology (1 and 2 Thessalonians, Philippians and Philemon)". In Jouette M. Bassler, ed. *Pauline Theology* Vol. 1. Minneapolis: Fortress Press.

Yoder, John Howard 1994. *The Politics of Jesus*, Second edition. Grand Rapids: Eerdmans.

Young, Kerry 1999. *The Art of Youth Work.* Lyme Regis: Russell House.

Young, Robert undated. *Analytical Concordance to the Bible.* Iowa Falls: Riverside Book and Bible House.

Youth for Christ undated. *YFC.* Corporate Brochure. Halesowen: YFC.

Zerner, Ruth 1999. "Church, state and the 'Jewish question'". In John de Gruchy, ed. *The Cambridge Companion to Dietrich Bonhoeffer*. Cambridge: Cambridge University Press.

Ziesler, John 1990. *Pauline Christianity*. Oxford: Oxford University Press.

Printed in the United Kingdom by
Lightning Source UK Ltd., Milton Keynes
138885UK00001B/24/P